Working for Wildlife

University of Toronto Press /Toronto & Buffalo

Working for Wildlife

The Beginning of Preservation in Canada

JANET FOSTER

© University of Toronto Press 1978
Toronto   Buffalo   London
Printed in Canada

Canadian Cataloguing in Publication Data

Foster, Janet, 1940–
  Working for wildlife

  Originally presented as the author's thesis,
  York University, 1971.
  Bibliography: p.
  Includes index.
  ISBN 0-8020-5399-8

  1. Wildlife conservation – Canada. I. Title.

QL84.24.F6   639'.9'0971   C77-001442-9

This book has been published with the assistance of grants from
the Social Science Research Council of Canada,
using funds provided by the Canada Council, and from the
Canadian National Sportsmen's Fund.

FOR JOHN

Contents

Illustrations

Preface

This book began as a doctoral thesis for the Department of History at York University, and during the course of my research I was grateful to a number of individuals for their assistance and support. I would like to take this opportunity to thank the Director General of Parks Canada for granting me access to early departmental files, and staff members of the Canadian Wildlife Service, the National Museum of Canada, and the National Archives, Washington, DC, for helping me locate government documents and records.

A very special thanks is due to Mr Hoyes Lloyd, who shared his recollections with me and offered many valuable suggestions during the early stages of writing, and Dr C.H.D. Clarke, a wildlife biologist whose long career in government service has made him familiar with many of the events and personalities described here. His insight, advice, and criticism were invaluable. A large debt of gratitude must go to my thesis advisor at York, Paul Stevens, who provided wise counsel in bringing the dissertation to completion. I was also grateful to Professors Ramsay Cook and Richard Storr for their comments and suggestions.

I became acquainted only very recently with Olive Fetherstonhaugh and Naomi Thompson, who very kindly gave me much additional information about their father, Maxwell Graham. Graham's granddaughter, Betty Salmon, also shared her early memories and sent me many notes and correspondence. I thank them for their generous co-operation.

The job of rewriting the thesis for publication was greatly helped by the work of my editor, Jean Wilson. She made it all the more enjoyable, as her enthusiasm for the subject helped to rekindle my own. I also thank Jean Houston, Executive Editor, University of Toronto Press, for her active support.

Grateful acknowledgement is made to the Ontario Arts Council, the Social Science Research Council, and the Canadian National Sportsmen's Fund for helping make this publication possible.

Lastly, I pay a loving tribute to my parents, John and Winifred Green, in gratitude for their lively interest and encouragement over the years, and for the long hours spent proofreading the final text and preparing the index. And to my husband John, a friend and a colleague, who not only helped this work in many unrecorded ways but who also shares a love of all things wild. To him this book is dedicated with affection and admiration.

JF

Working for Wildlife

1
Introduction

'We have only realized very late the importance of great truths – that the conservation of our game is as vital a subject for consideration and attention as is the conservation of any other of our natural resources.'[1] These words were spoken in 1919 by Arthur Meighen, Minister of the Interior, at the opening of a national conference in Ottawa on The Conservation of Game, Fur-Bearing Animals, and Other Wild Life. Such a statement, with all of its inherent wisdom, would have been unthinkable in 1885, yet it was reasonable and timely in 1919. Over a period of thirty-four years, a dramatic change in national attitudes, especially in that of the federal government, had been brought about through the determination, understanding, and foresight of a small group of remarkably dedicated civil servants who were able to turn their own goals of wildlife preservation into a declared government policy. The contribution they made to wildlife preservation, and to Canada's conservation history, has never been recognized, for the simple reason that their story has never been told.

The Canadian government had been slow to realize the importance of wildlife conservation. Unlike the broader movement for natural resource conservation that began in Canada during the early twentieth century, concern for wildlife did not have a clearly defined beginning. Wildlife was spelled as two words in these years and 'wild life conservation' implied a totally new concept for politicians, administrators, and civil servants. Because wildlife was not generally regarded as an important natural resource, policies for its preservation did not form major political planks of government administrations, nor did preservation policies take a prominent place within the conservation movement. Canada had no powerful Sierra Club in the nineteenth century and there was no well-based, influential National Audubon Society to direct public opinion and that of the government towards questions of pre-servation. While there was a growing number of regional field naturalists' clubs throughout Canada in the early 1900s, their interests were confined more to studies of local natural history than to campaigns for wildlife preservation on a national scale. There was no 'crusade' for wildlife in Canada as there later was in the United States, nor did public champions of the wildlife cause come forward to lead such a crusade. In the absence of a strong public movement in Canada, it was left to the federal government to develop an awareness of the need for wildlife conservation. This awareness was the result of a long, slow, evolutionary process of thought and recognition on the part of the government that did not begin until the early twentieth century.

What seemed to be a lack of concern on the part of the government in the nineteenth century can be attributed to a number of factors: the belief in the superabundance of wildlife resources; the presence of a wilderness frontier; the political climate of the National Policy, with its emphasis on exploitation and development; and the terms of the British North America Act, which placed natural resources under provincial jurisdiction. All of these factors and attitudes served to insulate the federal government from the need to think in terms of preservation.

The mistaken assumption that all North America's natural resources existed in an abundant, never-ending supply was widespread throughout Canada and the United States in the nineteenth century. It was an assumption that led to what Stewart Udall has termed the 'Myth of Superabundance':

It was the intoxicating profusion of the American continent which induced a state of mind that made waste and plunder inevitable. A temperate continent, rich in soils and minerals, and forests, and wildlife, enticed men to think in terms of infinity rather than fact, and produced an overriding fallacy that was nearly our undoing – the myth of superabundance.[2]

Canada had always been rich in natural resources, particularly wildlife. The wealth of the Atlantic fisheries first lured Europeans to British North American shores and it was the fur trade that largely deter-mined the course of exploration and development of the country. Beaver was the first species heavily exploited in the northern and eastern regions and for many years, even centuries, the British North American interior was regarded as little more than a storehouse and factory for the production of prime fur pelts destined for European markets and fashion houses. The continuous supply of pelts from the New World was believed inexhaustible, and even after the fur trade declined by the 1820s and 1830s (beaver had been hunted and trapped to the edge of virtual extinction in some regions), other valuable staple products rose to take its place. There seemed no end to the resource potential of the country.

Early European explorers and fur traders enhanced the myth of superabundance through their journals, which were filled with vivid descriptions of the variety and abundance of wildlife species. Alexander Mackenzie, who voyaged up the Peace River and across the arctic regions to the Pacific in 1793, recorded that the land was rich in wildlife. He noted that wildfowl, beaver, and hare were plentiful and that in every direction 'elk and buffalo are seen in possession of the hills and plains.' The country was so crowded with animals, wrote Mackenzie, 'as to have the appearance of a stall-yard from the state of the ground, and the quantity of dung which is scattered over it.'[3] Daniel Harmon, a fur trader who spent nineteen years with the North West Company, reported in 1800 that at Fort Dauphin, Manitoba, on the banks of the upper Red River, he saw buffalo in large numbers: 'I think I may with truth affirm, that there were in view on the surrounding plains, at least 5000 of them.'[4] The abundance of game on the prairie was also noted by Lewis and Clark, who led their expedition up the Missouri River in 1804. Crossing the Milk River in southern Alberta, they saw mule deer, elk, antelope, brown bear, beaver, and wild geese, while the buffalo 'were in such multitudes that we cannot exaggerate in saying that at a single glance we saw 3000 of them before us.'[5]

John Palliser's expedition of 1857 also sighted 'immense herds' of buffalo. At his camp on the Souris River in Manitoba, Palliser recorded that the whole region was covered with buffalo in bands varying from hundreds to thousands. 'So vast were the herds that I began to have serious apprehensions for my horses,' he wrote, 'as the grass was eaten to the earth as if the plain had been devastated by locusts.'[6] And Henry Hind, who led his party into the same territory one year later, noted that Métis hunters from the Red River settlement killed thousands of buffalo in 'wanton revelry' as far west as the Saskatchewan River.[7]

Vivid descriptions of the varied mammal and bird life fill early pioneering accounts in eastern Canada as well. An 1867 tourist guide extolled the shore of the lower St Lawrence as unequalled anywhere else in the world for its number and variety of wildfowl.[8] Despite growing settlement, Upper Canada was still rich in wildlife of many species by the middle of the century. The Reverend Thomas McGrath wrote home to Ireland in 1833 that the woods of Ontario 'abound with bears, wolves, turkey, and partridge ... deer may be shot in the woods, hares and rabbits are in abundance.'[9] Another settler wrote how wild pigeons came in April and were 'shot in the thousands – no fine for shooting, everyone may help himself without scruple or interference with the property of another.'[10] There was a plentiful supply of game for all. Anna Jameson recalled in 1838 that 'I stopped the horse and looked around and on every side, far and near – east, west, north, and south, it was all forest – a boundless sea of forest within whose leafy recesses lay hidden as infinite a variety of life and movement as within the depths of the ocean.'[11] British North America indeed appeared rich in what seemed an unlimited, self-perpetuating, superabundance of wildlife.

The belief was closely related to the recognition that Canada possessed a vast frontier – the largely unexplored hinterland of the Hudson Bay Territory and Rupert's Land, purchased by the Dominion in 1868. It was an enormous area, stretching from Labrador on the east to the Rocky Mountains on the west, and from the northern watershed of the St Lawrence River to the southern watershed of the Arctic Ocean, a total of 2,300,000 square miles. A report in 1870 on the route between Lake Superior and the Red River settlement described the newly acquired territories as 'a region which forms no inconsiderable portion of the American continent and which is unsurpassed in the variety and extent of its natural resources, by any other area of equal dimensions on the earth's surface.' It was a 'beautiful and fertile land of vast proportions ... rich in the products of the chase, in fisheries, and probably in mines.'[12] Few Canadians doubted that the frontier held the promise of potentially rich agricultural land, that it contained vast forests and mountain regions teeming with wildlife, cloaked in valuable timber stands, and concealing untapped mineral resources. The very presence of such a frontier instilled in Canadians, and in Canadian politicians, the belief in a great national destiny based on the riches of natural resources. In the words of Lord Dufferin, who visited the Northwest in 1877, 'when the Dominion of Canada came to these vast regions, she was no longer a mere settler along the banks of a single river, but the owner of half a continent – in the magnitude of her possessions, in the wealth of her resources, in the sinews of her national might – the peer of any power on earth.'[13]

The prairie and northern regions of this new frontier, regions over which Ottawa retained jurisdiction and complete control of resources, were still quite wild by the 1870s and there was scarcely an imprint of settlement. This was still the land that had so impressed Alexander Mackenzie when he first saw it, 'green with exuberant verdure, its gently undulating hills and valleys covered as far as the eye could see, with vast herds of buffalo and elk, with their young frisking about them.'[14]

But to a few seasoned explorers and trained observers, the land was not quite the same. There had been significant changes. Settlement was still as sparse as it had been in Mackenzie's day, but there was a growing scarcity of wild game. John Palliser had recorded seeing 'immense buffalo herds' in 1857, but just three years later there are repeated references in his journal to the expedition's difficulty in acquiring enough game to augment its food supplies. He noted that in 1855 York Factory on Hudson Bay had received 20,000 buffalo robes and skins for trade goods and he speculated from this that wild buffalo herds had to be decreasing. 'It's well known,' he wrote, 'that on the southern prairie they are becoming very scarce; while in the country of the Saskatchewan, notwithstanding that the contrary opinion is held by many, they are also decreasing.'[15] James Hector, who accompanied the expedition, lent weight to Palliser's speculations. Travelling north from Jasper House to the Smoking River, a branch of the Peace River, he looked across the same plains Alexander Mackenzie had crossed sixty years before. Sadly, Hector commented on the changes that had occurred:

Until a few years ago, these prairies supported large bands of buffalo and elk. When we compare the description given by Sir Alexander Mackenzie of the prairie country along the Peace River, with its vast herds of buffalo and elk, when he passed in 1793, with the present northern limit of the large herds of these animals, at least three degrees of latitude further south, the change is very striking; and still more so if it is true, as the hunters say, that the disappearance of the large quantities of game has only taken place within the last twenty years.[16]

Palliser and Hector attributed the decline in wild game to fire, disease, the increase in demand for food and furs and, in particular, to the introduction of firearms. In the upper Columbia Valley, Hector judged from the great number of antlers on the ground that elk must have been very numerous at one time. But the open nature of the woods, and the very limited elk range in the valley itself, must have made the animals easy prey when Indians acquired guns. Stoney Indian guides who accompanied the expedition told Hector that game was so scarce that 'only the best hunters can make sure of killing.'[17] Indeed, in Palliser's introduction to his report, he claimed that the fur trade was in decline because hunters had such difficulty existing in the bush for long periods at a time. 'First-rate hunters have frequently told me,' he wrote, 'that such hard and constant labour in pursuing thickwood animals for the support of themselves and their families left them neither courage nor time to devote to their traps.'[18] Hector and Palliser both knew by 1860 that wildlife conditions in the Northwest were undergoing serious changes, but their reports sparked little interest. Confederation was the order of the day and another thirty-four years would pass before any legislative attempts were made to halt the decline in wildlife population numbers in the Northwest.

The years after 1878 were not marked by prudence or caution, but rather were coloured with the triumph of John A. Macdonald's National Policy: protective tariffs, national economic development, and transcontinental expansion. For the next ten years, political and economic issues were the major considerations as settlers, citizens, and politicians began building a new nation. Few paused long enough to think in terms of safeguarding or conserving the 'unlimited' resources of the continent. As settlement and railways hungrily pushed their way west, 'the aim of our legislators was to clear the ground for general farming purposes and in so doing to dispose of the most valuable timber to the best advantage ... these resources were held to be inexhaustible and therefore in no need of protection, apart from making sure that those who exploited the timber did not monopolize it.'[19] Under the banner of the National Policy, the emphasis was on development, expansion, and exploitation for the good of the nation.

There was yet another reason why the government at Ottawa showed little awareness of the need for wildlife conservation policies. The British North America Act of 1867 made no mention of 'wildlife,' but it was assumed that wildlife, like other natural resources, would be the responsibility of the individual provinces.[20] The five eastern provinces and British Columbia would thus handle their own game problems, while Ottawa assumed responsibility for the Northwest Territories, which then included Manitoba, Alberta, Saskatchewan, and the distant northern regions of Canada. The federal government also held jurisdiction over a strip of territory running through British Columbia's Rocky Mountains, land surrendered by the province for the promise of a railway line. Since wildlife in the Northwest was believed to be abundant, self-regulating, and self-perpetuating, it seemed that there was little need for the federal government to do anything about protection. But government members might well have studied the provincial experiences, for what happened to bird and mammal species within provincial boundaries during the nineteenth century would eventually happen to wildlife species throughout the whole Dominion.

All the British North American provinces had game legislation on their provincial statute books, and the Ontario government in particular had gained considerable experience in handling questions of wildlife administration within the province. Significantly, and of even greater importance, the Ontario government had learned very early the necessity for wildlife conservation, a lesson that only experience had taught.

Ontario's forests, the natural habitat for much of the province's wildlife resources, came under the woodsman's axe and farmer's plough during the early nineteenth century. Valuable timber stands were cut and the land was burned over to make ready for farm and settlement. Few settlers missed the trees. Forests were usually regarded as obstacles to development, elements to be feared, or combated, or simply as something that 'blocked the settler's view.'[21] Anna Jameson observed that 'a Canadian settler hates a tree, regards it as his natural enemy, as something to be destroyed, eradicated, annihilated by all and any means. The idea of useful or ornamental is seldom associated here with even the most magnificent of timber trees.'[22] In the backwoods of Upper Canadian society, farmers and woodsmen were the true 'pioneers of progress' as the virgin wilderness was transformed into a 'fruitful garden.'[23]

But something was lost in Ontario's transformation from wilderness to garden. With the clearing away of the forests, the spread of settlement, and the building of roads and railway lines, wildlife suffered a crucial loss of habitat. At least one species, however, benefitted from the forest clearing. White-tailed deer followed the woodsmen's axe, attracted by the increase of new growth, their essential browse, that clear-cut logging methods created. But many other birds and mammal species suffered from loss of habitat and indiscriminate killing by growing numbers of settlers. Elk (wapiti) were approaching extinction by 1850, the wild turkey became extinct well before the end of the century, ducks and geese were killed in large numbers during their spring and fall migrations.[24] Public opinion, finally aroused by the slaughter of the passenger pigeon, demanded action from the provincial government.

Ontario's first game protective legislation went 'on the books' as far back as 1762 when General Thomas Gage, Military Governor of Canada, declared a closed season on partridge (ruffed grouse) in Upper Canada. This was followed by a wolf bounty in 1793 (presumably to protect deer as well as settlers' livestock), and in 1821, a closed season on deer. The first comprehensive Upper Canadian game law was passed in 1839, establishing closed seasons on a number of game bird species, and in 1856 the game laws were rewritten and extended to include fur-bearing animals. Insectivorous and other small birds regarded as beneficial to farmers' crops were also protected through legislation in 1864. But, faced with what sportsmen considered a grave crisis by the 1880s, the government set up a Royal Commission on Fish and Game to review the wildlife situation in the province. The Commission's report, published in 1892, chronicled the experience of Ontario and illuminated the fate of its wildlife:

On all sides, from every quarter, has been heard the same sickening tale of merciless, ruthless, and remorseless slaughter. Where but a few years ago game was plentiful, it is hardly now to be found; and there is great danger that, as in the case of the buffalo, even those animals which have become so numerous as to be looked upon with contempt will soon become extinct. The many places where game formerly abounded, large cities stand today. The clearing of the land, the cutting down of the forests, the introduction of railways, the ravages of wolves and the indiscriminate hunting of the human assassin and the use of dynamite and nets have all contributed to the general decrease of game and fish of this land. This is indeed a deplorable state of affairs. [25]

Public opinion and sportsmen's representations had forced the Commissioners to realize that if something was not done very quickly, Ontario's fish and game would be destroyed and 'what had been for years a sportsmen's paradise, known all over the world, and furnishing game and fish in abundance ... would be no more.'[26] As a result of the Commission's findings, the provincial government broadened and strengthened Ontario's Game and Fish acts, set up a new Game and Fisheries Board, and hired full-time game wardens. By the end of 1892, there were 392 deputy game wardens on the government payroll. Ontario's wildlife resources also benefitted from the establishment of Algonquin (1893) and Rondeau (1894) provincial parks; both parks were designated wildlife preserves.

Ontario had learned, to its cost, of the need for wildlife conservation. But in another sense the province had experienced the passing of a wilderness frontier, with all that this implied for its wildlife inhabitants.

The United States had suffered a similar loss of wildlife species that fell before the westward advance of civilization. The virtual extermination of the buffalo and passenger pigeon was the most spectacular in its thoroughness, and when wild bird plumage began to adorn women's hats, terns, egrets, and some species of shorebirds were also pushed close to extinction. William Hornaday, President of the American Bison Society and prominent American author and preservationist, warned that it was a fallacy to think of wildlife in terms of abundance; that no species was so great in numbers that it could not be exterminated by man. In 1913, looking back over the fate of America's wildlife, he wrote: 'It is our duty to heed the lessons of history and not rush blindly on until we perpetrate a continent destitute of wild life.'[27]

The perspective from Ottawa during the nineteenth century, however, was altogether different. The federal government had not witnessed at first hand the sudden ending of a frontier, nor had it become aware of the loss of wildlife on the same dramatic scale. The lands under federal jurisdiction changed as settlement followed the railway's steel tracks through the 1880s, but although animal life was threatened by loss of habitat and depredations by hunters, settlers, and Indians, the decline in wildlife numbers did not arouse the attention or immediate concern of government. Only one branch of government acknowledged the changes taking place in the western interior. In a handbook on Canada published by the Department of Agriculture in 1886 for the Colonial and Indian Exhibition in London, a report stated:

With the advance of settlement, animal life retreats. The western plains, so lately thronged with herds of elk and antelope and roamed over by countless herds of bison, are yearly required more and more for human pasture, instead of nature's feeding ground. Hills, valleys, forests, and meadows everywhere are alike coming under man's control, thereby rapidly pushing to the verge of extinction many species of animals which were formerly abundant.[28]

But having noted this fact, the publication nevertheless reassured its readers that 'there is still an abundance of game, and the migration of wild fowl saves them from the universal destruction which threatens quadrupedal life.' The myth of wildlife superabundance was as strong and healthy in government thinking as ever it had been. However, the government did move in 1894 – after much persuasion by individual members of the Northwest Mounted Police – to enact legislative measures to limit the kill of some wildlife species in the Northwest, notably buffalo. However, these measures were not adopted to protect an intrinsically valuable wildlife resource for its own sake, but to safeguard a dependable food supply for native peoples.

The truth is that the government knew very little about wildlife, which perhaps best explains its apparent lack of concern in the nineteenth century. Scientific studies of animal behaviour, and the interrelationship between species and their dependence on habitat, would have to wait until the twentieth century. Broad theories of wildlife management were not developed until well into the 1920s and 1930s; few biologists or zoologists were attached to government departments, and the first dominion ornithologist was not hired until 1918. While the Canadian Geological Survey had conducted numerous explorations and scientific investigations after 1873, little was known about native fauna beyond the numbers of different species and 'interesting commentaries on their importance.'[29]

When wildlife was considered at all by the government in the nineteenth century, it was seldom viewed in terms of conservation or preservation. It was generally looked upon as a food supply, a source of recreation through fishing and hunting and, much later, as a substantial producer of tourist revenues. When arguments were raised for the preservation of a particular wildlife species, they were seldom enhanced with aesthetic or sentimental persuasions, but firmly couched in the commercial and economic considerations of the day. For a young, undeveloped nation growing up in an exploitive age, this is hardly surprising. As a member of the Parks Branch declared in 1920, 'Conservation cannot be successfully carried on without money':

We must show the authorities that wild life is as much a natural resource as iron or timber or wheat and that as such, it is capable, under proper administration, of being a constant source of revenue.[30]

An uninhabited frontier, the myth of superabundance, an era of exploitation and lack of knowledge about wildlife, the political climate of the National Policy and the division of powers under the British North America Act – all of these factors and attitudes within government and among the Canadian people generally, obstructed and delayed the advent of wildlife conservation in Canada.

There was no formal concern for wildlife preservation expressed by the federal government in the nineteenth century, yet, during the closing years of that century and throughout the first two decades of the twentieth century, an awareness began to evolve and take shape in government thinking. The realization was dawning that Canada's wildlife resources were not unlimited and that certain species, far from being superabundant, were declining into extinction. With this realization came a growing sense of responsibility on the part of the federal government to preserve and protect Canada's wildlife resources. That responsibility was voiced and discussed during the first National Wild Life Conference, convened by the government, in 1919. Three years later, the responsibility was formally assumed and wildlife conservation became part of regular government policy.

What brought the government to a realization of its responsibility for wildlife conservation? One searches through voluminous ministerial records and manuscript collections of both Conservative and Liberal administrations in the hope of finding evidence that prime ministers or cabinet members initiated programs for wildlife conservation. But one searches in vain. The concept of wildlife conservation neither originated nor evolved at this high level of government. Rather, it was at the level of the senior civil servant that the awareness was born, and that new concepts emerged and took shape. Civil servants, members and heads of those departments most concerned with wildlife matters, made and carried out day-to-day decisions and gave recommendations that greatly influenced the course of government policy. It is through their work that the evolution of a growing sense of responsibility within government towards wildlife conservation is revealed.

Canada was fortunate to have a handful of far-sighted, resourceful, dedicated civil servants who turned their own goals of wildlife preservation into government policy. Howard Douglas, appointed Superintendent of Rocky Mountains Park in 1897, was one of the first civil servants to realize the importance of wildlife both as a tourist attraction and as a valuable national resource. Robert Campbell, Director of the Forestry Branch, Department of the Interior, drew attention to the important relationship between forest reserves and game preserves. After 1908, he took steps to familiarize the government and the Forestry Branch with better methods of wildlife protection on all Dominion forest reserves. James Harkin, appointed Commissioner of Dominion Parks in 1912, had a clear and unfailing vision of what wilderness, parks, and wildlife signified for the Canadian people in terms of both aesthetic and economic importance. As Parks Commissioner, he became custodian of what he believed to be Canada's true heritage, given to her in trust for future generations. Maxwell Graham, self-appointed Chief of the parks' three-man 'Animal Division,' personally and almost singlehandedly undertook the responsibility of preserving pronghorn antelope in the west and wood buffalo in the north. His efforts helped to advance a policy of wildlife preservation throughout the Dominion. And Gordon Hewitt, Dominion Entomologist with the Department of Agriculture, Consulting Zoologist to the dominion government, and life-long crusader for wildlife conservation, was the most energetic and effective advocate of wildlife preservation within the Canadian civil service. The International Migratory Bird Treaty, the Migratory Birds Convention Act, and the revision of the Northwest Game Act can all be attributed directly to Hewitt's influence and untiring efforts.

How was it that these few men seemingly escaped the influence of all the late nineteenth-century factors and attitudes that hindered the development of a wildlife consciousness? What explains their beliefs, convictions, and actions? The answer is not easy to find. None of them were political leaders, cabinet members, or even prominent public figures. They left behind no neatly filed manuscript collections in the Public Archives at Ottawa. No biographies were ever written about them and their counterparts today know little about these earlier civil servants. But from correspondence still scattered among old government files, from their published departmental reports, and from talks they gave before the Commission of Conservation and various wildlife organizations, something can be gleaned of the influences that underlay their beliefs and actions.

All of them were deeply influenced by the American example and experience: the loss of the frontier, the impact of civilization with its resulting decline in wildlife numbers, and the establishment and success of American national parks. Howard Douglas's determination to protect buffalo on Canadian reserves was based, in part, on the knowledge that the United States's buffalo herds had been exterminated in the wild before the end of the nineteenth century. James Harkin's beliefs in wilderness values were well grounded on the philosophy and writings of the American wilderness preservationist, John Muir. Indeed, the Parks Commissioner lost few occasions to quote the American author at length in his departmental reports to the Minister of the Interior on the need for wilderness areas and the importance of dominion parks. Both Douglas and Harkin were closely informed of developments in the American wildlife protection movement, well under way in the United States after 1911. When American wildlife preservationist William Hornaday published *Our Vanishing Wildlife* in 1913, he sent copies to Harkin, Douglas, and to all the superintendents of Canada's dominion parks. And in later years, Canadian civil servants were frequent speakers before the North American Fish and Game

Protective Association, the American Game Protective and Propagation Association, and the International Association of Game, Fish, and Conservation Commissioners. Even more significant was the relationship between Canadian senior civil servants and their American counterparts. Both Harkin and Hewitt worked closely with members of the United States Biological Survey, keeping them well briefed on the development and progress of wildlife legislation in Canada. Often, they confided in them more readily and more easily than in their own ministers, seeking their advice on issues pertaining to park development and wildlife administration. This relationship proved highly beneficial to both countries when the international treaty for migratory bird protection was under negotiation.

With the exception of Hewitt, none of these civil servants had any formal training or background in the biological sciences. Their knowledge of wildlife and the need for conservation was based on practical experience gained in their official positions and on information gathered and passed on to them by colleagues in other government departments. There was an active sharing of ideas and frequently they met and dealt with each other on a common ground that extended beyond their official government functions. In a number of instances, Hewitt and Harkin belonged to the same local naturalists' clubs and international game protective associations. There is no question that wildlife preservation was as much a personal commitment for these men as it was a professional preoccupation. At a time when there was little understanding at the government level about the plight of wildlife in Canada, this handful of senior civil servants recognized the need for wildlife protection. Through experience gained 'on the job,' and from ideas based on their own understanding and personal convictions, they charted a steady course that led the federal government towards a responsible role in wildlife conservation.

2

Parks, Resources, and the Role of Wildlife

Although the government's concern for wildlife preservation was slow in developing, there was a strong interest in the subject of natural resources in the late nineteenth and early twentieth centuries. Two movements were under way in North America during this period in which the Canadian government was directly involved: the establishment of national parks and the conservation of natural resources. The government's policies in dealing with these new issues not only highlighted its attitude towards 'wildlands' and conservation generally, but also demonstrated a lack of knowledge and concern for wildlife. A brief exploration of both the origin of national parks and the government's involvement with natural resource conservation will provide a backdrop against which the efforts and achievements of Canada's senior civil servants must be viewed.

Today, national parks are acknowledged wildlife sanctuaries, but when the first parks were established in the 1880s, this was not their primary function. A clause in the Rocky Mountains Park Act called for the 'preservation and protection of fish and game, [and] wild birds generally,' but creation of a wildlife reserve in the Rocky Mountains was not the intention of John A. Macdonald's government. Parks were to be 'commercial assets,'[1] sources of revenue to a government foundering in economic depression and burdened by debt from building the Canadian Pacific Railway. From the outset, the parks' chief function was to popularize and help promote the CPR; the railway, in return, was to bring in a steady stream of passengers with their tourist dollars. As Macdonald's Minister of the Interior confided to him in 1885: 'It is of the greatest importance that the mountain and BC sections of the CPR be made as popular as possible.'[2] One way to make them popular was to establish scenic tourist resorts and parklands along the railway line.

The Canadian government did not pioneer in the creation of national parks but closely followed and carefully emulated the American example. The first American to conceive of a 'national park' was the artist George Catlin. Catlin was a frequent traveller through the American west, where he witnessed firsthand the decline of wildlife numbers before 'the appalling appearance of civilized man.'[3] In 1832, on one of his many trips through the wilderness, the artist dreamed of a day when the American government, through 'a great government policy of protection,' would preserve the land and its wildlife in a park, 'a nation's park, containing beast and man, in all the wild and freshness of nature's beauty.'[4] That same year, the government set aside the Arkansas Hot Springs as a National Reserve, not to preserve the beauty and wildlife as Catlin had envisioned, but to safeguard the valuable hot springs from commercial exploitation. Forty years later, more hot springs were discovered, this time in Wyoming, and Catlin's dream came true. With the establishment of Yellowstone National Park in 1872, Americans had the first national park on the North American continent and, indeed, in the world.

Part of the park's origin lay in the discovery of mineral springs and the realization, by government members, of their commercial value and importance. But Yellowstone was also a superb two-million-acre tract of virgin wilderness, a land still hunted by bands of roving Indians (much to the consternation of early park administrators, who feared for the safety of visitors). Yellowstone was reserved as 'a public park or pleasure ground for the benefit and enjoyment of the people.' It was to be under the exclusive control of the Secretary of the Interior, who would make regulations for 'the prevention from injury and spoilation of timber, mineral deposits, natural curiosities, or wonders within the park and the retention of their natural condition.'[5] He also was to oversee the construction of buildings, bath houses, roads, and bridle paths.

As defined under the Yellowstone Park Act, all the timber, water power, grass, and potential mineral resources in the vast park were withdrawn forever from commercial exploitation, 'a piece of legislation,' wrote John Muir, 'that shines benignly amid the common dust and ashes history of the public domain.'[6] Such a wilderness reservation was possible in 1872 only because most private interests were not looking hungrily that far west and no railway lines passed within hundreds of miles of Yellowstone.[7] The battle over resources within the park, seemingly under the exclusive control and protection of government, would come later. For the present, the mountains, scenic splendours, and hot springs were reserved for the benefit of the American people.

Although natural resources and wilderness scenery were carefully safeguarded by clauses of the Yellowstone Park Act, wildlife protection was not so well defined. The clause in the Act relating to wildlife prohibited only the 'wanton destruction' of fish and game, not the destruction itself. And the fact that only the killing of game for 'gain and profit' was prohibited left the way open to sportsmen, explorers, travellers, and even park officials to kill wildlife species for sport or food.[8] As Yellowstone was created out of the wilderness (unlike Canadian parks, which later were established along the railway line), it was fully expected that most campers and visitors would have to depend on wildlife resources for food in order to survive in the new national park. The killing of game was prohibited in 1880, but with no money for rangers' salaries, there was little hope of enforcing the regulation even had the Superintendent been willing:

Elk, deer and other game being driven by storm into the sheltered glens and valleys, we were enabled to secure an abundant winter's supply of fresh meat, and also fine hides of three bear, wolf, and wolverine. Although severe and dangerous, hunting in the park was excellent sport and the only recreation I enjoyed during the season.[9]

Contrary to park regulations, park employees and political appointees killed game in Yellowstone National Park for sport and profit, which resulted in a general slaughter of the park's wildlife during the early years of its administration. This slaughter continued until the 1894 Lacey Act prohibited all hunting and killing of game within the park boundaries. It thus took twenty-two years to make Yellowstone a wildlife preserve as well as a public pleasure ground.

The origins of Canada's first park reserve also lay in the discovery of mineral hot springs. Canadian Pacific Railway workers discovered the springs in a cave along the railway line in 1885. Peter Mitchell, a former member of Macdonald's Conservative government, learned that there were applications to deed the land and quickly pointed out the commercial potential of the springs to the Prime Minister:

They are the only hot springs so far as I know yet discovered in the Dominion and their value in my opinion can scarcely be estimated and should not be allowed to

go into the hands of a private speculator but should be owned by the government
as a National Sanitarium in the same way as the hot springs of Arkansas are ...
for the United States.[10]

Once the existence of hot springs was determined, government
members lost little time in securing them for the Dominion. William
Pearce, Superintendent of Mines with the Department of the Interior,
visited Banff in September 1885 and found that three 'entrepreneurs'
had staked out claims and were busily engaged in developing the hot
springs for commercial purposes. According to Pearce's own account,
he was given a bad reception by the three, two of whom were prospec-
tors in the area and the third a CPR section foreman. On his return to
Ottawa, Pearce strongly urged the government to step in immediately
and make the springs a federal reservation.[11] Macdonald's Deputy
Minister of the Interior, Alexander Burgess, shared Pearce's suspi-
cions of the entrepreneurs and confided to Macdonald that any railway
involvement was 'typical of CPR people who are evincing a disposition to
grab everything in the Northwest, and apparently desire that everybody shall be excluded from these hot springs except themselves.'[12]
Two months later, Thomas White, the Minister of the Interior, also
journeyed to Banff. In a subsequent confidential report on the Northwest Territories, he stated: 'it would be a great misfortune to permit the
springs to get into the hands of any of these claimants.'[13]

There was little doubt that the hot springs had considerable commercial significance. 'The springs are of great value,' reported White,
'and being situated amidst the grand scenery of the Rocky Mountains
and within easy access of the CPR, are certain to become a popular
resort for people afflicted with diseases, rheumatism, and other trou-
bles.'[14] The order-in-council passed in November 1885, reserving
Banff Hot Springs, clearly revealed the government's purpose:

Whereas near the station of Banff on the CPR line, in the Provincial District of
Alberta, NWT, there have been discovered several hot springs which promise to be
of great sanitary advantage to the public, and in order that proper control of the
lands surrounding these springs may remain vested in the Crown, the said lands
surrounding these springs and in their immediate neighbourhood, be and are
reserved from sale, or settlement, or squatting.[15]

The ten acres of land around Banff Hot Springs were to be developed
as a health resort with the added attraction of clean air and mountain
scenery to lure the tourist as well as the afflicted. Visitors would travel

in large numbers to the park via the newly completed railway, providing it with a certain financial return. The beneficiary, of course, was the CPR. What was reserved in 1885 was not a 'wilderness' area similar to Yellowstone National Park, nor a wildlife reserve. The ten acres of land at Banff were set aside to preserve a valuable natural resource that could be exploited in the interests of the government and the railway.

Railway officials were understandably delighted with the park reservation, which offered unlimited commercial possibilities to the company. The CPR's General Superintendent hinted to Van Horne in 1886 what some of those possibilities included:

There is no question in my mind that if the ground could be reserved at once for park purposes at Banff and accommodation erected there, that we would have a number of passengers to and from that station. When there in February, there were in the vicinity of 40 invalids at the springs, and many more would go could they obtain the necessary hotel accommodation.[16]

Well before the end of 1886, several hotels were built on the reserve, bath house construction was under way, a sanitarium was being erected, and the CPR was drawing up blueprints for the Banff Springs Hotel.[17] The Deputy Minister had every reason to write exultantly to Macdonald that the park was likely to become 'the greatest and most successful health resort on the continent.'[18] And in his annual report to the Minister of the Interior he noted happily that all operations necessary to make the reserve 'a credible park' were in progress.[19]

The legislation to establish Banff Hot Springs as a dominion park came before Parliament in 1887.[20] Under the bill, the proposed reserve was enlarged from the original ten acres to an area of 260 square miles. The expansion was credited to George Stewart, a member of the Dominion Lands Branch who had carried out topographical surveys of the area and found regions of unsurpassed beauty in the surrounding mountains and valleys.[21] Members on both sides were in favour of preserving the hot springs and mountain scenery, particularly if they were capable of producing commercial revenue. The Liberal member for Perth South, James Trow, believed that Banff was worthy of reservation because such scenery existed nowhere else on the continent.[22] His colleague from Perth North, Conservative member Samuel Hesson, was glad the government had made an effort to preserve a resort for the Canadian people. 'I have no doubt,' he said, 'it will be sufficiently pleasant and valuable, as to induce those in search of health or recreation to spend the money in their own country which hitherto they have been in the habit of spending abroad.'[23] The benefits of the springs for Canada, he hinted, were of a kind 'that we cannot fully realize today.'

If there was little opposition in the House to the concept of a national park, what did rouse the ire of a number of opposition members was the fact that so much money, a total of $46,000, had been spent on the reserve between the time it was first set aside through order-in-council in 1885, and when the bill to establish the park was introduced to Parliament; money spent 'without the proper sanction of Parliament.' 'In many English speaking communities,' Richard Cartwright charged, 'it has always been understood that before public money is spent by Ministers of the Crown, the authority of Parliament should be obtained for it.'

I do not think there is anything in the Act of Parliament which authorizes the issue of Governor General's warrants which justifies the expenditure of $46,000 of public money on this public park without the authority of Parliament.[24]

Cartwright concluded that the money had not been spent properly, but George Casey, the Liberal member from Elgin West, went even further, accusing the government of 'unconstitutional dealings.'[25] And John Kirk, the opposition member from Guysborough, did not understand why the government was building hotels for tourists in the first place:

I do not see that the Government should go into the business of hotels at all. Why should they go into the business of preparing public parks as a resort –for whom? Not for the people of Canada, not for the people who pay the taxes, but for the wealthy people of the cities of the Dominion and the cities of other countries.[26]

The very close relationship that existed between the government and the CPR clearly bothered some opposition members. There were frequent charges of 'speculation,' 'monopoly,' and 'exclusiveness' made during the debate. George Casey surmised that the CPR was speculating with the government; 'they are going in snacks on the profits as well as certain private speculators, and the reservation is partly for the railway company and partly for private individuals.'[27] Alfred Jones, the Liberal member from Halifax, attacked the government in the same vein, pointing out that since seventy or eighty million dollars had already been given to the CPR for railway construction, any further expenditure should be borne by the railway company and not by the Canadian government:

The financial burden is such that we cannot afford to throw away money on such a project. We have had large deficiencies; there is depression existing in many parts of the Dominion ... the people of the Dominion will look with much apprehension at the inauguration of a policy such as this looking forward to a large expenditure.[28]

But Donald Smith, the independent Conservative member for Montreal West, and one who, by his own admission, was an interested party to the railway interests,[29] defended the CPR's involvement. He justified the government's taking immediate action to develop the springs in 1885 because their 'curative properties' had been recognized only recently. Speed was of the essence and the fact that many sufferers already had been 'relieved' and that people 'have gone there cripples and severe sufferers and have been restored to health' more than justified the government's acting without waiting for parliamentary sanction.[30] In answer to the charge that the CPR and not the government should bear the cost of developing the reserve, Smith told members the railway was building a large hotel on the site – at an estimated cost of $100,000 – 'not as a matter of profit,' he said, 'but with a view, when it has been made a success, of giving it over on the most reasonable terms possible to those who will manage it properly and make it a place of resort equal to any on the continent':

Anyone who has not gone to Banff, and from the plateau on which the hotel is to be built, has looked down on the fall immediately below, a fall of eighty feet or more with a large volume of water, who has looked on the reaches of the Bow River, and, on turning around beheld the mountains towering heavenward, and not felt himself elevated and proud that all this is part of the Dominion, cannot be a true Canadian.[31]

The strongest and most convincing case for establishing Rocky Mountains Park came from Macdonald himself. The Prime Minister eloquently defended the reservation, pointing out the natural beauties of the area, the many qualities that would make it a first-class health resort capable of attracting visitors from home and abroad. Establishment of the park promised 'large pecuniary advantage to the Dominion' and would enhance the prestige of Canada abroad. He looked to the day when the CPR would lay out a large town plot on the park reserve: 'Then there will be rental of waters; that is a perennial source of revenue, and if carefully managed will more than many times recuperate, or recoup, the government for any present expenditures.'[32] 'Recuperate too?' interjected Mitchell. 'Yes,' answered Macdonald, 'recuperate the patients and recoup the Treasury.'[33]

In spite of opposition arguments, there was never any doubt that the bill to establish Rocky Mountains Park would pass the House. Even Cartwright admitted that members on both sides agreed about the desirability of creating a national park,[34] only the question of 'unconstitutional' spending and railway involvement had belaboured the debate. The new national park was clearly regarded as a natural resource capable of exploitation and expected to produce large commercial revenues. In an 'age of bigness,' these were the values that counted most.[35] There was almost no discussion of the value or relative merit in preserving a 'wilderness' area. Development of a national park fitted easily and comfortably into the basic framework of the Conservatives' National Policy. In a period of economic depression and costly railroad construction, here was a resource which, if carefully managed and developed, would be capable of producing substantial revenues for the government, the CPR, and the Canadian people. As the Prime Minister put it, 'the government thought it was of the greatest importance that all this section of the country should be brought at once into usefulness.'[36] Wilderness alone was not useful, but the 260 square miles encompassing mineral hot springs could be 'made useful' to the Dominion in a highly commercial way. Clauses of the Rocky Mountains Parks bill provided that, far from the park being preserved in a 'virgin state,' the working of mines and development of mining interests within the park were allowed to continue, as was the pasturing of cattle and leasing of hay lands. Even timbering was not ruled out under the park regulations.[37] Only one MP – Samuel Burdett, the Liberal representative for Hastings – noted that Yellowstone National Park had been created an absolute reserve in the United States and asked the government if it now proposed to 'turn our park into a coal-mining corporation, or a lumbering corporation, or a hotel-keeping corporation.'[38] But the issue was scarcely discussed. Obviously, as revealed in the original order-in-council, the Commons debates, and the Rocky Mountains Park Act itself, park policy was commercial exploitation under the guise of 'usefulness' and 'utility.'

Although the Rocky Mountains Park Act contained protective regulations for wildlife, these were clearly subordinate to the Act's main purpose of promoting tourism. Clause 4f of the bill provided for the 'preservation and protection of game and fish [and] wild birds generally,' but the provision sparked little interest or debate in the House. Only Burdett raised the question of wildlife protection. Under Banff's

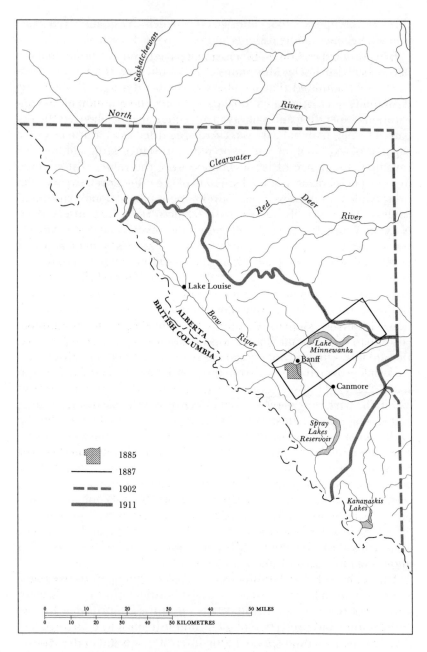

Rocky Mountains National Park (Banff) boundary changes

regulations, he noted, resource development was to be permitted. 'Allow coal miners and hunters and lumberers to frequent and work it,' he warned, 'and it ceases to be a national park and they would certainly destroy the game, and the fish, and the scenery, and all the beauties we have heard so much about.'[39] But few members from either side seriously debated, or fully understood, the contradiction between the park's general purpose and the specific clauses relating to wildlife protection. It was a tourist resort, not a wildlife sanctuary, that was being created in 1887.

Lack of concern for wildlife protection was also evident when the bill reached the Senate. Again, only one member seemed to understand the incompatibility between the park's purpose and the wildlife regulations. Senator Lawrence Power declared that 'the proposition to issue licenses for the pasturage of cattle and for hay lands is inconsistent with the main feature of the park – the preservation of specimens of wild animals indigenous to that portion of the country. Were we to have all these industries going on and cattle ranches in operation, it is quite impossible that we should be able to preserve, as we ought to, the wild animals of that region.'[40] But few Senate colleagues shared Power's concern. 'Surely,' Senator Robert Dickey exclaimed, 'the honourable gentleman does not propose that those treasures [resources] shall be locked up for all time to come merely because they happen to be within the limits of the park ... What more beautiful sight could there be in the recesses of the Rocky Mountains, on the East slope, where the warm Chinook winds and rich soil produce grasses that are succulent all year round – than an immense ranch of fine breeds of cattle.'[41]

On 23 June 1887, the Rocky Mountains Park Act passed both Houses of Parliament and Canada's first 'Dominion Park' came into being.[42] There were noticeable similarities and differences between it and the statute covering the United States's Yellowstone National Park. Both parks were set aside as public parks or pleasure grounds for 'the benefit and enjoyment of the people.' Their regulations covering development of the mineral springs, the erection of bath houses, and the granting of leases for public buildings were similar, but the commercial implications underlying the Banff reservation were far more pronounced than their American counterparts. Yellowstone, in 1872, was a virtual wilderness, far from towns or railways. The park owed its establishment not only to the existence of hot springs but also to the desire of a number of Americans to preserve that wilderness as wilderness.[43] Resource development in Yellowstone was prohibited; in Rocky Mountains Park, it was not only permitted, but actively encouraged.

Far from 'preservation,' the Canadian government's emphasis was on development, exploitation, and usefulness, the continuing program of the National Policy.

In spite of similarities between the Canadian and American park regulations, there was one surprising difference with regard to wildlife protection. Although the Canadian government did not entertain the notion of creating a wildlife preserve in 1887, the very wording of the Act went a long way towards establishing, in theory at least, the principle of wildlife protection. The Yellowstone regulations had prohibited only the 'wanton destruction' of wildlife, but, for some unknown reason, Canada's regulations included the clause referred to earlier, which provided for the 'protection and preservation of game, fish [and] wild birds generally.'[44] Granted, there were no enforcement clauses in the Act to support the protective regulations and no money allowed for a game guardian service or warden patrols; few would have recognized the need to protect wildlife anyway. But for George Stewart, the Dominion Lands Surveyor who became the park's first Superintendent in 1886, the fortuitous phrasing of the Act provided the basic framework on which to build a program of wildlife protection.

The Rocky Mountains Park Superintendent's annual reports to the Minister of the Interior in the early years after the park's establishment were devoted to detailed accounts of progress being made in park 'improvements.' Construction of roads, buildings, bath houses, and the leasing of town lots were all reported and commented on with painstaking thoroughness, while the CPR's hotel, already under construction in 1888, was heralded as 'an ornament to the park and a credit to the enterprising proprietors.'[45] Weather statistics and annual temperature readings were faithfully recorded and used as further inducements to vacationers. Much to Stewart's satisfaction, visitor numbers rose steadily as the reputation of Banff grew. The tourist class from Europe and Britain was increasing, and 'it is gratifying to find,' the Deputy Minister wrote, 'that the efforts of the Government of Canada to establish a health and pleasure resort in the heart of the Rocky Mountains amid scenery the grandeur and variety of which are not equalled anywhere on this continent, have been so warmly appreciated and so largely taken advantage of.'[46] Just one year after the park's establishment, visitors numbered 5822 and revenues from the bath houses totalled $976.20.[47] There was little doubt that by the end of the 1880s the park was fulfilling its original commercial function. Visitors were increasing and revenues were recouping the Treasury, as Macdonald had promised.

The government took steps to deal with the question of wildlife soon after the park was established. In 1886, W.F. Whitcher, a former Dominion Fisheries Commissioner, was sent out to report on the native fauna in the park and make recommendations for its management. Whitcher's report illustrated the basic assumptions that had characterized discussions surrounding establishment of the park; that wildlife, like the park, was a natural resource capable of profitable utilization. But his report also demonstrated the government's lack of knowledge and unfamiliarity in dealing with the whole question of managing and protecting wildlife on a Dominion reservation.

After conducting a limited survey of the park, Whitcher lost no time in reporting on the rapid decline of wildlife in the mountain regions. Where game had been plentiful, it was now scarce. 'Skin hunters, dynamiters, and netters, with Indians, wolves, and foxes have committed sad havoc,' he lamented, while the rapid development taking place within the park would 'further add elements of destruction.'[48] Wildlife species were 'part and parcel of ornaments interesting to visitors on every public reservation,' but Whitcher believed many species would not last much longer without vigorous protection.[49] Mountain sheep, goats, deer, and pronghorn antelope were annually slaughtered by Indians and hunters, he reported, and their protection would have to be carried out by park authorities. Such a program would necessitate hiring game wardens for the park and Whitcher recommended that police officers and forest rangers 'qualified by mountain experience and familiarity with animals' habits and haunts' be stationed permanently at Banff to 'secure the park against injury and destruction' and to enforce the park's protective regulations.[50] He also recommended that hunting in the park be restricted to certain 'open seasons' and then only for the purpose of 'immediate sport and domestic use.' Licences could be dispensed to bona fide hunters with prosecutions and heavy penalties levied against those hunting illegally.

It is surprising that Whitcher condoned hunting in the park at all. The Act's regulations did not specifically prohibit it, but obviously, Whitcher believed hunting could, and would, be continued. He had proposed as much to Stewart the previous fall when the boundaries of the new park were under discussion. Besides, there was good reason, in his opinion, to permit hunting:

I think it inadvisable to deny rational freedom in this particular within the boundaries of the Canadian reservation. Because it is quite controllable and it will remove every appearance of exclusive preservation from the protective measures to be rigidly enforced. It should thereby ensure public sympathy as a moral and material support to those officers charged with the duties of supervision and guardianship. [51]

To Whitcher's way of thinking, more people would be persuaded to accept the principle of wildlife protection in the park if they were allowed to hunt in special seasons and under controlled circumstances. Hunting could thus be made compatible with 'protection and preservation.'

Whitcher's report and recommendations are interesting, not for the knowledge of park wildlife they impart, but for the insight they give into contemporary attitudes towards wildlife. To ensure preservation of endangered species, he advised park authorities to 'balance nature' by weeding out certain animals considered by him to be useless, noxious, dangerous, or ferocious: the 'lupine, vulpine, feline, vermin that prey on furred and feathered game with a savage impartiality.' The list of candidates for extermination was a long one and, by today's standards, reads rather like the 'Who's Who' of predators. Heading it were wolves, coyotes, foxes, lynx, skunks, weasels, wild cats, porcupines, and badgers. Also included were eagles, falcons, owls, hawks, loons, mergansers, kingfishers, cormorants, and 'other inferior rapaces' (vultures, pelicans, buzzards, ravens, and crows were exempted on the grounds that they were 'useful as scavengers').[52] Fortunately for the park's wildlife inhabitants, few of Whitcher's recommendations were acted upon by park authorities. Far from authorizing open hunting seasons, an order-in-council in 1890 prohibited all killing in the park (although exceptions were made for mountain lions, bears, wolves, wolverine, lynx, and hawks, which could be killed under special authority of the Superintendent if they proved troublesome).

Whitcher believed that wildlife, like the park itself, was capable of being managed and 'improved.' The unnecessary species could be removed, protection for the 'good' animals through elimination of the 'bad.' There is the unmistakable impression drawn from his report that he regarded wildlife either as something to be hunted by sportsmen or as 'useful ornaments' to be enjoyed by park visitors. 'Plenteousness of wildlife,' he wrote at the conclusion of his report, 'would be a source of profit and pleasure to Canadians interested in its [the park's] development as a free popular resort for health and recreation ...':

There are recreative and attractive features about the prevalence of edible game in every new country that become in fact of the highest and most profitable utility, and which the progress of settlement and growth of trade serve greatly to enhance.[53]

The fact that Whitcher recognized that wildlife species were declining in the west and acknowledged the need for some kind of wildlife protection is significant. That the need and recommendations were justified in terms of profit, utility, and commercial potential is more a reflection of Whitcher's time than of Whitcher himself.

Protection of the park's wildlife was the responsibility of the Superintendent, George Stewart, but during the early years nearly all his reports dealt more with the development of the park as a credible tourist resort than with its establishment as a wildlife preserve. This was hardly surprising. Creation of the park had been a new and costly adventure for the government and it would have to be shown that the park was capable of paying for itself many times over to justify increasing expenditures. Stewart's first responsibility was to develop the park as a revenue-producing public playground.

Limited funds, and limited staff, necessarily confined Stewart's sphere of activity and interest to the immediate Banff townsite area. To encourage wildfowl, he ordered wild rice from Ontario planted in ponds and lakes around Banff. He also realized that something would have to be done to make the reservation more attractive to sportsmen, deprived as they now were of hunting privileges within the park. The lakes and streams were well adapted to fish propagation and Stewart recommended that a fish hatchery be constructed at Banff; the prospect of good fishing would help compensate sportsmen who 'were disappointed with the existence of the park.'[54] But Ottawa wasn't ready to embark on such a grandiose scheme as a fish hatchery, and Stewart's recommendations fell on deaf ears. With expenses for the first six years totalling $141,254, many MPs no doubt were sceptical of any proposal involving further expenditures on Rocky Mountains Park.[55]

An early proposal came from Alexander Begg to build a zoological display at Banff, a fenced enclosure where varieties of game could be put on public view. Begg also thought a herd of wild buffalo, 'now extinct in Canada,' would be an attractive and valuable addition to the park.[56] A similar proposal for a territorial museum came from Edgar Dewdney, Lieutenant-Governor of the Northwest Territories. Such a museum could exhibit territorial products and wildlife species native to the region. And, of course, Dewdney added, 'with mining information also given from here [the museum], an impetus would be given towards development of our quartz mining ...'[57] Later, the government did provide funds for construction of a territorial museum, but this was the only major innovation bearing directly on wildlife that was undertaken during Stewart's eleven-year tenure as Park Superintendent.

The Park Superintendent had little time or opportunity to become acquainted with the park's wildlife inhabitants. There were few roads or trails leading through the vast interior of the park. Although Stewart sympathized with the protective aspects of park regulations and made a concerted effort to uphold the preservationist principle, his job was made more difficult by the sheer size of the park. Its ill-defined boundaries encouraged poachers. Bands of Stoney Indians camped just beyond the park limits were the subject of most complaints and Stewart advised in his first report that Indians be excluded permanently from the park.[58] Banff was also a major outfitting centre and the CPR actively organized hunting parties into regions beyond the park boundaries. With large numbers of hunters crossing the interior of the park and no enforcement officers to uphold the protective regulations, there were numerous violations. The absence of warden patrols and lack of government money to inaugurate such a protective service further hampered the Superintendent's efforts at wildlife protection.

Stewart was sufficiently convinced of the park's popularity and commercial success by 1894 that he urged an extension of park boundaries further up the Bow River Valley. 'The time has therefore arrived,' he wrote, 'when an additional tract should be included in the bounds of Rocky Mountains Park, particularly when this tract contains scenery and other attractions not excelled in any other part of the American continent.'[59] He argued for a park expansion in terms of greater wildlife protection; an extension would create a much larger game preserve to be controlled by park authorities. This was a surprising recommendation in view of the fact that Stewart had great difficulty enforcing protective regulations on the park reserve as it was then constituted. He cited Ontario and Quebec as two provinces possessing larger game preserves than the Dominion's, and the fact that Ontario had established Algonquin Provincial Park the previous year was not lost on the Superintendent of Rocky Mountains. But it was a bad time to ask for a park expansion. Although visitors were still coming to the park during the depression years of the 1890s, their numbers were down. The government was not prepared to undertake the management and expense of an even larger park reserve at this time and all Stewart's urgings came to nought.

Three years after he had proposed an extension of the park, Stewart was dismissed as Park Superintendent. The Department announced officially that complaints had been received in Ottawa regarding his administration, but there is reason to suspect that political patronage rendered him a casualty of the 1896 federal election, which brought the Liberals to power.[60] During his tenure, the commercial potential of Rocky Mountains Park was ensured even if revenues did not equal expenses in 1897. But neither the park staff nor the government knew much more about the park's wildlife than was contained in Whitcher's 1886 report. The protective clauses of the Rocky Mountains Park Act relating to wildlife were recognized and it was understood that enforcement of the regulations would have to be carried out vigorously if game was to be protected on the reserve. But there were no funds made available to inaugurate a warden patrol service or to hire game guardians, as Whitcher had recommended. Greater understanding of wildlife and increased measures for its protection would have to wait until the country, and the government, came upon more prosperous times.*

Concern for wildlife protection had not taken a prominent place in the establishment of Rocky Mountains Park, nor did it play a large role in the government's concern for natural resource conservation which developed during the early years of the twentieth century. While the need for forest, mineral, soil, and water conservation was clearly recognized, the government showed little understanding or appreciation of the plight of birds and mammals. Both Canada and the United States had undergone many changes by the beginning of the twentieth century. Western expansion, railway construction, the spread of settlement and agriculture, and the growth of urbanization and industrialization had all changed the land. The change was far more apparent in the United States than in Canada and it was there that the movement for natural resource conservation began.

* Two other Dominion parks were established by the end of the nineteenth century. Yoho, an area of ten square miles in the vicinity of Mt Stephen, and Glacier, ten square miles at the summit of Roger's Pass, were reserved through an order-in-council in 1886. Both parks were set aside to 'preserve the timber and natural beauty of the district,' but their creation also followed White's advice to Macdonald in 1885 to make the BC and mountain sections of the CPR 'as popular as possible.' Both parks were later extended in size, Yoho to 828 square miles in 1901, and Glacier to 700 square miles in 1903.

As early as the 1870s, concerned American foresters began to speak out against the unbridled exploitation and waste that had characterized the 'Manifest Destiny' years of American expansion. The rich western forests suffered most at the hands of timber merchants and lumber barons who, operating on a 'get rich quick' philosophy, stripped the forests bare.[61] The consequences of such reckless destruction were immediate and far-reaching: rivers, lakes, and streams flooded and silted up without the forest's protective mantle, hillsides eroded, and each year valuable topsoil washed away in spring runoff. Settlers, careless railway work parties, and hissing sparks from railway locomotives were responsible for countless fires which destroyed many hundreds of square miles of forests.

Lumbermen and foresters launched a campaign to save forest wealth and formed the American Forestry Association in 1875. Association members recognized the need for government regulation and control of the forest industry. They urged that forests be reserved, areas of land set aside by government with entry and use prohibited. Such a policy of forest reservation was inaugurated by the Harrison administration in the 1880s, and in 1891 President Cleveland signed the General Revision Act, which allowed the President to set aside forest reserves for water supply and public park purposes.[62] But it was not until the end of the century, when a trained forester came forward with new theories of better land use and efficient forest management, that a true conservation movement began in the United States.

Gifford Pinchot was the first American forester to train specifically in 'forest management.' Educated in Europe, where theories of scientific forest management were well advanced in the nineteenth century, Pinchot returned to the United States and was appointed Chief Forester with the Department of Agriculture in 1898. He soon disagreed sharply with the established government policy of forest reservations. Forests, he argued, should be used, not reserved. Under programs of tree planting, selective cutting, and reforestation, Pinchot demonstrated that trees could be harvested efficiently and regularly like any other agricultural crop on a sustained yield basis; forests could be protected but still used to their full capacity.[63] Two years later, a Bureau of Forestry was established in the Department of the Interior and Pinchot was appointed Bureau Chief. Thus began a new era of scientific forestry techniques in the United States.

Pinchot was not a preservationist. Forests were of no value to him unless they could be effectively and economically used; he cared little for the aesthetic aspects of nature. Trees themselves were not important, only the good use they could be put to. Nor was he moved by considerations for wildlife or the recreational aspects of national parks. 'He always had a blind spot to wildlife and wilderness values,' writes Stewart Udall; 'to him, untrammelled wilderness was a waste.'[64] Pinchot's approach to forest reservations, and the conservation of all natural resources, was businesslike and strictly utilitarian:

The principles which govern the conservation movement, like all great and effective things, are simple and easily understood ... The first principle of conservation is development, the use of the natural resources now existing on this continent for the benefit of the people who live here now. There may be just as much waste in neglecting the development and use of certain natural resources as there is in their destruction. [65]

Pinchot's utilitarian views were challenged by another strain of conservationist thought in the late nineteenth century, that of the 'preservationists,' led by writer-naturalist, John Muir. Muir's approach to wilderness and parkland concepts was purely aesthetic, his beliefs well grounded in the transcendentalist philosophy of Emerson and Thoreau. Love of nature – nature untouched, unused, and unspoiled – was a form of religious worship for Muir and the preservationists and they looked far beyond the purely commercial value of trees. For Muir, wilderness was the natural home of all Americans, the fountain of spiritual and moral rejuvenation where the tensions and pressures of civilized life, 'the stupefying effects of the vice of over-industry and the deadly apathy of luxury,' could all be soothed and washed away amid the beauty of a more natural world to which every man belonged. 'Everybody,' he wrote, 'needs beauty as well as bread, places to play in and pray in, where Nature may heal and cheer and give strength to body and soul.'[66] By the end of the century, Muir had become the champion, defender, and publicist for wilderness, and he organized his band of followers into the powerful Sierra Club, an organization that spearheaded the drive for more national parks and more wilderness reservations. For the next two decades, the conservation issue in the United States was dominated and characterized by the controversy between 'non-use' preservationists and 'wise-use' conservationists.[67]

The conservation and preservation movements brought home to many Americans a realization of the waste and destruction of their natural resources that had already occurred. By the early 1900s, Americans were ready to be concerned about their environment, about changes wrought by urbanization and industrialization, and about the loss of abundant resources on a frontier they were now told was gone. They were receptive to new conservation principles of utility, efficiency, and scientific resource management. When Theodore Roosevelt became President in 1901, Pinchot found a strong supporter of his theories of forest management and conservation. Together, he and Roosevelt launched a conservation movement that became a major plank in the Republican administration and one of the central issues of the 'Progressive Era.'[68]

Canadians were not immune to developments south of the border; both Pinchot and Muir had a profound effect on Howard Douglas and James Harkin, Canada's Dominion Parks commissioners. The Canadian government had acted as host for the American Forestry Congress at Montreal in 1882 and was familiar with forestry issues and problems that were under discussion. Canada had suffered similar waste, inefficiency, and destructive logging methods and government members were well aware of the importance of forest protection, particularly in the light of numerous forest fires caused by railroad construction. Two years after the American Forestry Congress, the first Forestry Commissioner in Canada was appointed in the Department of the Interior to study new techniques of tree planting and forest protection.[69] The government also adopted a forest reserve policy similar to the American, and throughout the 1890s numerous forest reserves were set aside by departmental order of the Minister of the Interior. A special Forestry Branch was created by the Department in 1899 and a year later the Canadian Forestry Association was formed. In 1906, the Association held the first Canadian Forestry Convention in Ottawa.

The issues and ideas discussed at that convention stimulated new interest in Canada's natural resources and helped influence the direction taken by the conservation movement. In his opening address, Prime Minister Wilfrid Laurier, President of the Convention, deplored the great harm done to Canada's forest wealth, particularly by railways:

If you take the train at Halifax and go to Vancouver, in every province of the Dominion where there is timber, in Nova Scotia, in New Brunswick, in Quebec, in Ontario, in British Columbia, you will see miles and miles of what was once beautiful forest and which is now nothing but parched and blackened timber, a monument to the destructive power of the railway locomotive.[70]

Laurier spoke of the need to establish a 'large forest domain' under government control, of the need to protect forests and to understand better their relationship to water supply, and of the need for greater public awareness of the hazard and destructiveness of forest fires. He referred to France and Germany, where methods of tree planting and reforestation were well advanced, and urged the adoption of better forestry techniques for Canada. 'It is not fair to the country,' he said, 'it is not fair to us who are living and still less is it fair to the generations who come after us that we should allow the destruction of the forests to go on year after year by cutting down of the trees and make no effort whatever to replace what is thus taken away. The trees are a crop like any other growth.'[71]

It is not surprising that Gifford Pinchot was the honoured guest at the 1906 convention, for both the American and Canadian governments were following the 'wise use' concepts of the Chief Forester. Pinchot spoke of the 'timber famine' facing the United States and stressed the need for better resource policies in both countries. He reiterated the importance of forest conservation, concluding that 'forestry with us is a business proposition':

I have no interest in a forest that is not of use. If our forests are to stand unused there, if all we get out of them is the knowledge that we have them, then, so far as I am concerned, they disappear from my field of interest. I care nothing about them whatever. But use is the end of forest preservation, and the highest use.[72]

The holding of the Forestry Convention in 1906 stimulated new interest in forest conservation at the public, academic, professional, and governmental levels. Most of its recommendations were implemented by the dominion and provincial governments, including a Forest Reserves Act, passed by Parliament that same year. Frank Oliver, the new Minister of the Interior in Laurier's government, explained that the bill was designed to maintain a permanent supply of timber and to conserve water resources through protection of forests. When Conservative Frederick Monk asked if the bill was modelled on any American legislation, Laurier cited instead the resolution passed by the Forestry Convention recommending such a forest reserve policy.[73] Schools of forestry were subsequently established in the University of Toronto (1907) and the University of New Brunswick (1909), and several provincial governments created forest services. Concern for timber protection and water supply, and the development of new forest conservation techniques and principles followed the broad outlines of the American conservation movement. But what Canada lacked in 1906 was the preservationist side of the American movement. There was as yet no Canadian John Muir to argue for the preservation of natural beauty or to plead the moral necessity of creating forest reserves and national parks for the benefit of future generations.

The movement for the 'wise use' of natural resources was well under way. Two years after the Forestry Convention, President Roosevelt wrote to Laurier inviting Canadian representatives to attend a National Conservation Conference in Washington on 18 February 1909. The Americans had held two conservation conferences already, a Conference of Governors that conferred with the President the previous May on conservation issues, and a National Conservation Commission that was organized to compile inventories of American natural resources.[74] Roosevelt told Laurier that it was evident that resources were not limited by national boundaries and that the need for conserving them 'is as wide as the area upon which they exist.'[75] The purpose of the conference was to consider areas of mutual concern and the invitation, taken to Ottawa personally by Pinchot, was readily accepted.[76] Conservation was a matter of growing importance to the government and Laurier replied to the President that 'this is a subject as to which the two countries are equally interested.'[77] Three delegates were assigned to represent Canada in Washington: Sydney Fisher, Minister of Agriculture; Clifford Sifton, MP for Brandon, Manitoba, and former Minister of the Interior in Laurier's Cabinet; and Henri Béland, MP for Beauce, Quebec.[78]

The Conservation Conference agreed on a list of resource priorities, drawn up as a formal Declaration of Principles:

1 GENERAL; *resources were to be developed, used and conserved for the future, in the interest of mankind.*

2 PUBLIC HEALTH; *various jurisdictions should legislate against water pollution.*

3 FORESTS; *forest reservations should be established; there should be full-scale forest inventories; facilities for professional and technical education as well as for practical instruction should be expanded. The following measures should be encouraged; afforestation, reforestation, protection of forested land at the headwaters of streams, public ownership of forested land, protection of land better suited for forest growth than for other purposes, reforestation of private land, increase in fire protection services, strict regulation of cutting.*

4 WATERS; *the multiple use of streams and water sources should be studied; domestic and municipal use should be given top priority; navigation on the*

inland water ways should be developed under public control; there should be no more water power monopolies in perpetuity and the licensing of water power rights should be strictly regulated.

5 LANDS; *measures should be taken to ensure productivity and prevent monopoly. Scientific information on the preservation of soil productivity should be widely distributed. There should be legislation to provide public control over non-irrigable arid lands, to restore their value etc. Works should be constructed for the prevention of soil erosion.*

6 MINERALS; *fuel wastage to be avoided; the use of water power in lieu of exhaustible fuels should be promoted; surface rights and under rights should be distinctly separated. There should be research into technological improvements to eliminate waste. Public control should be established over mineral fertilizers.*

7 GAME; *there should be legislation to ensure game preservation and the protection of bird life.*

8 COMMISSIONS OF CONSERVATION; *each participating country should have commissions of conservation, similar to those set up in the United States.*

9 WORLD CONFERENCE; *a similar conference on a world-wide scale should be held under the sponsorship of the President of the United States.*[79]

The Declaration was not a treaty between governments or countries taking part in the conference; nor did it commit any one country to follow a particular line of action. It was merely a framework of suggestions that governments could follow to attain more efficient measures of natural resource conservation on the North American continent. As Robert Young, secretary for the three Canadian delegates, told Sifton: 'While the Federal Government took part in this conference there is no thought or idea of any infringement or interference with the rights of the provinces within the Dominion. The Declaration fully recognizes provincial, state, and national authorities.'[80] But he added that it was hoped the principles embodied in the Declaration would be commended to all government authorities engaged in natural resource administration.

The recommendation that each country establish a Commission of Conservation was not new to the Canadian delegates. Two and a half weeks before the Washington conference, Opposition leader Robert Borden had proposed creation of a Natural Resources Committee in the House of Commons. Borden believed that Parliament had not taken enough initiative in the conservation movement but had allowed outside influences, notably American, to focus public interest and attention. He applauded the achievements of the 1906 Forestry Convention and the work of the Forestry Branch in the Department of the Interior, but felt it was time Parliament took a more active role. Too much government work was being taken over by Cabinet members, he said, and, as the power of Cabinet increased, the 'influence of Parliament declines.' Borden believed that by establishing a committee to look into natural resources and 'earnestly striving to do some work of value in the public interest,' much of the influence lost by Parliament, 'Parliament as a Parliament and not as a partisan Parliament,' could be restored.[81] Borden noted there was already a parliamentary committee on agriculture engaged in non-partisan work. While he recognized that agriculture was the principal basis on which Canada's future wealth depended, he cautioned members not to be blind to the fact there were other resources – mines, fisheries, forests, minerals, waterways, and waterpower – whose development and conservation were of equal importance to the Canadian people. In many cases, the extent of these resources was not even known. Borden suggested a committee be established by Parliament, with various sub-committees, to determine the nature of Canada's natural resources and to advance measures for their development and conservation. Because this was a matter of public importance, Borden stressed to members that the committee should be totally non-partisan: 'Some initiative should come from Parliament, and the members of this Parliament, without regard to party, sinking for this purpose all partisan considerations, should take up this work and endeavour to accomplish something for the good of the country.'[82]

Three months after the Washington Conference, Parliament established the Commission of Conservation as a direct result of the recommendation made in Section 8 of the Declaration of Principles. Sydney Fisher, who introduced the bill, stated that its purpose was to create a permanent body to investigate Canada's natural resources and to submit recommendations for their development and conservation. Reminding members of the resolutions passed at the Washington Conference, he admitted that 'the government had judged that it is wise' to accept their recommendations.[83] There was little argument in the House over the need for natural resource conservation. Even Opposition member Frederick Monk declared that Fisher was 'carrying coals to Newcastle and preaching to the converted' on the issue. While acknowledging the great 'impetus' given to the conservation movement by President Roosevelt, Monk stated that he was sorry Canada had not been the first country to set an example in regard to natural resource preservation.[84]

The structure and non-partisan composition of the Commission was briefly outlined by the Minister. It was to be composed of representatives of both levels of government with federal and provincial governments granted the statutory right to membership. The ministers of the Interior, Agriculture, and Mines and the members of each provincial government charged with natural resource administration were declared ex-officio members.[85] There were sound, practical reasons for including provincial delegates. Except in the prairie provinces, natural resources came under provincial jurisdiction as defined by the British North America Act. Any attempt on the part of the Dominion to conserve natural resources in Canada would ultimately depend on provincial agreement, support, and co-operation. Twenty commissioners were to be appointed to the Commission by the Governor-General-in-Council and were to include at least one professor from each province in which there was a university.[86] This was designed to bring to Commission deliberations a high level of scholarship, scientific knowledge, and practical administrative experience and skill.[87] The Governor-General-in-Council would also appoint one of the Commission members as Chairman. In this instance, Clifford Sifton was chosen, which was to prove an excellent choice. Sifton was a practical businessman, a former Minister of the Interior with a knowledge of resources, and had been one of Canada's representatives to the Washington Conference. He was also a figure likely to command respect from members on both sides of the House.

Creation of the Commission was not costly, in spite of Opposition charges made during debate on the bill.[88] Appropriations were to come from Parliament each year but were to cover only members' travelling expenses to and from the annual meetings. No permanent staff members could be hired by the Commission and members themselves were not permitted to take salaries or fees. Assistants and special consultants could be hired for specific projects but their costs would come out of the general appropriations voted by Parliament, which, for the first year of operation, was set at $22,000 – $10,000 for members' expenses and $12,000 for maintenance of a small office staff.[89]

Although Opposition members raised a few arguments over the cost of the Commission to the Dominion, the possible duplication of government work, and the potential conflicts with provincial authorities, there was no serious opposition to creation of the advisory body. Laurier defended the bill by explaining that Canada and the United States had realized only within the previous few years that much of the resource wealth on the continent had been lost through 'not paying more attention to the laws of nature.' In that respect, he said, the conservation of natural resources 'is altogether a new idea.'[90] On 12 May 1909, the bill to establish the Commission of Conservation passed third reading. The advisory body that was created closely followed the principles that were laid out in the Washington Declaration but it was also given the non-partisan qualities that Robert Borden had recommended to Parliament three months earlier.

The Commission was unique, intended to be an independent, autonomous, objective, and fully non-partisan body that would explore all questions pertaining to natural resource conservation in Canada. To ensure its non-partisan nature, the Commission was established not as part of usual government machinery for which the party in power is politically responsible, but as a body responsible only to Parliament as a whole. It would report to the House from time to time through the Minister of Agriculture, but was not responsible to him, nor to any other minister or government department. The Commission was to be totally independent of the normal administration of government affairs.[91] This independence was designed to guarantee the non-partisan objectivity of Commission investigations and recommendations. Few MPs in 1909 appeared to grasp the implications of the independent body they were creating. The issue of responsibility did not come up during the debate, but by 1913 Martin Burrell, the Minister of Agriculture, was compelled to admit in the House that when he took office, he learned that he was to have something to do with the Commission but 'I found that it was not a department or a branch in any department, but that the Minister of Agriculture was made an intermediary between the Conservation Commission and Parliament in Council ... So far as I am concerned, I have no control over it.'[92]

The Commission was given no executive or administrative powers; its function was purely advisory, its duty to collect and disseminate information on natural resources and make recommendations to Parliament for their more efficient development and conservation. As Sifton told members gathered for the first annual meeting in 1910: 'We can only study, investigate, advise. The governments concerned must take the responsibility of accepting or rejecting what we recommend.'[93] But the Commission's mandate was broad. It could undertake any investigation, in or out of Canada, and report on any matter considered by its members to be related to conservation.[94] This mandate gave the Commission an independence and freedom of action that was to arouse increasing government jealousy and hostility.

Commission members were divided into small committees along the lines of those suggested in the Washington Declaration of Principles: Public Health, Forests, Waters, Lands, Minerals, and Game. Each committee was to compile accurate inventories of the resources for which it was responsible. As Sifton explained: 'The beginning of all proper investigations is the ascertainment of the facts, and there is no country that I know of where it is more urgently necessary in the public interest that the natural resources be tabulated and inventoried than it is in Canada.'[95] Sifton told the Commission he had heard the view expressed frequently that what Canada needed was not conservation but exploitation and development. He argued that this view was founded on a misconception that the Commission would have to overcome. 'If we stand in the way of development, our efforts will assuredly be of no avail either to stop development or promote conservation. It will not however, be hard to show that the best and most highly economic development and exploitation in the interests of the people can only take place by having regard to the principles of conservation.'[96]

Sifton's views were close to those of Gifford Pinchot regarding conservation, embracing 'wise use' concepts of development and exploitation. 'Conservation,' he told the Canadian Club in 1910, 'means the utilization of our resources in a proper and economical way' for the benefit and advantage of the Canadian people.[97] As Minister of the Interior from 1896 until 1905 and chief architect of western immigration and settlement policies, Sifton was fully aware of the importance of natural resources for Canada. He recognized the demands for development, but he also understood the necessity for conservation. 'Our resources are not illimitable. No matter how great the natural resources of any country may be, when a large and active population sets itself to develop them it very soon becomes evident that they are far from being illimitable.'[98] He was convinced that the Commission of Conservation could exert 'powerful influence' in leading the country towards a better utilization of its natural wealth. The Commission could 'strengthen the hands of all who are desirous of following progressive policies':

It can help render the labour of investigations in the various branches of scientific thought available for the service of the country. It can be the vehicle by which enlightened and educated men can bring an influence directly to bear on the administration of affairs. In a word, it can, if it will, be the embodiment of public spirit and advanced thought.[99]

During these years of awakening concern for natural resource con-servation, the question of wildlife protection was seldom raised. The subject was not discussed during the 1906 Forestry Convention; cer-tainly no one suggested establishing forest reserves for the protection of game, and there was little understanding of the importance of forest habitat for various wildlife species. The Forest Reserves Act, passed that same year, contained the provision that reserves were 'to protect, as far as the Parliament of Canada had jurisdiction, the animals, fish, and birds within the boundaries of such reserves,' but more likely the intent of this protective clause was to safeguard the forests by prohibiting entry to sportsmen and hunters (who might cause fires) than to pre-serve the indigenous wildlife. Although the Conservation Commission included a Committee on Fish, Game, and Fur-Bearing Animals, the emphasis was on the commercial fisheries aspects of Committee inves-tigations and reports. Indeed, during the first two annual meetings Sifton consistently referred to the committee as the 'Fisheries Commit-tee' and it was clear where the Commission's chief interests lay.

Early Commission projects were analyzing fishery resources in Canada, compiling statistics on commercial fishing, preparing useful summaries of dominion/provincial laws and regulations governing fisheries, and investigating the state of Maritime oyster and lobster industries.[100] A paper on 'Fur Bearing Animals and How to Prevent their Extinction' was read to the Commission in 1910 by F.T. Congdon, MP for Dawson, Yukon Territory, but the main thrust of his appeal was based on the economic value and importance of fur pelts. The fur trade, like the fisheries, was a major industry in Canada. Investigations were also conducted into fur farming, a new and profitable business in Canada during the early twentieth century.

For the first three years of the Commission's existence, wildlife investigations seldom went beyond economic studies of fish and fur-bearing animals. These resources were commercially valuable to the provinces and the Dominion and most committee recommendations were devoted to advancing measures for their more efficient utiliza-tion. As Sifton stated in 1910, utilization was the end goal of conserva-tion and there was little discussion by Commission members on the need for protection or conservation of those wildlife species whose value was not primarily economic. The preservationist side of the conservation movement had not been born yet in Canada. But the few individuals who were to help develop a concern for wildlife protection within the government, the Conservation Commission, and Canada as a whole, were already on the scene.

ABOVE The main street of Banff, Alberta, 1888. *Canadian Pacific Railway*

BELOW Banff Railway Station during the late 1880s. *Parks Canada*

ABOVE Log building used as an office by Howard Douglas when he became Superintendent of Rocky Mountains Park (Banff) in 1897. The photograph was taken in 1937, but the building is no longer standing. *Parks Canada*

BELOW The hot springs pool, Banff, 1880s. *Public Archives of Canada*

ABOVE The customary mode of transportation across the Canadian west in the days before the railway. *Public Archives of Canada*

BELOW 'Windy,' the oldest warden cabin in Rocky Mountains Park, was built in 1911. *Archives of the Canadian Rockies, Banff, Alberta*

Plains bison, Manitoba. *John Foster*

OPPOSITE TOP By the early 1880s, Canada's buffalo herds were gone from the western plains. Only scattered bones marked the tragic end of a once superabundant resource. *Archives, Royal Canadian Mounted Police*

OPPOSITE BOTTOM Buffalo bones awaiting their final journey across the prairie. They were used in the manufacture of fertilizer and the refining of sugar. *Public Archives of Canada*

ABOVE Michel Pablo, who sold one of the last wild buffalo herds to Canada in 1906. *New York Zoological Society*

TOP The small band of cowboys hired to help round up the Pablo buffalo herd in 1906. *Public Archives of Canada*

CENTRE The round-up in progress. *Public Archives of Canada*

BOTTOM The arrival of the first 200 American buffalo at Lamont, Alberta. *Public Archives of Canada*

Howard Douglas (second from left), camped in Montana to supervise the round-up and shipment of the buffalo to Canada. *Archives of the Canadian Rockies, Banff, Alberta*

OPPOSITE TOP Loading the animals on to the train at Lamont for shipment to the new buffalo park at Wainwright, Alberta, 1909. *Ontario Archives*

OPPOSITE BOTTOM Unloading the buffalo at Wainwright. *Ontario Archives*

ABOVE LEFT Maxwell Graham, one of Canada's first wildlife preservationists, at Peace Point on the Peace River, 1922. *Courtesy Maxwell Graham's family*

ABOVE RIGHT Maxwell Graham, *left*, near Foremost, Alberta, where he successfully fenced in a small herd of wild pronghorn antelope in 1915. The protected area became Nemiskam National Antelope Park. *Public Archives of Canada*

Pronghorn antelope. *Canadian Wildlife Service*

Edgar McHugh, who deeded a portion of land for creation of
Nemiskam National Antelope Park. *Canadian Wildlife Service*

3
Preservation:
The Beginning of an Idea

Howard Douglas was appointed Superintendent of Rocky Mountains Park in 1897 and was among the first in government to comprehend the role and importance of wildlife in a dominion park. As Superintendent of Canada's first national park, he was in a good strategic position to influence government thinking about wildlife preservation.

There seemed little in Douglas's background to qualify him for the office of Park Superintendent or to foretell his developing interest and concern for Canada's wildlife species. Born in Halton, Ontario, in 1853, he worked on the family farm until he was twenty-one, but his real interests lay in commercial ventures. He ran the general store in Bronte for four years and then opened a coal and wood business in Hamilton. In 1882, he moved to Calgary, where he continued his enterprise for another fifteen years. After George Stewart was dismissed from Rocky Mountains Park in 1897, Douglas either was offered or applied for the position of Park Superintendent.

When Douglas took over as Superintendent a fortuitous set of circumstances coincided with his arrival. The economic depression that had burdened the 1890s was lifting, the park was already a proven commercial success, a new Liberal government was ensconced in Ottawa, and a concern for natural resource conservation was emerging within the Department of the Interior. All of these factors produced a changed climate of opinion and lent material support to Douglas's efforts and innovations.

It did not take him long to realize that visitors came to Rocky Mountains Park not only to enjoy the mineral springs and mountain scenery, but also for the opportunity to see wildlife. In his estimation, animals were becoming the most attractive and interesting feature of the park and he worked to make Rocky Mountains a wildlife display centre as well as a wildlife refuge. An animal paddock was built, similar to the one proposed by Alexander Begg during George Stewart's administration of the park, and four buffalo were donated to it by a Toronto lawyer in 1898.[1] Plains bison were almost extinct in Canada and Douglas soon realized the commercial potential of any surviving animals as a tourist attraction. Sixteen more buffalo were donated to the park by Lord Strathcona in 1899, and by 1906 the total number of buffalo in the animal paddock had increased naturally to fifty-one.[2]

Douglas was convinced that Rocky Mountains Park could become a true wildlife preserve if it was stocked with indigenous wildlife species which, he hoped, would breed and multiply under the park's protective policies. On his recommendation, the park acquired mountain sheep, angora goats, elk, mule deer, and moose by the early 1900s, and the Deputy Minister himself was reportedly endeavouring to obtain reindeer, muskox, and wood buffalo from the Athabasca District.[3] Douglas also engaged the services of William Magrach of Rat Portage, Manitoba, to import caribou and moose from northern Ontario. Unfortunately for Douglas's plans, however, Edwin Tinsley, Ontario's Chief Game Warden, took a dim view of these activities, regarding the export of game a clear violation of Ontario's Game Protection Act (which, no doubt, it was). After only one successful delivery was completed, Tinsley threatened Magrach with legal action, informing him that a full report was being sent to the Department of the Interior with 'such comments as Mr Douglas' conduct deserves.'[4] But this did not dampen the Park Superintendent's enthusiasm for obtaining more wildlife species for Rocky Mountains. He corresponded with the United States Secretary of the Interior to obtain buffalo from Yellowstone National Park and suggested in his 1903 departmental report that the government consider importing European game birds.[5]

The number of wildlife species in the animal paddock at Banff continued to increase dramatically under Douglas's supervision, and proved a constant attraction for park visitors.[6] As Douglas explained in his first annual report, the money brought into Canada each year by visitors more than justified the money spent on developing the park.[7] The Deputy Minister of the Interior frequently commended the success of the animal preserve and noted in 1905 that park revenue more than doubled the amount required for expenditure and maintenance.[8] Douglas had every reason to be pleased with the park's wildlife acquisitions, which he viewed as an asset both to the park and to the country as a whole:

I consider the money spent in looking after and maintaining them, as well as any additional money that may be spent in rendering Banff more attractive as a place of call for the travelling public by procuring other animals that are indigenous to our country and climate ... will prove not only a present but permanent valuable investment, and add to the wealth of the Dominion generally.[9]

Shortly after becoming Park Superintendent, Douglas began to press for an expansion of Rocky Mountains Park. In his first report, he urged such an expansion in the interests of greater game and fish protection. George Stewart had advanced a similar argument for park expansion in 1894, but his recommendations were all but ignored by the Conservative government. Douglas's proposal however, elicited quite a different response from the Liberal administration. Deputy Minister Alexander Burgess informed Clifford Sifton, the new Minister of the Interior, that Douglas's suggestion was 'well worthy of serious consideration' and that the matter was being taken up by the Department. Burgess also added that the proposed extension would require very little expenditure, but would 'help ensure the success of the animal preserve experiment.'[10] Times, indeed, had changed.

There are a number of reasons why the government was prepared to look more favourably on an extension of Rocky Mountains Park in 1897. The depression was over, visitor numbers were increasing, and with park revenues rising to overtake expenditures, Rocky Mountains was justifying its establishment. In 1901, Douglas could report with some pride that the park was 'fulfilling the purpose for which it was set aside.'[11] The park's wildlife preserve policy, or the 'animal preserve experiment' as the Deputy Minister called it, also was proving successful and Douglas took every opportunity in his annual reports to draw the Minister's attention to the increasing wildlife numbers within the park, particularly the buffalo, which were reproducing steadily, and to emphasize their growing importance as a tourist attraction.

Douglas was not the only one to be concerned about wildlife protection in the Rocky Mountains or to recommend an extension of the national park. Since the early 1880s, detachments of the Northwest Mounted Police had been extending their patrols from the southern prairies northward into the forested interior of Alberta and Saskatchewan.[12] Along with their customary reports on the movement and location of wildlife species came warnings and deep misgivings about the true condition of mammal and bird life in the Northwest. Through daily execution of their patrol duties, members of the police force had the opportunity to witness at first hand the decline of wildlife in the Northwest Territories, to crack the myth of superabundance.

Police Commissioner Lawrence Herchmer advised the Minister of the Interior in 1889 that game, contrary to its believed abundance, was rapidly vanishing. Elk had almost disappeared, he wrote, bears were being killed in large numbers, antelope were steadily becoming scarce, and, in the whole of the territory, only six buffalo were known to exist. Herchmer admitted that previous winters had been hard on wildlife, but blamed Indians and whites for contributing to the decline by hunting and trapping out of season.[13] His concern was echoed by his assistant, who reported to the Minister that wild fowl were becoming scarce because Indians and half-breeds robbed the nests of eggs, and market hunters – 'becoming rife in this country' – killed large numbers of birds for shipment east.[14] One year later, Superintendent John McIllree of E Division, Calgary, reported that game continued to decrease in an alarming manner. He understood from his officers that there were few mammal species left in the mountains and that Stoney Indians were destroying the remaining deer in the foothills.[15] In a similar report, the Superintendent of the force's Saskatchewan District put the case for wildlife protection more bluntly:

If something is not done, and done quickly too, to prevent the wholesale destruction of game, a few years must see the end and the half breed and the Indian of the north must lose a source of income and food which has hitherto been his greatest standby, and [for] the thick bush Indian, his very existence.[16]

There were no game regulations covering the unorganized territories of the northwest. Outside of the provisional districts controlled by the Northwest Council, there was no legislation to protect wildlife against depredation by sportsmen, market hunters, and Indians. Police Superintendent McIllree told the Minister of the Interior in 1892 that he had been in the territories for many years and had watched the game closely. He warned that unless very different methods of protection were enacted and enforced at once, game in the Northwest would be a thing of the past. Recognizing the success of Rocky Mountains Park as a wildlife preserve, he urged the Minister to add a large tract of country to the park. 'These animals have found the park a safe retreat,' he wrote, 'they breed here, unmolested, and are a source of interest to the tourist.'[17]

Not since John Palliser's report of 1863 had the case for wildlife protection in the Northwest been stated so clearly and forthrightly. The warnings and recommendations of the NWMP were compiled and sent off to Ottawa each year in the force's annual reports. Finally, they brought action, not in an extension of Rocky Mountains Park, however, but in an Unorganized Territories Game Preservation Act passed by Parliament in 1894.[18] The Act, applied to the district of Keewatin and those territories not included in the provisional districts of Assiniboia, Alberta, or Saskatchewan, went a long way towards correcting the immediate abuses to wildlife. Under the Act's regulations, the killing of buffalo was prohibited for six years, with no exceptions; closed seasons were established for a number of bird and mammal species, and the use of poison by trappers and the taking of wildfowl eggs at any time were also restricted. However, the Act did permit native people, as well as travellers, explorers, and surveyors to take mammals (except buffalo) and bird eggs, a stipulation that must have disappointed many members of the police force.

The main purpose of the Act was to preserve the wildlife food supply of the northern Indian and Innuit peoples. Passage of the Act through Parliament in 1894 did not signify that the government or members of Parliament had developed a sudden concern to protect all of Canada's endangered wildlife species. The protective legislation was designed not to preserve wildlife species for their own sake, but to safeguard an economic resource on which native people depended. As Mackenzie Bowell, a member of the Senate, succinctly put it:

The object of the Act has been to assist the native people who would, in the event of the extermination of the animals, either starve to death or make their way out to the settled parts and become wards of the country.[19]

Administration of the Act was placed under the Department of the Interior, but enforcement of its regulations was entrusted to the members of the NWMP. No branch of government was better informed or better qualified to handle the question of wildlife protection at this time.

The realization that wildlife, contrary to popular belief, was not a superabundant resource in Canada's northland and that there was need for greater protective measures lent strong support to Douglas in his campaign for the expansion of Rocky Mountains Park. The principle and policy of game protection on a park preserve had proved beneficial to many species in the Rocky Mountains and it could be argued that an extension of the park would bring protection to larger numbers of birds and mammals. A member of the NWT Legislative Asssembly, Alfred E. Cross, wrote to Sifton in 1899, declaring that as big game animals were rapidly being exterminated in the Territories, measures should be taken at once to ensure their preservation. Cross's solution was to extend the boundaries of the park and create 'an extent of country large enough for game to breed in and to have a National Park that the Dominion could be proud of.' He added that a large park could easily be maintained as it was already surrounded on three sides by detachments of the NWMP.[20] William Pearce also threw the weight of his influence on the side of the park expansionists. It was his understanding that Stoney and Kootenay Indians were responsible for wildlife destruction in the west, and he believed that if this were allowed to continue it would mean the certain extermination of many big game species. He too proposed an extension of Rocky Mountains' boundaries, but cautioned Sifton that if the reserve took in any portion of the western summit of the Rockies it would necessitate co-operation with British Columbia. But, he added, 'I do not anticipate there would be much trouble on that score, as I think there is a general feeling that it is a laudable object to protect what game we have.'[21]

Douglas was the most persistent in voicing arguments for the park expansion. He took up the issue in each of his annual reports and in a memorandum to Sifton stressed that speed was of the essence, since the Territories would soon be divided up into provinces and 'it would then be difficult to procure land for national park purposes.'[22] He told Sifton the park was too small and that all the other American national and Canadian provincial parks were far larger than Rocky Mountains which, he complained, was less than one-tenth the size of Yellowstone. He argued that if the park were expanded to take in a greater portion of the Rocky Mountains it would not only be a larger wildlife preserve, but also a popular centre for mountain exploration which would bring even more visitors to the park.[23] Creation of a larger park also would bring several small lakes at the headwaters of the Bow River under government control, lakes that were well stocked with fish.[24]

No doubt the government was convinced by the merit of the arguments for expansion and by the proven commercial success of the park. In 1902, Parliament, deeming it 'expedient in the public interest to enlarge the boundaries of the national park,' passed an amendment to the 1887 Rocky Mountains Park Act.[25] The limits of the park were extended from the 250 square miles originally reserved in 1887 to 4900 square miles. In the House of Commons, Sifton justified the park expansion:

I may say that the number of visitors to the Park is increasing very rapidly, and it is found that it is likely to become a place of very considerable resort especially

*for the American tourist. We have a thriving herd of buffalo there and a num-
ber of other animals, such as moose, elk, a couple of varieties of goat, and we are
trying to get together a collection of animals that will be attractive.*[26]

Douglas now found himself in charge of a national park that covered
a huge area of the Rocky Mountains, but a park whose boundaries were
ill defined. Provisions of the Rocky Mountains Park Act had not provided for a warden service and poaching on the reserve was a continual
problem. Douglas acknowledged that game on the eastern slope of the
Rockies, plentiful twenty years before, was now almost gone. He recommended that Stoney Indians be compelled to hunt only on their
reserves but he also recognized that a rigid and thorough system of
game protection was urgently needed.[27] Douglas was unable to prevent
poaching in the more remote regions of the park and advised the
Minister in 1906 that he was arranging for a permanent patrol service
and constructing small cabins throughout the park to serve as warden
headquarters. He further recommended that two game wardens be
appointed to operate in the British Columbia and Alberta sections of
the park and suggested that they could also function as fishery and fire
control officers. 'I have had trouble maintaining the law,' Douglas
admitted in his 1906 report, 'but I have been unrelaxing in my efforts
to preserve the varieties of game which abound in the park.'[28]

Douglas made the protection of wildlife his major concern. He came
to believe that game was the true property of the state and that he had a
duty, as Superintendent, to preserve it and to educate the public on the
need for greater protection.[29] But he never lost sight of the larger
purpose the park was to serve as a revenue-producing tourist resort for
the Canadian people. To satisfy the government's commercial interest,
he reported annually on the development of trails and tote roads, the
success of the hotels and hot springs, the increasing revenue, and the
rising national and international popularity the park was enjoying.
During the first four years of his administration, annual visitor numbers climbed from 5087 to 8156, a good indication of the park's
success.[30]

The Superintendent saw little contradiction or inconsistency between wilderness preservation and development within a national
park. After the expansion of Yoho Park in 1902, Douglas noted how
the Canadian Pacific Railway, 'with commendable foresight and enterprise,' lost no time in building a chalet, and he welcomed the discovery,
by railway workers, of a large anthracite deposit in the vicinity of Banff
in 1904, for this would enhance still further the commercial value of

the park.[31] By 1908, Douglas was reporting on the success of Bankhead Coal Mines and Exshaw Cement Works, operating within the park. He reported, with some pride, that the cement works controlled 12,000 acres of land and that their output amounted to 2600 barrels of finished Portland cement a day.[32] (However, he did recommend that the government refrain from granting any more timber and mining licences in the park as work parties were having an adverse effect on the park's wildlife.) On the other hand, taking a leaf from John Muir's notebook, Douglas eulogized the beauty of untouched, unspoiled wilderness:

None of nature's landscapes are ugly so long as they are wild; and much must be in great part wild. The steady long lasting glaciers in the mountains and the rocky canyons must in general, along with the mountains, be always wild.[33]

But as Superintendent of a park whose object was to provide a 'pleasure ground' for the Canadian people, Douglas also believed that wilderness must serve the general public. Directly quoting Muir, he wrote in his 1903 departmental report: 'All the mountains are still rich in wildness and by means of good roads are being brought closer to civilization each year; the wildest health and pleasure grounds are made accessible and available to many a lover of wilderness who without them would never see it.'[34] Unfortunately, neither Muir nor Douglas could possibly have known that by the 1970s roads would become the major threat to the very wilderness both were endeavouring to preserve.

Douglas knew that national parks and wildlife preservation policies would have to enjoy full government support and that the way to win support was to demonstrate that both parks and wildlife were valuable attractions, that policies for their care and protection could become commercially viable propositions. By 1906, Rocky Mountains Park was an acclaimed commercial success in terms of tourist revenues and Douglas had shown that wildlife within a national park was as much a part of the park's attractions as the hot springs, mountain scenery, and mineral resources. Wildlife was accounting for much of the park's growing popularity and thus paying for itself many times over.

Douglas had been interested in acquiring buffalo for the park ever since his appointment in 1897. The small herd donated by Lord Strathcona in 1899 proved to him the enormous value of buffalo as a natural curiosity. He also felt it his duty to preserve wildlife species that were, or had been, indigenous to the Canadian west. Such species, he believed, were a permanent valuable investment which added to the national wealth of the Dominion. In 1906, Douglas was suddenly presented with a rare opportunity to secure a large herd of plains bison. The account of his efforts to influence and persuade the Canadian government to buy the Michel Pablo buffalo herd, the last great herd reputed to be in existence, is a story all but ignored and forgotten by resource historians. Yet, in the history of Canadian wildlife conservation, it forms an important chapter.

The American bison was the most visible manifestation of the superabundance of wildlife that once existed in North America. Buffalo roamed over a third of the continent and estimates of their numbers before 1800 vary greatly from a high of 60 million guessed at by Ernest Thompson Seton to a more conservative estimate by biologists today of between 20 and 30 million. Journals and diaries of early explorers and fur traders note sightings of 'immense herds,' 'teeming myriads,' and 'countless numbers.' It is small wonder that, confronting herds that stretched across and covered the prairie as far as the eye could see, men could not imagine the day when buffalo would no longer darken the western plains. William Hornaday, writing on the extermination of the buffalo in 1889, claimed that some Indian tribes believed the animals came out of the ground, so abundant were their numbers, and that the supply was 'necessarily inexhaustible.'[35]

The supply was far from inexhaustible. The inexorable westward push of the American frontier, the introduction of barbed wire fences, the loss of prairie habitat, and the relentless pursuit by Indians and growing numbers of whites equipped with modern repeating firearms destined the buffalo to almost certain extinction. But it was the American transcontinental railways that divided the great herds and brought carloads of market hunters pouring into the west that telescoped the slaughter and final extermination of plains bison into a matter of a few years. From 1873 to 1875, an estimated 6,750,000 buffalo were killed, and by 1884 the American wild buffalo herds had ceased to exist.[36]

Americans were not unaware of the slaughter. Joel Asaph Allen wrote *The American Bison, Living and Extinct* in 1876 immediately after the southern buffalo herd had been wiped out, and Richard Irving Dodge followed with *Plains of the Great West* in 1877. But the best history and detailed description was contained in a lengthy article by William Hornaday which appeared in the United States Natural History Museum Annual Report for 1889. Hornaday was head taxidermist for the museum and travelled west in 1886 to locate some buffalo specimens. He hunted for two months but found only a few scattered herds left. 'With such a lesson before our eyes,' he wrote, 'confirmed in every detail by living testimony, who will dare to say that there will be any elk, moose, caribou, mountain sheep, mountain goat, antelope, or black-tailed deer left alive in the United States in a wild state fifty years from this day, aye, or even twenty-five years?'[37]

Hornaday began working for the preservation of what few buffalo there were left on the American plains, and with the help of other dedicated wildlife preservationists founded the American Bison Society in 1905. Through Society efforts, Congress was persuaded to establish a National Bison Range in western Montana, where remaining buffalo could benefit from full government protection. 'It may fairly be supposed,' Hornaday surmised, 'that if the people of this country could have been made to realize the immense money value of the great buffalo herds as they existed in 1870, a vigorous and successful effort would have been made to regulate and restrict the slaughter. But as yet the American people have not learned to spend money for the protection of valuable game, and by the time they do learn it, there will be no game left to protect.'[38]

British North America had enjoyed a similar abundance of plains bison, the animals providing the basic food support for Métis, Blackfoot, Cree, and Assiniboine Indian tribes on the western prairies. In the years after 1820, large hunting parties annually left the Red River settlement in search of buffalo, until, by the late 1850s, there were few herds remaining in southern Manitoba. Henry Hind recorded one such Red River hunting expedition in 1849 numbering 700 Métis, 200 Indians, 603 carts, 600 horses, 200 oxen, and 400 dogs.[39] Captain Palliser found such an abundance of buffalo along the South Saskatchewan River in 1857 that 'the grass was eaten to the earth, as if the place had been devastated by locusts,'[40] while Cecil Denny, moving west with the NWMP through Saskatchewan in 1874, noted that the farther the troupe travelled, the more plentiful the buffalo became. 'We came to places where, as far as the eye could see, untold thousands were in sight; the country being fairly black with them ... these immense herds were moving north and there seemed no end to them.'[41] But four years later, Denny reported that only a few buffalo were found near Fort Walsh and in 1879 he concluded that the day of the buffalo on the plains was over.[42] John Macoun, a botanist with the Geological Survey, substantiated Denny. 'Where the hills were covered with countless thousands in 1877,' he wrote, 'the Blackfeet were dying of starvation in 1879.'[43] Just five years after Denny made his initial observation of the giant herds, buffalo had gone from the Canadian prairie.

There had never been a large-scale extermination program for buffalo on Canadian territory, yet the immense herds disappeared as totally and as completely as they had in the United States. Despite the Hudson's Bay Company's opposition to settlement, which delayed the opening of bulk transportation routes, and the high cost of exporting buffalo by cart and water routes from the west, which discouraged heavy commercial exploitation of the herds, buffalo numbers declined substantially on the prairies after 1870.[44] One reason for the decline can be found in the heavy exploitation by American hide hunters and whiskey traders who crossed over the border in pursuit of remaining buffalo herds on Canadian territory. Traders persuaded the Blackfeet and other plains Indians to hunt to excess, promising cheap alcohol for the countless numbers slain. A New York tannery developed a superior leather from buffalo hide in 1871, which increased still further the demand for buffalo robes. This new development also introduced the hide hunter, described as 'the most prolific wildlife killer the world had ever seen.'[45] His only interest was in the hide, and the rest of the buffalo, once utilized by the Indian for tents, food, clothing, utensils, canoes, and ornaments, was left to rot on the plain. A good hide man was reputed to kill more than a hundred animals in a single day.

The Canadian prairies also had to support increasing numbers of American Indians during the 1870s who came into the 'great white mother's land' in search of peace denied them by the American authorities. Nearly 3000 entered the Cypress Hills region in 1876, and in 1877 Chief Sitting Bull with a band of 1000 Sioux also sought refuge, followed by a remnant of the Nez Percé tribe led by their indomitable war chief, White Bird. The Blackfeet, resenting this sudden invasion of their territory, appealed to the NWMP to protect their traditional hunting grounds between the Cypress Hills and the Rocky Mountains. An ordinance was passed the following year forbidding the 'wanton destruction' of buffalo, the killing of animals under two years of age, and the slaughter of females. But, as Denny observed, the regulations were impossible to enforce due to the vastness of the country and the multitude of Indians relying on the buffalo for food. Further restrictions would have only increased their hardship. One year after it was passed, the ordinance was repealed.[46]

A police report for 1879 admitted that the Sioux invasion and the Indians' heavy dependence on the plains for support had completely upset the calculations the different treaties were based on, namely, that the Indians could subsist on buffalo until they became self-supporting. There were too many Indians and too few buffalo. The Sioux killed great numbers and the report concluded that it was doubtful the buffalo herds would ever return to their former numbers.[47] Denny reported that for the next few years Indians continued to leave their reserve in large numbers, searching for the vanished buffalo:

It was hard to make them believe that they were gone forever and for years they believed they would re-appear. They had a legend that the buffalo came originally from a hole in the ground in the centre of a lake in the north, and that on the advent of the white man they had re-entered it and would ultimately re-emerge. [48]

The wild buffalo herds had gone from the southern Canadian prairies by the time the Canadian Pacific Railway was completed in 1885. There were only bleaching bones in the country through which it passed. A tourist who took one of the earliest trips on the railroad in 1888 recorded his observations:

All through today's journey, piled up at the leading stations along the road, were vast heaps of bones of the earliest owners of the prairie – the buffalo. Giant heads and ribs and thigh bones, without one pick of meat on them, clean as a well washed plate, white as driven snow, there they lay, a giant sacrifice on the altar of trade and civilization ... [49]

But the traveller was not deeply troubled by the sights he saw on his journey westward. The buffalo symbolized only a land that was a 'wild and useless waste,' he wrote, but the train's whistle meant 'education and religion, law and order, and best of all, the grass supporting men, women, and children, instead of herds of beasts.' His views reflected the attitude of most North Americans in the nineteenth century. Indeed, the author concluded that the buffalo departed life just at the right time, when 'utilitarianism marks everything, for every white bone is worth money when used as fertilizer or in connection with refining sugar.' Fortunately, Howard Douglas saw the importance of buffalo in quite a different light. Realizing the value of plains bison both as a wildlife species and as a tourist attraction, Douglas was determined to obtain more buffalo for Rocky Mountains Park.

News of a large buffalo herd in Montana and of its owner's willingness to sell reached the Canadian government by a circuitous route. Benjamin Davis, an agent with the Canadian Immigration Department in Montana, met Michel Pablo on his travels through the American state in 1905. Pablo was a Mexican halfbreed who, together with his partner, Charles Allard, had acquired a small herd of ten plains bison in 1883 from a Pend d'Oreille Indian called Samuel Walking Coyote. Ten years later, they bought the remaining animals in Buffalo Jones's herd at Omaha, which numbered twenty-six pure plains bison and eighteen hybrid catello, a cross between buffalo and domestic cattle. Their herd, reproducing regularly and successfully each year, ranged freely on Allard's ranch near Ravalli in western Montana. Allard, however, died in 1896 and by 1902, Pablo found himself sole owner of a herd numbering well over 360 animals. It soon became evident that he needed more buffalo range, but the American government seemed reluctant to give him any more land; in fact, he thought they were trying to 'freeze him out' by opening to settlement the Flathead Reserve the herd was grazing on, and Congress balked at the cost of purchasing the herd for the government. Pablo asked Davis if the herd could be moved to a comparable range in western Canada.[50]

Davis immediately notified J. Obed-Smith, Immigration Commissioner in Ottawa, of Pablo's request and the Commissioner, in turn, passed the word on to his Superintendent, W.D. Scott:

It occurred to me that perhaps some of the Departments of the Government are desirous of acquiring some of these animals for the Banff National Park and as this appears to be a valuable herd and has been brought up in a district very similar to what we have in the west, it affords an opportunity to secure a desirable bunch of these animals from one owner.[51]

The message filtered through to the Department of the Interior, but Deputy Minister William Cory, believing Banff already had enough buffalo, replied that the government was not interested in purchasing any additional animals for the park.[52] The matter seemed closed. But in March 1906 discussions opened again. Davis wrote to the Immigration Commissioner that Pablo was now desperate to move his herd and wished to drive them up into western Canada. If the Canadian government would give him range and water lands in the mountains, Pablo promised that the herd would not interfere with farming lands. All he wanted to know was whether or not the government would allow the buffalo herd to enter Canadian territory duty free. Davis emphasized that this was the 'only wild herd' left in existence on the North American continent and hinted that Pablo was open to a reasonable sale.[53] Once again, messages passed back and forth between the departments of Immigration and the Interior. Without committing himself either way, the Deputy Minister instructed Davis to find out what price Pablo wanted for his buffalo herd.

Howard Douglas was promptly sent down by the Department of the Interior in June 1906 to examine the herd in Montana and to prepare estimates of the cost should the government decide to buy it. His report was enthusiastic. The animals were all pure-bred, he claimed, and numbered close to 350. Pablo was asking $200 a head for the whole herd, a price Douglas considered cheap:

I am sure there will be a howl from the Americans should the government decide to purchase them. They are within sixty miles of Yellowstone National Park and if the Americans knew we were negotiating for the herd, they would close in at once on them. [54]

Douglas enclosed a rough estimate of the total cost of the herd, the price of delivering them to Canada, fencing, caretakers' fees, and other necessary contingencies, all of which amounted to $95,150, a staggering amount of money even by present-day standards but one which Douglas considered a good investment. There was no mistaking that he wanted his government to buy the herd. 'It would be a great advertisement for Canada,' he told the Secretary for the Interior, 'for with the wild buffalo in the north [wood buffalo], Canada would own 8/10 of all living buffalo.'

The Deputy Minister of the Interior supported Douglas's recommendation, although he was slower to share in his enthusiasm. But events speeded up considerably by early 1907 when Cory learned that the American Bison Society was planning to acquire the Pablo herd. The Deputy Minister suggested to his Minister, Frank Oliver, that Douglas be ordered to proceed immediately with the purchase. [55] With the recommendation accepted, Douglas was dispatched to Montana once again. This time he was authorized to conduct financial negotiations on behalf of the Canadian government and to supervise the round-up and shipment of the herd by railway from Ravalli, Montana, to Alberta.

Once in Montana, Douglas confided to the Deputy Minister that Pablo was suspicious and afraid of being cheated, but was reportedly worth $250,000 and 'will carry out the agreement to the letter.' Douglas also told Cory that Pablo had a grievance against the American government and would prefer selling to the Canadian government just to get even. Douglas suggested a legal contract be sent to Montana covering the negotiations and that after the contract was signed, a draft of $10,000 be made payable to Pablo, the balance to be paid by the government upon delivery of the herd. Aware of the importance and significance of the buffalo purchase, Douglas cautioned Pablo to say nothing of the sale and warned Cory that no publicity should be made until the bargain was completed, for 'I am positive if the papers in the States were to get the information we might as well abandon the whole matter.'[56]

In spite of Douglas's attempts to cloud the sale in secrecy, the news leaked out, to both the *Montana Great Falls Daily Tribune* and the *Missoulian* newspapers. Davis wrote to the Deputy Minister that the Americans were 'much put out' when they learned Canada was to have the entire herd and warned the Deputy Minister that 'if they can't buy buffalo perhaps they can steal some of ours. They will probably attempt something of that sort but I shall watch things pretty closely and see that we get what belongs to us.'[57] Canadian fears were doubtless exaggerated. An article in the Annual Report of the American Bison Society in 1907 stated that Pablo could not be blamed for selling his herd to Canada. The Society understood his difficulty in maintaining the buffalo and believed he would have preferred to keep them in the United States, but found no opportunity to sell to the government. The editorial concluded that 'the cost of the range will not be as great as the loss to the nation of the herd that has been sold.'[58] The United States's loss was Canada's gain. Nonetheless, the Department of the Interior took necessary precautions. Asked in the House of Commons why an area in the Moose Mountains had not been selected to house the buffalo, Frank Oliver replied: 'When I heard of the resentment that was felt locally against the removal of the herd from Montana, I thought it would be doubtful policy to place such a large herd within what you might term easy reach of the boundary line.'[59]

Round-up and shipment of the buffalo began and proceeded very slowly throughout the summer and autumn of 1907. Pablo was seventy years old but well up to a task that would have defeated far younger men. Standing six feet tall, he reportedly still spent most of his waking hours in the saddle and had a voice that could easily match the angry bellow of a captured buffalo bull. Even so, the job of catching 350 wild animals that had roamed freely for generations, corralling and loading them into waiting railway cars, could tax even Pablo's energy and resources.[60]

Pablo brought together a small band of cowboys, led by Charles Allard, Jr, and later advertised an offer of five dollars a day plus room and board to any cowhand who would help move the herd. He soon had a small army of seventy-five cowboys. But according to one eyewitness, things went far from smoothly:

Neither Pablo nor anyone else anticipated difficulty with the buffalo. In fact, their characteristic shambling, head-down gait as a small bunch trotted into the railroad yard that first morning made them look humble and hopeless. Few of the cowboys could put much enthusiasm into the whoops with which they urged the huge beasts along. And when the first old bull started up the runway into a cattle car, some onlookers looked away.

They quickly looked back. With scarcely a break in stride the old bull and his followers smashed through the stout planks of the other side of the car and trotted back up the valley.

For a moment the spectators stared at the splintered cattle car. Then they set up a shout of mixed cheers and laughter.

"Hey Pablo," some wit yelled, "is them what you call vanishing buffalo?"[61]

Pablo remained unperturbed. He merely constructed more corrals and headed out once again to resume the round-up.

In July, Douglas wrote to Oliver that he had learned the Americans were offering Pablo $500 for every buffalo not shipped, but, as Canada's contract called for the entire herd, Douglas believed the government should take all the animals.[62] What neither Douglas nor the Minister realized then was that the entire herd was considerably larger than the estimated 350 animals contracted for. By late summer, Douglas was compelled to revise his earlier estimate and prepare a new total cost sheet. He notified his department that another $40,000 minimum would be needed. Prime Minister Laurier prepared a memorandum for the Governor-General-in-Council, stating that there were more buffalo than originally believed and requesting an additional $75,000 to cover added costs and transportation. Laurier thought that it was in the public interest to grant the money immediately.[63] A year later, Oliver argued in the House that the increased expense was justified. He claimed that Canada was getting the herd at a price the country could well afford and that 'if we are able to corner the market by getting the whole herd that fact will appreciate the value of what we have.'[64]

Purchase of the Pablo buffalo herd began to assume national importance for the Canadian government and it became a question of national pride to acquire all the animals, whatever the cost, and the cost steadily mounted. It was to be another two years before full delivery was completed, but, as Oliver declared in the House: 'This is the only considerable herd that there is anywhere' and 'they are of value as a natural curiosity.'[65] Even a Montana daily newspaper admitted that the Canadian government's enterprise in buying the herd had 'out-Yanked the Yankees.'[66]

Meanwhile, the round-up was continuing successfully in Montana. Pablo, ever in search of better methods to corral the animals, had built a twenty-six-mile long fence from the banks of the Flathead River in the middle of the valley to the corral at Ravalli. It formed a huge funnel and up it Pablo succeeded in marshalling 180 buffalo cows and calves. But that was all. The bulls carefully evaded the trap. The following spring, Pablo was forced to design an even better method, this time a V-shaped barricade a mile long set up in the centre of the valley. Its sides narrowed down until they opened right onto the banks of the Flathead River at a point where it entered a steep-walled canyon. There was a small beach on the opposite side of the river and Pablo reasoned that the buffalo, once entering the V, would be forced to travel its length, cross the river, and come out on the beach. From there, they could be easily captured and crated for transit. His reasoning soon proved correct and many more buffalo were successfully shipped to Canada by the fall of 1910. But it was hard work and there were many buffalo, at least 400, that were never captured.[67]

Finally, in 1911, almost four years after negotiations had first begun, delivery of the Pablo herd to Canada was completed and Canadians were the proud owners of 703 plains bison. The cost of the animals alone, outside of the transportation and fencing, amounted to over $140,000, but there was no criticism expressed by parliamentarians on either side of the House. Acquisition of the buffalo had been in the national interest. Pablo died three years later, but he had the satisfaction of knowing that the American Congress had declared the southern edge of the Flathead Reservation in Montana the National Bison Range. It covered 18,000 acres and was home to the 'outlaw' buffalo that had escaped the round-up.[68] Additional range land was all that Pablo had asked for in 1906 and perhaps if Congress had been a little more aware, and a little more willing, Pablo would never have sold his wild herd to Canada and it would have been Canada's loss instead.

Once the herd arrived in Canada, a section of land between the Canadian Pacific Railway and the Grand Trunk Pacific near Wainwright, Alberta, was set aside for creation of 'Buffalo National Park.' The railways, particularly the Grand Trunk Pacific, were understandably delighted with the prospect of a new park, wishing to have their railway lines identified as closely as possible with the now famous herd.

Indeed, the Second Vice-President of the Grand Trunk Pacific, urged Oliver to put up buildings that 'will identify the Buffalo Park with our railway,' but was told in reply only that the park entrance would be 'convenient' to the railway station.[69] Railway officials clearly hoped that Buffalo National Park would benefit their railway lines as much as the creation of Rocky Mountains Park had benefitted the Canadian Pacific Railway.

The Canadian government won strong praise from the American Bison Society for permanently protecting the plains bison, but most of the credit for the herd's acquisition belonged to Howard Douglas. He, more than anyone else, had learned the importance of wildlife, and its cash value to the government in terms of tourist dollars. It was his belief in the importance of the herd to Canada, not only as a 'natural curiosity' but as a relic of the former herds that once covered the plains of western Canada, that convinced the Deputy Minister and the Minister of the Interior to embark on negotiations for their costly purchase. Once committed, members of government realized the national significance in obtaining the herd. 'Save for the actions of the Canadian Government,' Douglas wrote in 1911, 'these relics of the countless monarchs of the plains would have been doomed to certain extinction.'[70]

By 1912, Douglas could look back on a successful administration of Canada's parks and wildlife. The value and reputation of the parks had grown since the establishment of Rocky Mountains Park in 1887, far surpassing the wildest expectations of those earlier members of Parliament. There were six national parks in Canada by 1908, together covering large territories in the west, and all of great and growing importance: Rocky Mountains (1887), Glacier/Yoho (1886), Waterton Lakes (1895, forest reserve), Jasper (1907), Buffalo (1908) – a total of 11,136 square miles of 'protected forests and refuges for many varieties of rapidly disappearing game.' Realizing the need for better administration of what was quickly becoming an important new resource, the government placed park administration under the Forestry Branch in 1908. Douglas, described as 'eminently qualified for the job,'[71] was appointed Commissioner of Canada's Dominion Parks, a just reward.

As Superintendent and then Commissioner, Douglas had established the policy of wildlife preservation throughout the dominion parks and had made government aware of the vital importance of continual protection. New regulations were passed through an order-in-council in 1909 providing for the employment of game and fish guardians who would also serve as forest fire protection officers, as Douglas had recommended.[72] Warden patrols almost totally eliminated poaching, and regulations were later passed which prohibited the carrying of unsealed firearms in all dominion parks. In 1911, Douglas reported to the Minister that 'game laws and regulations have resulted in an increase of game and they have less fear of man.'[73]

Douglas's policies had been both successful and influential. Among civil servants, he was the first to become concerned about wildlife at a time when the concept of wildlife preservation was evolving. He understood that economic arguments alone would justify increased park appropriations and greater wildlife protective measures, and he persuaded the government to embark on a course of park and wildlife protection by demonstrating that the result would be increased tourist revenues. Rocky Mountains Park was his shining example. When it was established in 1887, there were only 3000 visitors; by 1912 the annual attendance totalled 73,725.[74]

By the time Douglas left office in 1912,[75] wildlife preservation had become a policy in dominion parks. Rocky Mountains and all the other parks were, at last, true wildlife refuges as well as public playgrounds. Largely because of the groundwork laid by Douglas during the fifteen years of his administration, the new Parks Branch that was created in 1911 was in a far better position to deal effectively and efficiently with the question of wildlife protection in Canada.

4

Towards Better
Administration

The administration of Canada's national parks had become much more complex by 1911. From 1887, when Rocky Mountains Park was established, until 1908, the parks had been administered by their individual park superintendents under the direction and authority of the Minister of the Interior. This was a satisfactory arrangement, since there were only a few, small parks in the late nineteenth century. By 1908, however, there were six, and they were all proving to be of significant national, and international, importance. Accordingly, they were placed, for administrative purposes, under the Forestry Branch and came under the supervision of Forestry Superintendent Robert Campbell. At this same time, Douglas was designated Commissioner of Dominion Parks in the Forestry Branch. The arrangement was only a temporary one. The problem of administration remained, and by 1911 the Minister, Frank Oliver, was convinced that the parks were in need of even better management.[1] The solution was to create a completely separate Parks Branch and appoint a Dominion Parks Commissioner to head the new administrative body. This was accomplished shortly after the important Dominion Forest Reserves and Parks Act was passed by Parliament in May 1911.[2]

Under this Act, a number of dominion lands throughout British Columbia, Alberta, Saskatchewan, and Manitoba were withdrawn from sale, or occupancy, and set aside as Dominion Forest Reserves under the control and direction of the Forestry Superintendent. But the Act had two larger objectives: to establish a 16,000,000-acre forest reserve on the eastern slope of the Rocky Mountains and to reduce the areas of the three dominion parks located within the forest reserve – Rocky Mountains, Jasper, and Waterton Lakes parks. Under the new legislation, the forest reserve was to be administered by the Forestry

Branch, but the park reserve areas were to come under the Parks Branch.[3] No one argued with the need for greater forest protection and conservation in Canada. The Act was designed to create a forest reserve large enough to conserve timber and water supplies and to ensure regulated production and reforestation of timber, to 'harvest our crop of timber, and re-produce that crop,' as Oliver declared in the House.[4] Such a reserve on the eastern slope of the Rockies had been advocated in previous years by William Pearce,[5] the Canadian Forestry Association,[6] the Conservation Commission, and the Minister of the Interior, who was well aware of prairie farmers' dependence on the Rocky Mountains' timber and water supplies.[7]

One month after the Act passed Parliament, the three dominion parks located in the huge reserve were reduced in size through an order-in-council. Rocky Mountains Park, formerly an impressive 4900 square miles, was reduced to 1800; Jasper was cut from 5000 square miles to 1000; and Waterton Lakes was reduced from 54 square miles to a mere 13.[8] A number of government members believed that the parks, as originally constituted, were too large to patrol and protect adequately and park reductions were held to be in the interests of better management and more efficient administration.[9] But the decision to reduce the boundaries soon sparked an angry response from conservation groups in both Canada and the United States.

There were two new government attitudes revealed during debate on the Forest Reserves and Parks bill. Implicit in the discussions was the recognition that the government was going to take a much firmer hand with regard to commercial activities and resource development within the parks. Indeed, at one point Oliver stated: 'It may as well be understood from the beginning that it is not proposed that these parts of reserves set apart for purposes of recreation shall be primarily places of business. There will be no business there except such as is absolutely necessary for the recreation of the people.'[10] The Minister's statement was in surprising contrast to the policies underlying Rocky Mountains Park in 1887, which had not only permitted, but actively encouraged, resource development within the park reservation. Oliver stated during the opening debate on the Forest Reserves and Parks bill that regulations governing the park reserves would 'look to the enjoyment by the people of the natural advantages and beauties of these particular sections of the reserves.'[11] The success of Rocky Mountains Park no doubt had convinced the government of the importance of recreation and scenic attractions in all the Dominion parks, a recognition that was clearly evident during debate in Parliament.

The government also demonstrated a new and surprising concern for wildlife protection in the Rocky Mountains Forest Reserve. According to the Minister of the Interior, the whole of the reserve was to be a game preserve and he promised that 'we intend to patrol these reserves and exercise our right of proprietorship in the protection of game.'[12] When one opposition member pointed out that the provinces retained jurisdiction over game administration, Oliver gave quick assurance that the government would come to an arrangement with the provinces regarding any general law dealing with game. 'The whole purpose of setting aside this reserve,' he announced in the House, 'is to preserve the game':

Therefore, any law of the province that contemplated the prevention of the killing of game at some time will be acceptable to the Dominion. We will operate within the provincial laws and there will be no conflict.[13]

The government's concern for wildlife protection on the huge Rocky Mountains Forest Reserve in 1911 is all the more startling when it is remembered that in 1906, during debate on the first Forest Reserves bill, there had been little discussion of wildlife in Parliament and no one suggested establishing forest reserves to protect game. Yet, five years later, the Minister was stating firmly that the whole purpose of setting aside the Rocky Mountains reserve was to protect the game! The explanation for this apparent new concern for wildlife protection expressed by government members is not difficult to find. Since 1906, members of the Forestry Branch, and particularly Forestry Superintendent Robert Campbell, had developed a keen and active interest in the question of game protection.

Robert Campbell was born in Ontario in 1867. He was educated at Ottawa's Collegiate Institute and entered government service in 1887. He served as Private Secretary to both the Deputy Minister and the Minister of the Interior and was later appointed Chief Clerk in the Timber and Mines Branch. In 1907, he succeeded Elihu Stewart as Forestry Superintendent in the Department of the Interior. Campbell had been impressed by the increase of wildlife under the protective policies of dominion parks. It was his conviction that a similar increase could be achieved on all forest reserves by declaring them game preserves and enforcing protective regulations. The subject was brought to his attention in 1908 when the Manitoba Game Protective Association requested that the government prohibit hunting in the Riding Mountain Forest Reserve.[14] A year later, residents in the vicinity of the Spruce Woods Forest Reserve, Manitoba, also petitioned for game protection.[15] Both reserves had been set aside under the 1906 Forest Reserves Act and although the earlier legislation prohibited hunting on the preserves, there were no specific regulations drawn up under the Act for game protection and no means provided for enforcing the protective principle. Campbell considered the petitions and reported to the Minister that he was taking steps to put the Forestry Branch in a better position to deal effectively with game protection in all forest reserves.[16]

Campbell studied Dominion Park regulations and drew up a list of similar measures for game and fish protection to be enforced by members of his branch in all forest reserves.[17] Under his proposed regulations, all hunting, trapping, killing, and wounding of birds and mammals was strictly prohibited, and it was forbidden for anyone to carry firearms into the reserves except duly authorized forest rangers. Daily bag limits were set for fishermen and they were restricted from using seines, nets, fish traps, or explosives. Any person found violating the protective regulations was subject to penalties under the 1906 Forest Reserves Act. Campbell submitted his proposals to the Minister in 1909 and later that same year they were adopted and proclaimed, by order-in-council, for the Moose Mountain, Beaver Hills, and Pines Forest reserves in Saskatchewan.[18] Within the next two years, both the Saskatchewan and Manitoba governments followed the federal lead and recognized all Dominion Forest reserves within their provinces as Provincial Wildlife reserves. Eventually, Campbell's stringent regulations were enforced in all Dominion Forest reserves and the Forestry Superintendent noted that as a result of protection, wildlife numbers were increasing steadily.[19]

Campbell's experience and success in turning forest reserves into effective game preserves might well have had strong influence within the government. Under the Dominion Forest Reserves and Parks Act of 1911, all forest reserves were declared game preserves with authority vested in the Governor-in-Council to make regulations for the 'protection of the animals, birds and fish therein.' Responsibility for wildlife on the forest reserve areas was given to the Forestry Branch, which was becoming increasingly familiar with wildlife protection.

Canada was the first country in the world to set up a government organization devoted solely to the management and development of national parks. The establishment of the Parks Branch in 1911 and the appointment of James Harkin as Dominion Parks Commissioner marked a significant advance in park and wildlife administration.[20] It was the beginning of a new era of far-reaching protective policies initiated from within government that would lead to greater protection of parks and wildlife throughout the Dominion.

The Parks Branch was established shortly after passage of the Forest Reserves and Parks Act. Consisting of only seven members, the branch was hardly an impressive body, but Harkin was to bring to it, and to the government, a totally new sense of purpose and direction.[21] There seemed little in his background to equip or qualify him for the job of Dominion Parks Commissioner. By his own admission, he doubted his ability to administer the new Parks Branch, for 'I knew nothing about parks or what would be expected of me.' Born at Vankleek Hill, Ontario, in 1875, Harkin was educated in Ontario and Michigan before working as parliamentary correspondent with the *Montreal Herald* and *Toronto News*. In 1903, he was appointed Private Secretary to Clifford Sifton and Frank Oliver, consecutive ministers of the Interior in Laurier's Liberal cabinet. Although Harkin was unfamiliar with park policy and administration, he did understand politics and from his close association with both ministers of the Interior had developed a keen awareness of the importance of natural resources and the value of park reservations. Frequently his departmental reports reflected his own journalistic training, as proposals for park development and protection were advanced with colourful enthusiasm, persuasion, and a steady persistence that stood the fledgling Parks Branch in good stead during the first years of its existence.

Most of Harkin's early innovations called for large expenditures and he had to find a way to get the money he needed from a government that reportedly thought of national parks as little more than 'tulip beds and roses.'[23] Harkin was as aware of the commercial importance of national parks as Howard Douglas had been before him and he also knew that only the parks' proven commercial success would ensure a continuous flow of appropriations from Parliament. The Commissioner was impressed by the millions of dollars spent each year by tourists on the European and North American continents and he instructed his staff to find out how much revenue was annually produced from tourist travel.[24] He corresponded with members of the United States Department of the Interior, requesting information on the economic value of tourism. 'There is no doubt,' he confided to the Chief Clerk there, 'that this aspect in itself justifies the money spent on National Parks quite outside of other considerations of their value ... it is an argument that is, of course, of assistance in securing appropriations.'[25]

The answers to Harkin's inquiries were startling. The combined annual revenue produced by tourism, for France, Italy, and Switzerland was $750,000,000. The state of Maine alone gathered in $40,000,000, while the money spent by Americans abroad in just one year came to the incredible sum of $400,000,000. To Harkin, these figures indicated that Canada, with 'incomparable scenic attractions,' could anticipate annual revenues reaching far into the millions.[26] This alone would justify continued and increased expenditures for park development. The Canadian Pacific Railway supported Harkin's assessment by reporting that the amount of money brought in by visitors to the Rocky Mountains each year was $50,000,000, a sum sufficient to pay the interest on the national debt, the Commissioner concluded.[27] Harkin published all the compiled tourist revenue figures in his departmental report and sent copies to each member of the House of Commons and Senate in 1913. Years later, he recalled that when park appropriations came up and were questioned in the House, Arthur Meighen defended the increase, quoting all Harkin's figures. Harkin believed that the economic value of all dominion parks was established at that moment.[28]

He saw that the development of national parks not only would give Canadians the chance to see incomparable scenery and enjoy recreation under the best possible conditions, but also would be a good means of keeping tourist dollars inside Canada. Foreseeing the day when adequate roads through all the mountain parks would bring in a huge tourist traffic, he wrote: 'What a revenue this country will obtain when thousands of autos are traversing the parks.'[29]

Although Harkin was quick to see large tourist revenues as a convincing argument for securing larger appropriations for park development, he did not view parks primarily in terms of their commercial values. He argued that park lands preserved untouched wilderness areas that were comparable to priceless works of art, created by nature in accordance with divine laws of harmony. 'Will we ever be able to educate the man in the street,' Harkin once asked, 'to realize that it is as much a desecration to mar this natural harmony as to draw a razor across the Mona Lisa?'[30] National Parks were to preserve the original landscape of Canada, to ensure that every Canadian, by right of citizenship, would own a share of unspoiled country. Indeed, parks had a truly patriotic mission to perform: to instill in all Canadians a love of the country and pride in its natural beauty. In his annual report for 1913, Harkin quoted the President of the American Civic Federation speaking on the subject of the value of park reservations. 'Change the word "American" to "Canadian",' he instructed the Minister, 'and the

concluding portion of his address crystallizes a thought of equal application to Canada':

*Our devotion to the flag begins in that love of country which its beauty has
begotten; it may end, at the last supreme test, in the beauty of soul that makes the
patriot ready to die for his country in battle – if just battle there may ever again be.*
    *So, I hold that in stimulating and safeguarding the essential virtue of patrio-
tism, the beauty of American parks stands forth as most of all worth while.*[31]

Harkin shared the philosophy of John Muir that sunshine, scenery,
and fresh air could strengthen the body and rejuvenate the human
spirit. He paid tribute to Muir for having clarified the purpose of
national parks and frequently quoted the American author in his
departmental reports on the need for park reservations:

*The tendency nowadays to wander in wilderness is delightful to see. Thousands
of tired, nerve-shaken, overcivilized people are beginning to find out that
going to the mountains is going home; that wilderness is a necessity and that
mountain parks and reservations are useful, not only as fountains of timber and
irrigating waters, but as fountains of life.*[32]

He maintained that man needed wholesome, outdoor recreation and
that national parks were essential for his physical, moral, and mental
well-being. 'The ultimate purpose of parks,' he wrote, 'is to provide
opportunities for wholesome play.'[33] The Commissioner recognized
that people needed to escape from the pressures and tensions of
modern life, to seek a life closer to nature where, in fresh air and
sunshine, the 'marvellous tonic properties of play' could be enjoyed to
the full.[34] He developed a theory around what he called the 'play spirit'
or 'play instinct' in man showing how, throughout human history, the
cultural flowering of nations was greatest when this spirit was at its
height. The 'Golden Age' of Greece, the age of European chivalry,
Elizabethan England, and the Italian Renaissance were examples of its
high development and, as a result, art, literature, learning, invention,
and discovery flourished.[35]
    Harkin believed that conditions of modern social and industrial life
had suppressed and perverted the play instinct by denying people
the time and opportunity to indulge in carefree recreation in the
outdoors:

To many people in cities, life means long hours of labour amidst the dust and whirr of wheels, an excessive nervous strain, and joyless, monotonous employ-ment; to many, life is a grind, a round of labour, a season of care, on top of which are conditions of overcrowding. The dangers that threaten, the evils which have been constantly increasing in industrial centres, are a degeneration in physical type, a deterioration in mental and moral quality.[36]

Life without the play spirit, Harkin warned, was a life without colour, vividness, joyousness, or liberty – all the qualities from which a nation's art and heroism stemmed. In his opinion, the national parks thus had to fill a vital and important role: to offer facilities for wholesome recreation that would physically and spiritually rejuvenate the Cana-dian people by building up their play instinct. 'National Parks are reservations of the wilderness,' he wrote, 'they constitute a national recognition of the necessity of recreation.'[37]

Harkin's belief in parks and wilderness values frequently bordered on the mystical: From the mountains, he believed, came emanations that elevated the mind and purified the spirit. In nature, man's 'wasted springs of vitality' were renewed, and only from nature could man come close to understanding the mystery of life. Parks existed so that Canadians could satisfy their hunger for nature and beauty, absorb the peace of the forests, steep their souls in the brilliance of wildflowers, and lose themselves in the sublimity of mountain peaks.[38] Such were the properties and capabilities of national parks and anything that impaired their natural beauty or interfered with their peaceful tran-quility was firmly excluded. Harkin opposed the sale of park lands for commercial purposes and under his administration many of the timber permits previously granted for Rocky Mountains Park were cancelled.[39]

The need to safeguard Canada's wild lands by establishing more parks was obvious to the Commissioner and he warned the Minister that the need for reservations would become more pressing as the population increased and life became more complex. 'Future genera-tions may wonder at our blindness,' he wrote, 'if we neglect to set them aside before civilization invades them':

The day will come when the population of Canada will be ten times as great as it is now but the national parks ensure that every Canadian ... will still have free access to vast areas possessing some of the finest scenery in Canada, in which the beauty of the landscape is protected from profanation, the natural wild animals, plants, and forests preserved, and the peace and solitude of primeval nature retained.[40]

Harkin's hopes, beliefs, and ideals filled the pages of his annual departmental reports to the Minister of the Interior during the early years of his administration. He had told Oliver he knew nothing of national parks, but in his understanding of the need for recreation and his appreciation of wilderness values he was far closer, in 1912, to our time than he was to his own.

Harkin's first efforts as Commissioner were directed towards opening channels of communication between Ottawa and Washington. Although the Americans did not establish their own separate Parks Branch until 1916, their experience with national park administration was considerably longer and broader than the Canadians'. Harkin corresponded with members of the Department of the Interior who were responsible for the American parks, suggesting a possible exchange of information, maps, publications, and annual reports relating to national park development in both countries. At least one American was more than willing to pool information. C.S. Ucker, the Chief Clerk in the Department, proposed exchanging lantern slides of American national parks with the Canadians. Unfortunately, his superior took a dim view of such an exchange. 'A large portion of the tourist travel to the Canadian parks comes from the United States,' he informed Ucker, 'and while I do not consider it advisable for this office to make a concerted movement in opposition to the Canadian Parks, I do consider it inadvisable for this office to have any part in advertising the Canadian reserves.' The advantage of such a slide exchange, he concluded, would lie entirely with the Canadians and 'I do not think this Department should take the initiative in bringing the matter to their attention.'[41]

Harkin and Ucker nonetheless carried on a steady correspondence, exchanging annual reports and consulting each other on mutual problems in park administration. The Canadian Commissioner sent Ucker a copy of the 1911 Forest Reserves and Parks Act as well as copies of Hansard with debates on the Forest Reserves bill, believing they would be of some help to the Americans in drafting their own legislation. Ucker in turn agreed to keep Harkin informed on progress of the American Parks bill (to establish a separate Parks Branch) and promised to forward Congressional debates on all subjects relating to park administration.[42] This was the beginning of a close association between members of the Parks Branch and the United States Department of the Interior that was to profit both countries on the subject of wildlife protection.

The most immediate problem Harkin confronted was the question of boundaries for Rocky Mountains, Jasper, and Waterton Lakes parks. All three parks were located in the Rocky Mountains Forest Reserve and under the order-in-council of 1911 their areas had been redefined and drastically reduced. There seemed good reason, at the time, for their substantial reductions. The boundaries of Rocky Mountains Park had never been clearly defined and the huge reserve had consistently suffered from poaching. The Chief Game Guardian at Banff thought that a complete system of protection over a smaller park area would be more effective in the long run than an incomplete system over a larger area. The solution to the problem, in his opinion, was to reduce Rocky Mountains Park.[43] He made his proposal to Robert Campbell in 1909 but Douglas, who was then Commissioner of Parks in the Forestry Branch, doubted that public sentiment would accept a reduction of the national park.[44] His doubts were soon justified.

Once the order-in-council was passed in 1911, a storm of protest broke. Under the terms of the legislation, Rocky Mountains Park was reduced by a total of 3100 square miles and it was not long before the opponents of the new boundaries let their feelings be known. The Alberta Game and Fish Protective Association strongly urged the Department to reconsider the matter for, 'if the proposed reduction takes place, it will nullify all the good work of the past in the matter of game protection.'[45] The Camp Fire Club of America, an organization founded by William Hornaday, was disappointed as well to learn of the alterations. Its Secretary wrote that members were at a loss to understand why Waterton Lakes Park had been decreased, since the need of game protective measures in that particular region of the country was 'too obvious to require argument.'[46] Officials with the Canadian Northern and Grand Trunk Pacific also bitterly protested the reduction of Jasper – the park having figured prominently in the railways' advertising campaign and tourist brochures – and they demanded an immediate restoration of the original boundaries.[47]

Howard Douglas had recognized the need to solve the boundary problem in Rocky Mountains Park while he was Superintendent, but once the order-in-council had passed he wrote to the Minister deploring the fact that so much territory had been cut out from the park:

We have been protecting this portion at considerable expense and care for the last ten years until it abounds with big game of all kinds. The animals in this area have become almost tame and it would be a suicidal policy to allow Indians and others to go in there during the open season and slaughter and kill what it has taken years to shelter and protect.[48]

Douglas proposed that the original park areas be maintained and administered as closed game preserves by park personnel. 'Our system of protection was getting into good shape the last few years,' he told the Minister, 'and I do not think poaching to any extent was carried on.' Should the original park areas be declared preserves and placed under park authority, he concluded, 'I am sure it would be appreciated by all who have the interests of fish and game at heart.'[49]

Clearly the reduction of dominion parks in 1911, carried out in the best interests of more efficient wildlife protection, had dissatisfied many, particularly those in the Parks Branch who possibly resented the Forestry Branch acquiring game protective jurisdiction over areas formerly administered as parks. It is small wonder that the boundary issue became the major problem to be solved by Harkin as soon as he became Parks Commissioner.

He acknowledged the protests regarding boundary changes in his first report as Commissioner and subsequently took the whole matter under close consideration. After careful study and much time spent in poring over old maps and departmental records, he concluded that the parks should be extended to their former size. He admitted to the Deputy Minister that 'areas of great value, from scenic, game-breeding, and other aspects, had been excluded from park protection.'[50]

One area in need of immediate attention was the southern portion of the original Rocky Mountains Park, withdrawn from the park reserve under the new boundary regulations. The Alberta Game and Fish Protective Association suggested that the area either be declared a game preserve under the Forest Reserves Act or be rejoined to Rocky Mountains Park and protected by members of the Parks Branch. Harkin tended to support their views, and wrote to the Deputy Minister in 1912 that 'the close proximity of a large Stoney Indian Reserve makes it increasingly imperative that game in this part of the Forest Reserve should have protection.'[51] Under the Forest Reserves and Parks Act, the Minister of the Interior had authority to proclaim certain areas of the Rocky Mountains Forest Reserve as game preserves, and in 1913 the Minister of the Interior in the new Conservative administration, William Roche, accepted Harkin's advice and declared the area a game preserve. The order-in-council described the preserve as a 'favourite haunt of deer and mountain sheep and goats' and concluded that it was necessary to afford these animals protection in their natural habitat in order to prevent their extinction.[52]

Having solved the problem of Rocky Mountains Park, Harkin

turned his attention to Waterton Lakes. The park was located on the eastern slope of the Rocky Mountains, just north of the international boundary. It was set aside in 1895 as a forest reserve, largely at the urgings of John 'Kootenai' Brown, a former trapper and hunter who was concerned about the declining wildlife numbers in the region.[53] When the reserve was given Dominion Park status in 1911, Brown was appointed Park Superintendent. He wrote to Harkin, informing the Commissioner that he had been in close contact with the Camp Fire Club of America and that the creation of an international wildlife refuge by joining Waterton with the American Glacier National Park was 'something wished for by true sportsmen and nature lovers.'[54] Describing the Waterton Lakes region in great detail and mentioning the many species of wildlife that found sanctuary there, Brown pleaded with the Commissioner to extend the park boundaries. Hornaday, president of the Camp Fire Club, had sent Brown a copy of his book, *Our Vanishing Wildlife*, and the Superintendent closed his letter to Harkin with a quotation from it:

The wild things of Earth are not ours to do with as we please. They have been given to us in trust, and we must account for them to the generations which will come after us to audit our accounts.[55]

Members of the Department of the Interior had been in correspondence with the Camp Fire Club in previous years over the boundary change to Waterton. Club members were particularly anxious to secure an extension of the park. Three months after Harkin received Brown's earnest request, he concluded that the Parks Branch was 'thoroughly in accord' with the Camp Fire Club's proposal. He explained to the Deputy Minister that although Waterton Lakes Park was a game preserve, its area was so reduced under the 1911 legislation that it was no longer large enough to protect the many varieties of wildlife that inhabited the region. Harkin suggested that the obvious way to create an effective preserve was to extend the boundaries of the park beyond their existing limits.[56] The Conservation Commission's Committee on Forests also recommended that the park be extended in the interests of game preservation and James White, the Commission's Secretary, sent a personal copy of its resolution to Robert Borden, the Conservative prime minister.[57]

The recommendation was accepted. In 1914, an Order-in-Council extended the boundaries of Waterton Lakes Park to cover an area of 423 square miles, creating a park far larger than the original fifty-four square miles set aside in 1895.[58] Harkin acknowledged in his annual report for 1914 that the decision to extend the park was the result of 'strong representations' made to the branch by the Camp Fire Club of America and other parties interested in the preservation of wildlife. The park area now reached the boundary line and, in conjunction with Glacier National Park, formed one huge international wildlife preserve.

Harkin by this time was convinced of the need to extend all the national parks and he proposed enlarging Jasper Park to 4400 square miles (from its current 1000 and former 5000). He argued that the park area was too small and narrow and the fact that it had undefined boundaries made the question of game protection and regulations 'a joke.'[59] Poachers and Indians easily penetrated the region. The boundaries should follow natural features, he advised the Deputy Minister, and should include the most beautiful scenery, located at present outside the park area.[60] Enclosing letters from railway officials desirous of the park's expansion, the Commissioner, as if to put the icing on the cake, promised Cory that 'the enlargement of Jasper will be to the Grand Trunk Pacific and Canadian Northern, what Banff was to the Canadian Pacific Railway.' And to convince the Deputy Minister still further of the necessity for immediately enlarging the park, Harkin added that 'a large area will attract and retain for a longer time tourists who bring into the country thousands of dollars and take nothing out.'[61] It seems the government needed little convincing in 1914 on the commercial importance of national parks. The same order-in-council that extended the boundaries of Waterton Lakes Park also extended those of Jasper.

Harkin recognized that the extension of national parks was essential for game protection in the Rocky Mountains, but he also knew that not all Canadians shared his views. Just as protests had risen from conservation groups when the park areas were reduced in 1911, petitions from hunters protesting the parks' expansion came in after 1914. 'Protests are bound to be made no matter where game preserves may be established,' Harkin admitted to a member of the Alberta provincial government who had received a number of angry letters and petitions. 'No person who has been in the habit of hunting in any park looks very kindly upon action which deprives him of such privileges.'[62] But Harkin told the provincial member that so far as the Parks Branch was concerned, the goal was to protect the wildlife of the Rocky Mountains and that even if a limited number of hunters were being deprived of their privileges, the larger interests of the Canadian people were being served by protecting the country's wildlife.[63]

The Parks Commissioner came to recognize, like Douglas, that wildlife had an important role within a national park and that birds and mammals were an attraction for tourists 'not even second to the grandeur of the mountain scenery':[64]

Many children today have never seen a wild animal unless in a circus, museum or zoo, and these can give him at best but a poor and partial idea of what a wild creature is like in its natural surroundings. To see a deer leading its fawn down to drink at some quiet lake, to watch a beaver building its dam, or black bear cubs chasing each other up and down a tall pine tree, a wild goat leading the flock across a knife-edge crag to their airy pastures near the snow line can give him a thrilling sense of kinship with nature, and teach him more of her wondrous ways than all the classes in biology ever can.[65]

There were also aesthetic and highly sentimental reasons for preserving wildlife that were closely bound up with Harkin's own personal philosophy of wilderness. 'The farther we have been from nature,' he once wrote, 'the more we need to get back to the natural and even primitive life. Such a life allows man to resume his relationship with wild animals, a relationship as old as man himself and which every man takes pleasure in renewing.'[66] Harkin shared the same fear as Hornaday that, as civilization encroached more and more on wilderness, national parks would soon become the only places left where wildlife could be found in a natural and pristine state. As Parks Commissioner, Harkin felt keenly his personal responsibility, and that of his branch, for wildlife protection on all park reservations and throughout the large, uninhabited regions of northern Canada. He quoted Hornaday's prediction that North America was rapidly becoming a gameless continent, and that unless protective measures were instituted at once many wildlife species would eventually go the way of the buffalo, the passenger pigeon, and the great auk.[67] If the Canadian government did not take prompt action, Harkin warned the Minister in 1916, Canada's wildlife species would suffer the same fate as that overtaking those in the United States. The buffalo had been saved 'at the last moment' by government action, but he recognized the need for greater protection of deer, moose, elk, and caribou:

Once an animal becomes exterminated it cannot be replaced. Forests may be cut down and burned but reforestation is possible; towns may be destroyed by fire but better ones may rise from the ashes. It is not so with our mammals and birds; creatures that have existed long before the advent of man disappear as a result of [our] waste and recklessness and we are poorer for their loss.[68]

Hornaday had estimated that barren ground caribou, in spite of their large numbers, would be 'swept away in 100 years or less' and that moose, unless protected, would also surely and rapidly disappear. 'These conditions emphasize the need of active steps being now taken,' Harkin told the Minister. 'Protective laws, while of great importance, must be supplemented by ample sanctuaries':

All the Dominion parks are wild life sanctuaries, and everything done in connection with the extension of parks ... will contribute in a most important and effective way towards the preservation of Canadian wild life. [69]

The Parks Branch was in a far stronger position after Harkin took office to deal effectively with questions of wildlife protection. The new branch included an 'Animal Division' that became responsible for many matters of game protection throughout the Dominion. Wildlife was still a relatively new concern for government, but Harkin's interest, like Douglas's before him, was not confined solely to national parks. Determined that North America should not become the 'gameless continent' that Hornaday had predicted, the Commissioner turned the attentions of his branch, and the Animal Division, to many wildlife species that were in need of protection – migratory birds, wood buffalo and fur-bearing animals in the north, and to the endangered prong-horn antelope on the Canadian prairies.

James Harkin, Canada's first Dominion Parks Commissioner and the first Canadian to understand the value of wilderness as a resource. *Public Archives of Canada*

The original staff members of the National Parks Branch shortly after creation of the branch in 1913. Maxwell Graham is seated second from the left and James Harkin is standing centre rear. *Parks Canada*

Gordon Hewitt, a dedicated preservationist and Dominion Entomologist with the Department of Agriculture. Hewitt was Canada's chief negotiator for the International Migratory Bird Treaty signed in 1916. *Public Archives of Canada*

The trade in wild bird plumage in the United States at the end of the
nineteenth century contributed to the decline in numbers of many bird species.
This hat is adorned with egret feathers. NAS *Photo, National Audubon Society*

Advertisement from Eaton's *Fall and Winter Catalogue*, 1902–3. *Archives, Eaton's of Canada Limited*

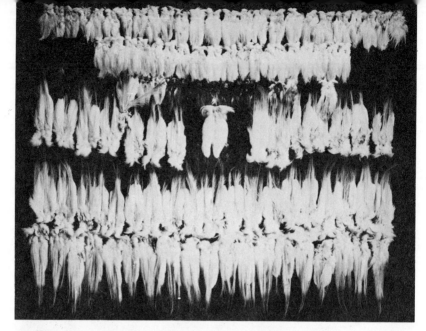

ABOVE Wild bird plumage seized by American authorities in the 1920s. The trade in feathers from protected species became illegal with passage of the Migratory Bird Treaty. NAS *Photo, National Audubon Society*

BELOW Hunters in a Kansas City bar in 1913. This picture clearly illustrates the need for bag limits and international hunting regulations. *New York Zoological Society*

5
Taking the Initiative

One of the major problems to confront the Parks Branch after 1912 was the declining number of pronghorn antelope on the Canadian prairies. The animals, believed by some writers to have been once as numerous as the buffalo, ranged in Canada on the grassland territory between Manitoba and the Rocky Mountains, and as far north as Edmonton, Alberta.[1] During the nineteenth century, their numbers rapidly declined with the spread of prairie settlement and loss of range land, the building of railways that hindered the animals' natural migrations, and increasing man-made range fires and indiscriminate shooting by whites and Indians alike. Writer-naturalist Ernest Thompson Seton reported the last one killed in Manitoba in 1881,[2] and by the 1890s pronghorn disappeared entirely from their former range in the north. Only a small remnant of the once numerous herds remained in southern Alberta and Saskatchewan. A disastrously hard winter in 1906–7 further reduced pronghorn numbers and their extinction in Canada became almost inevitable.

The Chief Game Guardian with the Saskatchewan provincial government, Thomas Willing, believed that of an estimated 20,000 antelope surviving on the North American continent in 1910, some 4000 were divided evenly between Alberta and Saskatchewan. Suggesting that 'we should learn something from the experience gained by the disappearance of the buffalo,' he proposed to Campbell that antelope preserves be established throughout the prairie provinces where the animals could be protected in captivity. Many areas of southern Saskatchewan were unfit for agriculture but would be eminently suitable for pronghorn. Willing advised Campbell that should the dominion government set aside such lands in southern Saskatchewan, the provincial government would declare them sanctuaries.[3]

Campbell supported Willing's proposal and informed the Deputy Minister of the Interior that the country frequented by antelope was being rapidly settled and that 'if reserves are not created immediately, the pronghorn will almost certainly become extinct.'[4] The following year, an area of land along the banks of the South Saskatchewan River north of Swift Current was set aside under authority of the Deputy Minister as a Dominion Forest Reserve. It was declared a game preserve by the Saskatchewan provincial government at the same time.[5]

Alberta's Chief Game Guardian, Benjamin Lawton, was also deeply concerned about the fate of the pronghorn. He reported that between 1908 and 1913, some 634 animals were legally shot in his province, while many others, no doubt, were shot illegally. After 1910, conditions in southern Alberta grew increasingly unfavourable for the animals as open rangeland was taken over by homesteaders, and antelope territory steadily dwindled. Lawton recommended that the provincial government introduce a closed hunting season to last for a number of years so that the pronghorn population could rebuild, but he also believed that the animals would soon be 'crowded out of existence' unless a reserve was immediately established.[6] He suggested that an area along the Red Deer River in the vicinity of Medicine Hat be set aside for this purpose as the land there was rough and totally unsuited to agriculture. 'I cannot too strongly recommend the establishment of such a reserve,' he concluded in his 1911 report. During the next few years, the provincial government did consider a number of measures for protecting the pronghorn, but although a five-year closed hunting season was adopted in 1913, the province took no further action towards establishing Lawton's proposed reserve.

As mentioned earlier, shortly after creation of the Parks Branch in 1911, a small Animal Division had been established within the branch to handle all specific questions relating to wildlife. It was headed by Maxwell Graham, who had entered government service as a clerk in 1906 and joined the Parks Branch in 1912. Graham was born in England in 1870 and was the son of Lieutenant-General Sir Gerald and Lady Jane Graham of Bideford, Devon. His father had distinguished himself as a young second lieutenant at the Crimea in 1854, winning the Victoria Cross in recognition of his bravery and humanity on the battlefield. Later successes during the China campaign of 1860 and in the eastern Sudan in 1884 brought him a hero's welcome in England. But military life did not attract young Maxwell and rather than follow in his father's prestigious footsteps, he sailed for Canada in 1897 at the age of twenty-two. He settled in Guelph, where he attended Ontario's Agricultural College, learning all there was to know about the newest scientific farming techniques. A few years later, he bought a farm near Magnetawan and his education was put to good use. With his wife and two small children, Graham readily adapted to life in the outdoors and the freedom of running his own small mixed farming operation. Northwestern Ontario was very much a wilderness frontier at the turn of the century and it was there that Graham's interest in birds and mammals awakened. During the long winter evenings, he frequently read aloud to his daughters from the works of William Shakespeare and Charles Dickens and later, he filled their imaginations with tales from Charles G.D. Roberts, Thornton Burgess, and Ernest Thompson Seton. But life in the backwoods of Ontario was hard on his young wife, and after six years Graham sold the farm and moved his family to Ottawa. Once he had found a job in government service, it was only a question of time until his growing interest in wildlife brought him eventually to the Parks Branch.[7]

Graham shared a similar commitment and enthusiasm with the Dominion Parks Commission towards preserving Canada's indigenous wildlife species and, shortly after the three-man Animal Division was created, he quickly appointed himself chief of it. The question of pronghorn antelope protection soon occupied his undivided attention. Members of the Parks Branch became convinced as early as 1909, while they were still under the administration of the Forestry Branch, of the urgent necessity to protect pronghorn. Many attempts were made to acquire the animals for the national parks, but staff efforts met with little success. The fleet-footed pronghorns with their superb telescopic sight were difficult to capture and adapted badly to captivity. Six of the nine introduced to Buffalo National Park died during the winter of 1910, their deaths attributed to confinement and lack of natural vegetation.[8] Graham joined Robert Campbell in his efforts to live-trap the animals, but by the end of 1912 he admitted to Harkin that success had eluded them. Twelve of the fourteen transported to Rocky Mountains and Buffalo parks died in the first year and survival of the remaining two was in grave doubt. At this point, Graham became convinced that it was impossible to preserve the animals in the existing national parks that were located far from the animals' natural environment. He seized upon the idea that if the species was to survive at all, the herds would have to be fenced and protected on their open rangeland in the wild.[9]

Harkin went along with Graham's theory and approached Ernest

Thompson Seton for his assistance in locating appropriate range lands in the west that could be reserved and fenced for pronghorn. Although the branch had its tiny Animal Division, it did not have any wildlife specialists or consultants on staff and there was good reason for Harkin to engage Seton's services. Seton was wildlife consultant to the Manitoba provincial government and had established an international reputation as a renowned author and naturalist. He was born in England but came to Canada with his family at the age of six. While growing up in southern Ontario and on the plains of Manitoba, Seton developed the skills of an artist and a life-long interest in wildlife. His first, and most famous, work, *Wild Animals I Have Known*, was published in 1898. In requesting Seton's assistance, Harkin explained to the Deputy Minister that saving the antelope was a matter of concern to all lovers of wildlife, but that efforts in national parks had failed. Seton, however, had recommended a range near Medicine Hat where the antelope could be enclosed and protected in the wild state. It was Harkin's intention to send him and Graham out to inspect the area for a potential reserve. Even if the range proved unsuitable, Harkin prudently added, 'the department can hardly incur fair criticism of action taken on the advice of such an undoubted authority – in the public estimation – as Mr Seton.'[10] One can only imagine the eager anticipation with which Graham looked forward to his first assignment. Here was a good chance to test his theory, and a golden opportunity to meet and spend time with a man whose works he had known and deeply admired for a number of years.

Seton and Graham set out on their inspection tour in the spring of 1914. The proposed reserve area, located in Alberta just north of Medicine Hat, was unfit for agriculture, but with its abundance of shrubs and plants was well adapted for antelope range. It was also in the same area that Benjamin Lawton had proposed for a reserve to the provincial government four years before. Snowfall was light, the climate moderate, and Seton predicted it would be easy to fence. The proposed territory was close to two railway lines, and a branch of the Grand Trunk Pacific was scheduled to run just a few miles to the north. Both buffalo and elk bones were found in the area, and the presence of black-tailed deer and mountain sheep further convinced Seton that it was good grazing land. Medicine Hat's leading citizens and neighbouring ranchers were reportedly in favour of the reserve, and with all the natural beauties of the area, 'the place will be celebrated in the northwest,' the naturalist concluded. Graham fully concurred in Seton's appraisal, adding that road and trails in the vicinity were well adapted for motoring, and recommended to Harkin that 'Canyon Preserve' be set aside immediately as a permanent antelope reserve.[11]

Seton and Graham took the opportunity to examine a second possible reserve area near Maple Creek in southern Saskatchewan. It covered 12,000 acres of valley, ravines, ponds, and upland meadows and was, in Seton's estimation, by far the most beautiful range land they had seen. Situated in the heart of 'old antelope country,' it contained a similar abundance of plant food to Canyon Preserve, and abounded in game animals and bird life. Even in the improbable event that antelope did not thrive in the region, Seton pointed out that the reserve could still be well used for buffalo, elk, deer, beaver, and all the many varieties of birds in the northwest. The owner of the land agreed to an equitable arrangement for transferring sections of it to the government and Seton advised Harkin to secure the area for an antelope reserve, wildlife sanctuary, and national park. 'I am convinced that there is not only a wonderful opportunity to save the antelope as you did the buffalo,' he wrote, 'but you can also secure the gratitude of posterity by establishing these parks as places of pleasure and health for the whole nation.' Indeed, so enthusiastic was Seton over the possibilities for Maple Creek Preserve that he personally offered, 'at great personal sacrifice,' to undertake development of it.[12] Graham advised Harkin in a separate memorandum not to underestimate Seton's enthusiasm. The American government had approached the famous naturalist more than once to undertake various projects for them, he wrote, but Seton was 'a good British subject and would be willing to do for Canada what he would not undertake for a foreign government.' Supporting Seton's recommendation for the reservation of Maple Creek, Graham impressed on Harkin the importance of getting a speedy decision from the Minister.[13]

Just two weeks after their recommendation went through, both proposed reserves – Canyon and Maple Creek – were set aside as permanent antelope parks. Maple Creek was subsequently fenced, but no one knows if Seton played a role in the early development of the reserve. With the assignment completed, Seton returned to New York and Graham to Ottawa. But a strong friendship had developed between the two men and Seton's personality and opinion was to exert a strong influence on Graham's wildlife work in the years ahead.

A year after creation of the two new reserves, Sergeant Tom Stevens of the NWMP reported to his Commanding Officer in February 1915, that a sheep rancher north of Foremost, Alberta, had discovered about 200 antelope on his range. The snow was very deep and the animals

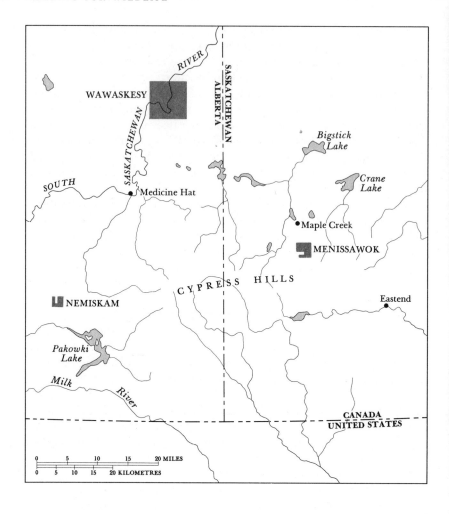

Wawaskesy, Menissawok, and Nemiskam National Antelope Parks

obviously starving, as they had overcome their natural fear of man and were feeding with the rancher's sheep close to the farm buildings. While the rancher took great pride in having antelope on his property, he had little feed to spare and Stevens believed that the government should do something to protect the herd.[14] Harkin received word of the pronghorn and recommended to the Deputy Minister that Graham go out to Alberta at once and corral the animals. 'This is an opportunity to capture antelope in quantity which may never come again,' he added in a postscript, 'and despite financial conditions is one that I consider the department cannot afford to overlook.'[15]

Graham promptly and eagerly returned to Alberta. The Canadian Pacific construction agent at Medicine Hat kindly gave him the use of a railway freight car which Graham fitted up as an office and bunkhouse. From there, with the assistance of two game guardians and a forest ranger from Cypress Hills, he set out to locate the antelope herd. His plan was to construct a corral near the animals and either entice or drive them into it. Once caught, the pronghorn could be quickly and easily transported to either of the new antelope reserves.

The job of finding and containing the antelope, however, proved more difficult than Graham had imagined. They found thirty-two pronghorn and had the corral almost completed when a warm chinook wind blew in the night, dispersing the entire herd. Undaunted, Graham hired seven professional riders and succeeded in finding the animals, now numbering fifty, located on a neighbouring ranch fifteen miles to the south. Graham realized he could not drive the animals back to the partially completed corral, but he also doubted they would thrive anywhere in a confined space. He shelved his earlier plans and decided to fence the surrounding five sections of land and completely enclose the herd in its wild state. The area covered five square miles and Graham estimated the fence would take at least a month to complete, but he assured the Parks Commissioner that the cost of fencing, labour included, would be well under $1500. He pointed out that the Foremost District, which was along the main line of the Canadian Pacific Railway, contained more antelope than any other region in Alberta, and concluded, 'we shall never have a better opportunity of cheaply making an all year [round] reserve for antelope.'[16]

Harkin, recognizing the need to protect pronghorns, supported Graham's endeavours from the beginning, but now he seriously doubted that Graham could fence the wild herd. 'If I were satisfied Graham could positively make good his guarantee,' he admitted to William Cory, the Deputy Minister, 'I would have no hesitation in recommending that the necessary authority be given to him.' But Harkin doubted Graham could hold the herd long enough to complete the fencing. Having no further advice on the subject and clearly reluctant to come to a decision himself, he left the matter up to the Deputy Minister, with the result that Graham was recalled at once and the project cancelled.[17]

Graham returned to Ottawa more determined than ever to test his theory for successfully preserving pronghorn. It was an opportunity too good to miss, and he soon convinced Harkin that the wild herd could be fenced and protected in the wild. The Parks Commissioner told the Deputy Minister that Graham's extensive knowledge about the habits of the antelope, and the fact that local residents agreed with his proposition, 'convinces me that this proposal is perfectly sound and would be good business.' Graham gave Harkin his word that the total cost would not exceed $1500 and the Commissioner pointed out to the Deputy Minister that a conservative estimate on the value of fifty antelope, 'at present prices,' was $2500. There could be economically sound reasons for protecting pronghorn antelope! Harkin recommended that, in view of all the factors involved and the threatened extinction of wild antelope in Canada, Graham be given permission to proceed with his plans for antelope preservation.[18]

For the third time, Graham returned to the west, where he found a disheartening situation. A neighbouring rancher who had been looking after the antelope for the Parks Branch was ill, and, in his absence, a band of roving Indians had killed a number of the antelope and driven off many others. Only twenty-one pronghorn remained in the five sections, but Graham was confident that the rest would eventually return.[19] 'If you are thoroughly satisfied you can enclose the remaining antelope,' Harkin cabled from Ottawa, 'proceed with fence.' The following day, the Commissioner wired Graham $1500.[20]

He hired a small group of local men and began work early in April, ordering specially woven wire fencing from Hamilton, Ontario, and more than 2000 cedar posts to support it. The fence had to stand at least five feet high with three strands of barbed wire running along the top to keep dogs and coyotes out of the enclosure. He sent detailed descriptions of his plans to Seton in New York and also wrote to Hornaday and the head of the United States Biological Survey asking their advice on the proposed height for the fence and on methods of attracting other antelope into the enclosure once it was erected.[21]

The work proceeded quickly and smoothly and by the end of four months, well within the allotted time, Graham had successfully fenced the five square miles. The fence went up so quickly and quietly that Hornaday later claimed Graham must have used 'padded hammers and velvet-headed nails.'[22] The land was owned by Edgar McHugh, who willingly deeded the portion the reserve was on to the federal government. Indeed, he offered, at no cost, to act as caretaker for the antelope. Graham was delighted with McHugh's spirit of co-operation and wrote to Seton that the rancher was a good British subject (even though he had originally belonged to the 7th Division of the United States Cavalry) and was 'a lover of all forms of wild life.' It was agreed that McHugh would use the enclosure for his livestock only during the winter. Graham thought this was an excellent idea, for the cattle's hooves would break through the crusty snow and enable the antelope to graze more easily, and as there would be no cattle there in the summer months, the vegetation required by the antelope would have a good chance to reach maturity and reseed itself. It was a good arrangement for all concerned.[23]

By the late summer of 1915, the wild herd of twenty-one pronghorn antelope was safely enclosed and the reserve was officially named Nemiskam National Antelope Park. The government's efforts to protect the pronghorn had not gone unnoticed. Hornaday commended Graham personally on his achievements and wrote a glowing tribute in the Annual Bulletin of the American Permanent Wild Life Protection Fund in 1917, crediting Canada with being the first country in the world to create a huge fenced preserve exclusively for the protection of the endangered antelope. The Alberta Game and Fish Protective Association congratulated the government and hoped that more reserves would be established, and Harkin praised Graham's work in an article he wrote on conservation in Canada for the American Game Protective and Propagation Association. 'It seemed a wild goose proposition to us at Ottawa, and we refused him permission,' the Commissioner admitted, 'but he was so insistent that he was finally authorized to go ahead.' Canada now had a herd of fifty antelope on the protected reservation and 'everything indicates the scheme is going to be a success.'[24]

Nemiskam National Antelope Park was held by members of the Parks Branch to be a decided success. In 1922, Nemiskam, Canyon Reserve, and Maple Creek were all given Dominion Park status and the future of pronghorn antelope on Canada's western prairies was secured. The antelope in Nemiskam increased to 180 in 1923, and by 1925, the reserve was home for 235 pronghorn.[25] So successful was their recovery that the reserve was abolished in 1947 and the land returned to the Alberta provincial government. Canyon Reserve and

Maple Creek, renamed Wawaskesy and Menissawok, were also abolished in 1930 and 1938 respectively and their lands returned to the provincial governments. There was no longer any need to protect pronghorn antelope.

Antelope protection was a singular achievement for the Parks Branch and signified Harkin's intention, and Graham's, to involve the branch and the government in far greater measures of wildlife preservation throughout Canada. 'All the Dominion Parks are game sanctuaries,' the Commissioner wrote in a memo to the Minister in 1914, 'but the question of game outside the parks is of vital concern.' Protective work with antelope convinced Harkin that creating sanctuaries and preserving species in the wild, in their natural habitat, was a sure way to 'give wild animals a chance.'[26] He was aware that caribou, muskox, wood buffalo, and many of the fur-bearing animals in the north were in need of protection and he told the Minister in 1914 that wildlife was too valuable a source of revenue to imperil. Harkin impressed upon the Minister of the Interior the urgent necessity of establishing more game sanctuaries throughout the northwest. In particular, he demanded protection for wood buffalo, a subspecies of plains bison that inhabited the remote, wooded northern regions of western Canada.

Wood buffalo were once numerous in northwestern Canada, ranging through the Athabasca District of central Alberta and Saskatchewan and north to Great Slave Lake in the Northwest Territories. Samuel Hearne wrote the first description of wood buffalo in 1772, noting their presence in large numbers in the lower Slave River region.[27] Sir John Franklin observed them on the north side of Great Slave Lake in 1820,[28] while Alexander Mackenzie (1789), Daniel Harmon (1808), and Sir George Simpson (1828) recorded their abundance along the Peace River.[29]

No one knows how many wood buffalo there were originally. Estimates vary greatly, one source placing their numbers at 168,000 in 1800.[30] Few white men other than explorers and trappers had frequented the northern haunts of wood buffalo, and most estimates, based on daily sightings, rumours, and native Indian memories, were purely conjectural. In any case, it would have been very difficult to judge numbers accurately. Unlike the prairies to the south, where buffalo could be sighted easily, the country inhabited by wood buffalo was heavily forested and the herds smaller and more widely scattered. Estimates of wood buffalo numbers were, at best, educated guesses.

There is no doubt, however, that wood buffalo were numerous in the early 1800s and that sometime during the nineteenth century their numbers began a steady decline. By the 1890s, they were brought to the verge of extinction. Journals and diaries began to note a growing scarcity of buffalo after 1860. Journeying down the Peace River in 1872, William Butler missed the 'giant forms' that 'no longer darken the steep lofty slopes';[31] John Macoun reported wood buffalo practically extinct south of the Peace River by 1875;[32] and Robert MacFarlane, remembering how plentiful buffalo were in 1863, observed that in the Athabasca region they had 'dwindled so greatly' in numbers that only a few individuals remained.[33] William Ogilvie sadly concluded in a report to the Senate Investigating Committee in 1888 that wood buffalo were 'nearly a thing of the past.'[34]

The causes of wood buffalo decline are much more difficult to determine than those of the plains bison. The animals never suffered the same systematic killing as the southern species and there were no railways or settlement patterns in the north to affect their migration routes or natural habitat. Following extinction of the plains bison, there was some exploitation of wood buffalo, but not enough to have been a significant factor in their decline. There is evidence from travellers at the time that a series of hard winters in the 1860s with deep snow and rain followed by freezing conditions was responsible for large-scale destruction of the herds. George M. Dawson, exploring the Peace River region in 1879, learned from Indians that the extinction of the buffalo was due not to the introduction of firearms and the active hunting carried on to supply the Hudson Bay forts, but to an excessively severe winter when the snow was 'over the buffalos' backs.'[35] At the same time, William Hornaday also heard that 'many thousands of buffalo' perished as a result of a fourteen-foot snowfall some years earlier.[36] The species depended on being able to feed through snow during long northern winters and unusually deep snowfalls or the formation of an icy crust (such as apparently formed during the mid-nineteenth century) prevented the animals from breaking through the surface to their food supply. It is likely that large numbers of buffalo starved to death on that occasion.

No doubt the harshness of the environment was a significant limiting factor on wood buffalo herds. As a more recent author concluded, wood buffalo did not live under optimum conditions as did the plains bison, and 'a series of difficult winters ... coming simultaneously with improved firearms in the hands of even a limited number of white men and native hunters would be sufficient to cause the near approach to extermination which occurred.'[37] This would seem the most logical explanation, given the written testimony and eyewitness accounts for the decline of wood buffalo numbers in the late nineteenth century. The animals were at the northern limit of a critical range; winters were a test of survival and any new or unusual predation would have had immediate and disastrous consequences for the species.

Concern for wood buffalo protection found expression by the 1890s. Little was known about wildlife in the Northwest Territories, but what scattered information there was came from explorers, members of the Canadian Geological Survey, Northwest Mounted Police detachments, and a few sportsmen and naturalists who ventured into the region. A series of Senate investigating committees into the resources of the NWT began in 1870, and during an 1891 meeting it was reported that wood buffalo were rare in the Athabasca. The committee advised protecting the few remaining herds before the species became totally extinct.[38] Three years after the Senate Investigating Committee Report, the Unorganized Territories Game Preservation Act was passed by Parliament. Divisions of the NWMP were the first to note the decline of wildlife in the northwest and the origin of the 1894 Act can be credited to police officers' concern for bird and mammal species in a land of supposed wildlife superabundance. The Act provided for increased wildlife protection throughout the territories by establishing closed hunting seasons for a variety of birds and mammals and strictly prohibiting the killing of wood buffalo for a five-year period.

Little was done in the way of enforcing the Unorganized Territories Game Preservation Act until NWMP Inspector Arthur Jarvis took the first patrol into the Athabasca region in 1897. Jarvis was ordered by Commissioner Lawrence Herchmer to report on the condition of the Indians there, but he was also instructed to obtain what information he could on a large herd of wood buffalo, reported to have been seen in the area of the Caribou Mountains, south of Great Slave Lake and near Fort Smith.[39] Estimates of the surviving numbers varied between one hundred and five hundred animals, and Jarvis was advised to locate the herd, determine its exact numbers, and see if the 1894 Game Act was affording them adequate protection.

Travelling down the Athabasca River, Jarvis learned of the large numbers of wood buffalo that formerly roamed through the region, but was told by Indians that the herds were now scattered and probably did not exceed 300 animals. Jarvis determined as best he could the range of the buffalo, and posted notices of game laws and closed seasons everywhere he travelled.[40] This resulted in the following year in the first conviction under the Act, when two Indian hunters were arrested and punished in Fort Smith for illegally killing wood buffalo. Commissioner Herchmer noted the example and claimed it had an excellent effect for, one year later, not a single wood buffalo had been killed.[41] Enforcement of the Game Act no doubt marked the beginning of a natural wood buffalo increase in the area. The Commissioner for the Department of Indian Affairs, who journeyed through the Athabasca in the vicinity of Caribou Mountains in 1900, estimated the surviving buffalo numbers between 500 and 575, a significant increase from previous years.[42]

Police officers were not the only ones concerned about wood buffalo protection in the Canadian north during the early twentieth century. In 1902 Madison Grant, a prominent member of the New York Zoological Society, wrote to Clifford Sifton, Minister of the Interior, noting that the period of wood buffalo protection under the 1894 Game Act was due to expire that year. The Society had learned from an unknown source that Indian tribes in northern Athabasca were planning a buffalo hunt with the object of 'destroying as many of the remaining buffalo as circumstances will permit' and Grant hoped the government would re-enact the closed season. He praised the success of the Canadian government in 'preserving order, and securing observance of its laws' and told Sifton that Canada furnished a noteworthy example for all other countries. The Zoological Society urged the 'extreme desirability' of extending protection to the wild bison still found in the Athabasca.[43]

The protective period for wood buffalo did expire in 1902, but MPs, no doubt influenced by the recommendations of the NWMP and the Minister of the Interior, passed an amendment to the 1894 Act which extended the closed season on wood buffalo to 1907. As before, members of the NWMP were appointed ex-officio game guardians and police detachments continued to penetrate the little-known regions of the Athabasca, gathering valuable information about the herds and haunts of wood buffalo, and determining the limits of their northern range.

The problem, however, became more complex in the early 1900s. Colourful rumours began to circulate that timber wolves were increasing throughout wood buffalo country. Stories told of great wolf packs attacking the buffalo herds and killing all the young calves. Reports that the buffalo herds were steadily declining in numbers due to fierce wolf predation reached both the Department of the Interior and the NWMP in 1906.[44] Police officers in the Athabasca region raised the wolf bounty from five to ten dollars, but Indians were reportedly superstitious about wolves and refused to kill them, regardless of the increased bounty.[45] Edward Preble, a naturalist with the United States Biological Survey, reported in 1904 that 'Indians are superstitious about wolves, and can scarcely be induced to kill them, much less skin or handle them, for fear of misfortune. The death of a child soon afterwards was supposed to have been the result of this rash act, in which the father had participated.'

The reports prompted another investigation by Inspector Jarvis in 1907. This time he was accompanied by Ernest Thompson Seton and Edward Preble. Operating out of Fort Smith, Jarvis and Seton quickly determined that buffalo were indeed decreasing, but not from wolf predation. Rather, it was the 'two-legged' poachers out of Fort Smith that were to blame. Seton summed up the situation with some humour for the Minister:

At Ottawa it was reported that the wolves were killing the calves, so the buffalo did not increase. At Winnipeg the wolves were so bad that they killed the year-lings; at Edmonton the cows were not safe; at Chepewyan the wolves, re-inforced by large bands from the Barren Grounds, were killing the young buffalo, and later the cows and young bulls. At Smith's Landing ... horses and dogs were now being devoured. Terrible battles were taking place between the dark wolves of Peace River and the White wolves of the Barrens for possession of the buffalo grounds!

'The wolves are indeed playing havoc with the buffalo,' Jarvis concluded, 'and the ravenous leaders of the pack are called Sousi, Kiza, and Squirrel!' (the names of three local Chipewyan Indians).[46]

Contrary to the many stories, Jarvis and his party found no sign of wolves on their expeditions out from Fort Smith. They did discover that the region abounded in bear, caribou, moose, and a great variety of bird life. They also established that the wood buffalo range was very limited and encompassed a wedge of territory between the Slave and Peace rivers and the Caribou Mountains. Predicting that without great-er protection wood buffalo would not last another five years, Jarvis recommended the appointment of resident game guardians to protect the herds. But, he added, 'it would be easy to secure greater protection by establishing the area as a national park.'[47]

Northwest Mounted Police Commissioner Aylesworth Perry, who had replaced Herchmer, supported Jarvis's conclusion and advised the Minister of the Interior that 'these are the last wood buffalo and it would be a thousand pities if they were exterminated.' Permanent police detachments were stationed at forts Smith, Vermilion, and

Chipewyan the following year to enforce game regulations, but Perry recommended in his 1908 report that a buffalo reserve be created in the Athabasca. Police patrols had established that the buffalo range encompassed some 9100 square miles and Perry observed that should a national park be established on the range, it would protect not only the buffalo, but all species of wildlife in the region.[48]

Between 1907 and 1911, the role of the NWMP in wood buffalo protection was substantial. Detachments gathered essential information on buffalo habitat, range, and approximate numbers and put forward the suggestion for a national park. Had their recommendation been carried out, it would have resulted in creation of the largest and most northerly national park established by the dominion government, a park created not as a 'public playground' but for the protection of an endangered wildlife species.

However, in 1911, responsibility for wood buffalo protection was taken away suddenly from the NWMP and given to the Forestry Branch of the Department of the Interior. It was Campbell's decision to make his Forestry Branch responsible for wood buffalo protection and probably his influence persuaded the Minister to sanction the transfer.[49] Forestry personnel were experienced in handling wildlife matters in dominion forest reserves, and it may have been that Campbell was attracted by the wooded region of the Athabasca with its herds of wild buffalo. There is little evidence to show from their reports whether NWMP officers were disappointed about the curtailment of their duties. The report for 1911 noted only that the two half-breed trappers hired by the NWMP to protect the herds were discharged in the summer and special supervision of wood buffalo was transferred to the government agent at Smith's Landing.

Campbell moved quickly to prepare for the takeover of wood buffalo protection by his branch. He hired a game guardian, George Mulloy, and an experienced trapper, Peter McCallum, in the early spring to take charge of the northern bison. Both men were to be under the immediate supervision of the department's representative at Smith's Landing, A.J. Bell, but were responsible to the Forestry Branch in Ottawa.[50] Mulloy was a former bank clerk who had taken a course in natural science from Ontario's Agricultural College. Experienced in surveying, he was expected to compile accurate maps of the region, while McCallum, his assistant, was to hunt and destroy wolves.[51] The animals were still firmly believed to be the major cause of buffalo decline, although no proof was furnished by the NWMP in all their years of patrolling the area.

The two men set off in the spring of 1911 to reconnoitre buffalo country, but from the very beginning they did not get on well together. Mulloy was considerably younger than McCallum and the old trapper seemed unimpressed by Mulloy's credentials or abilities. Most of their time was spent in bitter disagreement, while long letters filled with petty complaints against each other flowed back to departmental headquarters in Ottawa. Mulloy had no trapping experience of any kind, but was quick to find fault with McCallum, complaining that the old trapper's eyes were dim, that he lacked the ability to follow a track, and that he was unable to travel over rough terrain for any distance. 'I don't know why I should be hampered by an old fake like him,' Mulloy complained to Campbell, 'just because he's a friend of Mr Oliver [Minister of the Interior]. That same "pull" as he thinks he possesses has made him assume an air of authority and made him thoroughly obnoxious.'[52] A few of Mulloy's complaints were justified. McCallum's trapping experience was limited to beaver, mink, and other small fur-bearing animals.[53] No doubt he lacked the necessary technique and expertise to track and trap timber wolves, a difficult task for even the most experienced trappers. But the difference in age and background probably accounted for most of their disagreements. To the young, impatient Mulloy, McCallum was little more than 'a doddering old ex-carpenter.'[54]

Despite their disagreements, however, the survey continued throughout the spring and summer, providing solid information about the region and revealing that game was plentiful – moose, caribou, bear, beaver, partridge, and prairie chicken reportedly 'abounding everywhere.'[55] They also established the presence of two buffalo herds on the range, a northern and a southern, but had no luck estimating the total numbers in either herd. Contrary to belief, they found no sign of significant wolf predation and concluded that it was unlikely the animals were to blame for reducing buffalo herds.[56] But without knowing the numbers of buffalo in the region, neither Mulloy nor McCallum had any way of determining if, indeed, the herds were declining, much less what the cause of the decline could be.

Following completion of Mulloy's survey, Bell furnished a detailed report to the Department in January 1912. He noted the difficulty of protecting bison in the vast territory and suggested that, if the herds could be centralized, 'the annual expenditure would be greatly reduced and more effective protection afforded them.' Bell proposed fencing an area at the junction of the Slave and Peace rivers that was frequented by wood buffalo during the summer and winter months. Both herds could be worked into the protected range and the reserve would provide ample range for a number of years to come. Bell estimated the total cost of moving the herds into such an enclosure, exclusive of the cost of wiring, would be under $5130.[57] Campbell added to that cost the price of fencing the enclosure which, based on the price of fencing the Pablo buffalo herd, would amount to $103,562.[58]

The Deputy Minister of the Interior was as anxious as Bell and Campbell to safeguard the wood buffalo. He reported to the Minister that the animals were the last remnant of a species that 'once roamed in countless thousands' across the North American continent and that the Forestry Branch was making determined efforts to preserve them.[59] Campbell meantime assured the Deputy Minister that the bison were in good health, increasing naturally, and that there was little sign of wolf predation. Mulloy reported that Indians were 'too afraid of the NWMP' to kill the animals and Campbell confidently predicted in 1913 that wood buffalo numbers could reach as high as 500.[60]

Shortly after he had appointed himself Chief of the Parks Branch Animal Division, Maxwell Graham familiarized himself with the Forestry Branch's work in connection with the wood buffalo. Early in 1912, he brought the subject to Harkin's attention, summarizing the work done to date by both the NWMP and the Forestry Branch, and agreeing in principle with Bell's proposal to build a fenced enclosure. Graham estimated there were between one hundred and three hundred wood buffalo surviving in the Athabasca and recommended that their protection be entrusted to a government branch whose interests were bound up with the interests of wildlife, namely the Parks Branch.[61]

He was obviously excited over the prospect of creating a national park in the north and anxious that his branch should play a prominent role in its establishment. He defined the area inhabited by wood buffalo for the Commissioner, pointing out that the land was of little economic value but, possessing winter and summer ranges, would be an ideal location for a large buffalo reserve. The proposed sanctuary would also protect caribou, moose, deer, muskox, muskrat, marten, wolverine, mink, fisher, bear, fox, ermine, beaver, badger, otter, and lynx – all valuable fur-bearing animals in the economic sense, but some of them endangered through over-trapping and the indiscriminate use of poison. The reserve principle had been applied in East Africa with 'brilliant success,' Graham informed Harkin, and he also noted how a protected strip of land on either side of the Uganda Railway was 'absolutely swarming with game.' There was no reason why the same could not be accomplished in the Canadian north.[62] Graham believed that game laws in the Athabasca were not effective, since Indians were by nature 'wantonly destructive' and devoid of ideas of economy in killing. 'It is now generally conceded,' he told Harkin, 'that local inhabitants do not have divine right to pollute streams with sawdust, or destroy forests with axe and fire, or slaughter every living thing; for game and forests belong to all the nation.' The Indians of the Athabasca, Graham concluded, must be persuaded to leave the proposed area and a national park be reserved at once for the protection of all wildlife in the north.[63]

There was good reason in Graham's opinion why the Parks Branch should be given jurisdiction over wood buffalo protection in the north. Park personnel were responsible for wildlife in all the national parks and Graham pointed out that the Athabasca buffalo were the only herds of pureblood bison left on the continent. They compared favourably with the plains bison and it was Graham's belief that the buffalo stock in national parks could be improved and increased by introducing young wood buffalo bulls.[65] It was only natural, therefore, that the animals be placed under the jurisdiction and protection of the dominion Parks Branch.

Harkin took up Graham's suggestion and informed the Minister of the Interior in 1913 that a proposal was being prepared to establish a buffalo reserve in the district of Fort Smith. 'It is considered that if this area was somewhat enlarged and adequately protected,' he advised, 'it would become a natural breeding ground for fur-bearing animals':

These animals would soon learn they were protected in this area and as they would breed there under the most favourable conditions the overflow should in a short time serve to supply a very large contiguous district. [65]

The Parks Commissioner was aware that the protective period for buffalo under the 1894 Game Act was expiring again and that an amendment to re-enact the closed season was due to be introduced to the House of Commons in June 1914. But, as the time approached, Harkin advised the Minister that 'if you do not care to put the Bill through now, due to the late hour of the session, the same purpose could be effected by establishing the area in which the wild buffalo roam as a Dominion Park.' Park status to the area would automatically bring wood buffalo under park jurisdiction and Harkin added that the proposed reserve area was definitely known and 'could easily be de-scribed in an Order-in-Council creating it a Dominion Park.'[66]

Later, the Parks Commissioner had second thoughts on his note to the Minister, perhaps fearing he had overstated the plight of the buffalo. Anxious to check his facts more thoroughly, he instructed Graham to prepare a detailed report on the necessity of protecting the northern bison. Graham, eager to see protection of buffalo placed under the Parks Branch, hastened to comply and within forty-eight hours placed a report, compiled from 'authentic and conclusive evi-dence,' in the Commissioner's hands.[67]

Graham's report narrated the former abundance of wood buffalo and chronicled their steady decline throughout the nineteenth cen-tury. The 1894 Game Act was of limited effect and Graham recom-mended instead that the buffalo range be declared an absolute game sanctuary. 'This can best be done,' he concluded, 'by making such an area a national park.' A park would not conflict with future settlement and development of the Peace River Valley, he argued, but would save the wood bison from extermination and furnish a sanctuary for valu-able northern fur-bearing animals. Reassured by Graham's findings, Harkin passed the report on to the Minister of the Interior, and at the close of the parliamentary session William Roche recommended set-ting aside the wildlife reserve as a national park.[68] But the proposed reserve area was also a traditional Indian hunting ground and before any national park could be created in the north the matter would have to be submitted to the native people. At this juncture, in 1914, negotia-tions for the creation of Caribou Mountain National Park began to bog down.

During the next two years, the proposal to create the park was argued about by the Parks Branch and the Department of Indian Affairs. Inspector Henry Conroy of Indian Affairs strongly opposed the establishment of any wildlife reserve on Indian hunting territory. He questioned whether the region was, in fact, the natural buffalo habitat, and suggested the bison be driven to some other suitable range, arguing that if Indians were forbidden to hunt, wolves would become a serious problem for local communities in the north.[69] Harkin brushed Conroy's suggestion and objection aside. Only a few Indians hunted in the area, he countered in a memo to the Deputy Minister, and they did not possess any special treaty rights. As for the wolf problem, Harkin reminded Cory that Indians would not kill wolves because of their tribal superstitions. He told Cory the Parks Branch had sufficient proof that bison had been in the Fort Smith area for well

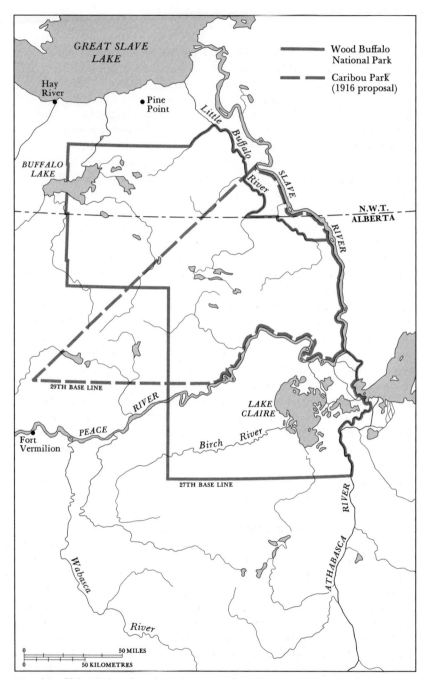

Wood Buffalo National Park and proposed Caribou Park boundaries

over 100 years, and that the reserve, 'like Algonquin Park,' could be a successful breeding place for wildlife. He added that the views of the Parks Branch were 'fully endorsed and concurred in by leading American and Canadian authorities' and concluded by suggesting that a member of Indian Affairs obtain a signed statement from Indian hunters 'waiving any fancied rights they may or may not think they possess to hunt and trap in that area.' He also reminded the Deputy Minister that the original order-in-council of 30 June 1914, recommending the reservation, was still awaiting submission to the Council. It was now April 1916 and he believed 'the time has arrived when steps should be taken to carry out the wishes of authorities everywhere on the conservation of game.'[70]

The proposal to establish a national park in the Fort Smith region was explained to local Indians by members of the Department of Indian Affairs. They were told why the government wanted the reserve, and that native peoples would benefit directly by the overflow of game from the protected park area. They were also assured that the government did not intend to deprive them of their livelihood. After discussing the matter among themselves, the Indian chiefs and headmen reported to H.J. Bury of the Department that the country was 'large and full of game.' If they were allowed a reasonable time to relocate their hunting grounds, they promised they would not claim compensation from the government.[71]

Harkin was impatient to establish the park as soon as possible, and shortly after receiving Bury's report he instructed Graham to draw up a proclamation creating Caribou Mountain National Park for submission to the Governor-General. Possibly as a significant recognition of legitimate Indian claims, Harkin hinted in a note to the Deputy Minister that not all national park regulations need apply to the area in question, but that the northern park could be subject to regulations formed by the Governor-General-in-Council.[72] It is likely Harkin was suggesting to Cory that Indians would be permitted to hunt for game other than wood buffalo in the same region after it was declared a national park.

Harkin and Graham were anxious to protect the bison by establishing a national park in the north. They used their considerable influence within the Department to persuade and convince the Minister of the necessity of establishing the reserve and provided him with the informal means by which it could be accomplished. But the order-in-council, drafted by Graham and submitted to the Governor-General in 1916, was not proclaimed and Caribou Mountain National Park was not created. Possibly World War I and lack of appropriations for park purposes prevented its establishment. However, after the war, Wood Buffalo National Park was established in 1922 within the same geographical limits as the earlier Caribou Mountain National Park.[73] But contrary to Graham's vision of a northern refuge for all species of wildlife, the park regulations permitted Indians to kill game other than wood buffalo within the new park. Harkin had hinted to the Deputy Minister that such a privilege might be granted and it was for Graham, perhaps, the price of obtaining a protected preserve for wood buffalo in 1922.

The negotiations for establishing a wood buffalo park in the years after 1911 emphasized Harkin's and Graham's growing commitment towards preserving Canada's endangered wildlife species. At the same time, the involvement of the Parks Branch also underscored their conviction that it should undertake sole responsibility for wood buffalo and, indeed, all wildlife protection in the Northwest Territories. Even while the Forestry Branch was administering the buffalo herds, Harkin began to exert his influence with the Deputy Minister, advising him that the Parks Branch was studying the question in great detail and was prepared to take over administration of the wild buffalo herds. It was not long before members of the branch were at loggerheads with the Forestry Superintendent. The occasion was the resignation in 1913 of George Mulloy, who finally had become fed up with Peter McCallum. While Campbell cast about for another warden, Harkin immediately contacted the Deputy Minister. Stressing how 'vitally concerned' his branch was in the welfare of the herds, Harkin recommended that they be placed under his jurisdiction for, he told Cory, 'the Forestry Branch cannot have the same incentive for jealously guarding them' as did the Parks Branch.[74] Little transpired as a result of Harkin's recommendation, however, but early in December Campbell began to marshal his arguments to justify the Forestry Branch's continued administration. Preservation of wildlife in the United States, he informed the Deputy Minister, was handled by the Forestry Branch, since most varieties of wild game were 'products of the forest,' and it was only natural that the dominion Forestry Branch handle all questions relating to game in Canada.[75]

Harkin disagreed emphatically with both Campbell's premise and conclusion. While the American Forestry Branch might have handled game preservation before 1900, he argued, the United States Biological Survey was responsible now and the Parks Branch Animal Division was doing 'comparable' work to the animal division of the Biological Survey. He denied that most varieties of wild game were products of the forest; antelope and plains bison clearly were not. 'This branch has had good experience with handling game protective matters,' he told the Deputy Minister, 'and should administer all questions relating to game protection.' Any area in Canada that was inhabited by valuable birds and mammals should be set aside as a game sanctuary and administered by the Parks Branch, he believed, but 'Mr Campbell takes the view that, because these animals are in the forests, the Forestry Branch should administer them.'[76]

It was Harkin's opinion that no matter where wildlife existed, in or out of forest reserves, those areas should be set aside and protected by the Parks Branch. As mentioned earlier, under the 1911 Forest Reserves and Parks Act, the Forestry Branch was responsible for wildlife protection in dominion forest reserves and the Parks Branch responsible for its protection in national parks. The Parks Commissioner, however, was implying that his branch should have sole responsibility for game in all forest reserves, dominion parks, and throughout the whole of the Northwest Territories. It is small wonder that Campbell was annoyed.

He again clarified his position. Members of his branch, he wrote, had taken up matters of game protection with provincial authorities, local game and fish organizations, and members of the Department of Indian Affairs as much as park personnel had done. 'I have no objection to Harkin enlarging the scope of his department,' Campbell warned, 'so long as he does not break down the forestry administration.' He reminded the Deputy Minister that when the Forest Reserves and Parks Act had been passed, it had been decided that both branches should handle game on dominion reserves: 'But that was apparently only a preliminary move on his [Harkin's] part toward trying to get a legal position from which he would work to get control of a large measure of the forestry administration as well as what is properly parks administration.' Campbell complained that Harkin's claim to 'special experts' in his branch added nothing to the argument, for scientifically trained men in forestry had a better knowledge of the theory and practice of game protection than the members or staff of the Parks Branch. 'It's rather far-fetched to equate a small offshoot from the Parks Branch with the United States Biological Survey,' he told the Deputy Minister, 'and claim equal expert knowledge.'[77]

The argument, however, was far from sound. Harkin denied that the Parks Branch equated their Animal Division with the US Biological

Survey, but stated that the Parks' Branch Division was staffed with good men who had taken the initiative on a number of occasions. 'I need only refer you to the written opinion of Mr Ernest Thompson Seton,' he told Cory, 'regarding the work of this branch in the preservation of the antelope.'[78] Maxwell Graham also entered the debate, presenting detailed proof that the Forestry Branch had neither the facilities, special knowledge, nor right to administer game preserves, 'any more than it has the right to administer the development of mineral resources or water powers.' Forestry personnel had been responsible for both park and forest reserves prior to 1911, but Graham charged that during that time no biological work had been undertaken, no data collected regarding birds and mammals, no direct supervision of wildlife initiated by forestry personnel, and no co-operation achieved with provincial authorities on the question of open and closed hunting seasons. 'Some members of the Forestry Branch may be scientifically trained in forestry,' Graham acknowledged, 'but none of them are scientifically, or specially, trained in biology and certainly not in zoology.' (Graham neglected to mention, of course, that neither he nor Harkin had any scientific training in the biological sciences either.) Members of the Forestry Branch, in Graham's estimation, were unfit and unqualified to handle the question of wildlife preservation. Their work with wood buffalo, he pointed out, was not effective and certainly would not be an argument for that branch being entrusted with further work in connection with the conservation of game animals; they had not even succeeded in trapping any wolves. 'The proposed branch to administer game,' Graham concluded, 'whether on forest reserves or not, should be the parks. Our Branch already possesses experienced staff.'[79]

The two-way battle continued through 1914 and well into 1915 with park and forestry personnel both claiming the right to administer wildlife on dominion reserves and throughout the northwest. Graham continually stressed the value of game and the importance of wildlife conservation, while Harkin took the position that foresters were not biologists and 'sufficient has already been said regarding the unfitness of foresters with the work of game conservation.' To strengthen his arguments further, Harkin cited all the individuals and organizations that had expressed approval of the branch's work over previous years and closed his final memo in 1915 with a summary of the effective game regulations in all the dominion parks.[80]

Throughout the continuing debate, the Minister had remained silent, receiving the steady flow of memoranda from Deputy Minister

William Cory, weighing the evidence and coming to his own conclusions. No decision was taken until 1917 and then Cory sent Campbell a short memo informing him that it had been decided to place wildlife protection in the Northwest Territories under the Parks Branch. No formal reasons were given. Campbell was merely instructed to transfer all his files on wood buffalo over to the Parks Commissioner, thus ending the Forestry Branch's involvement with wood buffalo and game protection in the northwest.[81]

The decision to make the Parks Branch responsible for wildlife protection in the north was a sound one. By placing wildlife under a single government branch, protective policies would achieve a uniformity, continuity, and long-term effectiveness. Certainly the past performance of the Parks Branch and Harkin's belief in the value and importance of wildlife to the Dominion augured well for future government wildlife policies. The decision also marked a victory for the Parks Branch and was a strong vindication of Harkin's, and Graham's, wildlife protection program. The Parks Commissioner was becoming committed to the sanctuary idea. He told the Minister of the Interior in 1914 that more protection was needed in the 'great hinterland of the north,'[82] and now that his branch had won jurisdiction over game in the northwest, Harkin could proceed with his plans for muskox and barren ground caribou preservation – wildlife resources he knew were endangered and in need of effective government protection.

6

Protecting an
International Resource

The Migratory Birds Convention Act, passed in 1917, was a landmark
in the evolution of the Canadian government's role in wildlife protection. During the previous years, a few specific endangered wildlife
species – plains bison, antelope, and wood buffalo – had been successfully protected by the federal government, but such protection had not
resulted in a continuing policy for wildlife preservation. In Canada,
most public lands, with the exception of national parks and military
reserves, came under provincial jurisdiction as defined by the British
North America Act. As provincial governments handled their own
game administration, there had been little apparent need for the
federal government to embark on a broad program of wildlife conservation. The question of migratory birds, however, presented an entirely new problem. Birds that summered in the high Canadian arctic
and travelled the length of the continent to winter in the southern
American states and Mexico were neither a national nor a provincial
resource and policies for their protection demanded direct federal
intervention to secure interprovincial and international co-operation.
The movement that carried the question of migratory bird protection
forward in both Canada and the United States became one of the most
important in the early twentieth century.

Public interest in wild birds developed early in the nineteenth century,
stimulated greatly by John James Audubon, the noted naturalist, artist,
and ornithologist. Audubon came to North America from Haiti in
1803 and travelled widely, visiting the coasts of Newfoundland and
Labrador, and the Gulf of the St Lawrence in the 1830s. His large

volumes, *Birds of America* and *Ornithological Biography*, were published in 1826. The emergence of bird-watching and naturalists' clubs was undoubtedly related, in part, to Audubon's works. The parent organization of the Thomas McIlwraith Field Naturalists' Club was one of the earliest in Canada, founded in 1863 and followed by the Ottawa Field-Naturalists' Club in 1879. Both societies had small but expanding memberships and were devoted to bird sightings, insect studies, botany, and detailed examinations of their areas' natural history.

In the United States, the first society concerned solely with the study of birds was the Nutall Ornithological Club, established in Cambridge, Massachusetts, in 1873. It provided an active centre for North American bird-watchers and ornithologists to come together, observe birds, and exchange notes and information. It was of primary importance, however, as the parent club of the American Ornithologists' Union.

The AOU went far beyond being a mere centre for bird-watching activities. There was a growing concern in the United States over the apparent decline in bird life. Farmers noticed an absence of insectivorous birds and reported increasing insect damage to crops and orchards as a result, while urban dwellers noted a significant decline in songbird populations. There was little understanding in the late 1800s about the importance of bird habitat. The draining of swamps and sloughs as settlement advanced destroyed vital nesting grounds for numerous species of waterfowl and shorebirds, while the growth of townsites resulted in a crucial loss of forests, the natural habitat of song and insectivorous birds. After the Civil War, famine was widespread in most southern states and songbirds, woodpeckers, and doves provided an all too easy food supply.[1] The passenger pigeon, like the buffalo, once a symbol of wildlife superabundance, was quickly approaching extinction, and following its disappearance hunters turned to the shorebird populations. Eskimo curlews, Hudsonian godwits, and golden plover were taken for food and fishing bait, practices that pushed all three species to the edge of extinction by the end of the 1880s.[2]

The belief in the superabundance of bird life led to the general slaughter of other species as well. By 1900, Labrador ducks, great auks, and passenger pigeons were extinct, while whooping cranes, wood ducks, egrets, and trumpeter swans joined the growing list of endangered species.[3] The absence of bag limits and uniform hunting seasons in the United States, coupled with intensive market hunting and regular spring shooting, took a heavy toll on bird numbers; but the dictates of fashion took the heaviest toll of all as milliners turned to the colourful plumage of terns, egrets, ibises, bobolinks, rails, and herons to adorn women's hats. A Committee on Bird Protection, set up in 1884 by the AOU to combat the destruction of birds for the millinery trade, reported two years later that in Norfolk, Virginia, robins, meadowlarks, blackbirds, thrushes, warblers, vireos, and waxwings were being sold as food by street vendors, while five million birds a year were systematically slaughtered for the millinery trade:

Among the smaller birds it is naturally the brighter coloured species that furnish most of the victims, especially the orioles, tanagers, grosbeaks, cedar wax-wings, bluebirds, meadow-larks and golden winged woodpeckers. Only their conspicuous abundance on hats and bonnets and their greatly decreased numbers attest the slaughter to which they are subjected. [4]

The Committee found the trade was so lucrative that many of the gunners and market hunters gave up their usual shooting to enter what had become a 'war of extermination.' It reported that in one season alone, over 40,000 terns were killed in the Cape Cod region and a million bobolinks and rails were slaughtered near Philadelphia in a single month, all for the sake of providing feathers for women's hats. Appalled by the increasing destruction of birds, and convinced that the American public was too apathetic or ignorant to take any action, the AOU set itself the task of awakening public conscience to the need for securing better protective legislation.

The problem was that there were no theories of wildlife management or conservation in the 1880s, and North Americans generally knew little of bird habits, food requirements, dependence on habitat, or annual migrations. 'There was a hazy kind of faith,' wrote one author, 'in the existence far north of our borders of a sort of mysterious duck and snipe factory that would turn out the required supply [of game] practically forever.'[5] The Audubon Society, founded in 1886 by Dr George Bird Grinnell, a member of the AOU, joined with the AOU in a campaign against the use of wild bird plumage in the millinery industry. But their task was made doubly difficult by the prevailing belief in wildfowl superabundance. One woman told a writer for the *Audubon Magazine* that 'there is a great deal of sentiment wasted on birds. There are so many of them they will never be missed, any more than mosquitos. I shall put birds on my bonnet.'[6]

Concern for bird protection became more widespread towards the end of the century as pressure for game legislation steadily mounted. More was known about birds, their habits, and annual migrations by 1900. Experiments in bird banding that began in Europe and were brought to America in the late 1890s revealed for the first time the

range and routes of bird migrations across the North American continent.[7] Once the patterns of migration were understood, the consequences of spring shooting, permitted in most American states and many
Canadian provinces, became evident; birds shot on their way north to
nesting grounds in the spring resulted in fewer birds returning south
in the fall. Greater knowledge of bird migrations led to more effective
and better based arguments for legislative protection. The AOU put
forward a 'Model Bird Law' as early as 1886 which was to serve as a
foundation for future legislation. It contained uniform game laws and
hunting seasons for all the states and territories (including the 'British
Provinces') and included a list of endangered species that warranted
permanent protection. But even the AOU recognized that 'the fault is
not so much a lack of laws, or inadequate legislation, as the absence of
nearly all efforts to interpose obstacles, legal or otherwise, in the way of
"free slaughter" .'[8]

The United States's first federal statute for bird protection, the
Lacey Act, was passed by Congress in 1900. It was designed to abolish
market hunting by banning the interstate transportation of birds and
wild game killed in violation of state laws, and by prohibiting the
importation of foreign birds that were regarded as destructive to
American agriculture or native birds. But the legislation did not stop
the importation of foreign bird skins and feathers for the millinery
trade, a practice that continued until well into the 1920s.[9] The Lacey
Act soon proved inadequate to curb abuses. There was profit to be
made in market hunting and too few officers to enforce the new
regulations.[10] The federal legislation did not prohibit either spring
shooting or local market hunting and pressure continued to mount for
more effective legislation.

A second bill for migratory bird protection was introduced to Congress by George Shiras in 1904. Song- and insectivorous birds were not
included in the bill's provisions, however, which led one author to
conclude that only game birds were considered important in 1904 and
that not until much later would bird lovers and the general public
'share the burden of battle.'[11] Although the Shiras bill was referred to a
Committee on Agriculture and praised by President Roosevelt, it failed
to pass the House and no further legislative action was taken in the
United States for the protection of migratory birds in the opening
years of the twentieth century.

The question of migratory bird protection was of great importance to
Canada but few government members or private citizens seemed con-

cerned about the issue. Nearly eighty per cent of all North American waterfowl nested on the Canadian prairies, and the western and northern territories constituted the chief breeding grounds for what is, indeed, an international resource. Abuses against birds and waterfowl were not so great in Canada as in the United States because the hunting population was considerably smaller. Although there were market hunters in Canada, particularly in the Windsor and Prince Edward County regions of southern Ontario, 'market hunting,' because of its dependence on fast transportation and easy access to large urban centres, did not develop into the same large-scale commercial business that it did in the United States. The Unorganized Territories Game Preservation Act of 1894 had provided some protection by establishing closed seasons for swans, ducks, and geese in the NWT, and prohibiting the taking of eggs by anyone except Indians, trappers, and explorers. After 1896, however, intensive western settlement brought by far the greatest pressures on waterfowl numbers as swamps and prairie sloughs were drained to make way for agriculture. Loss of habitat was undoubtedly the single largest factor in the decline of North American waterfowl populations, a fact that was little understood in the nineteenth and early twentieth centuries. Each of the provinces had game legislation on their provincial statute books and most had regulated, if not uniform, open and closed hunting seasons. But provincial legislation was difficult to enforce, particularly along the coastal regions and in the Gulf of the St Lawrence, where chains of small islands formed breeding colonies for thousands of cormorants, murres, gannets, and gulls. Newfoundland and Labrador fishermen traditionally salted down barrels of seabirds for food and bait, while commercial 'eggers' prowled the rugged St Lawrence coastline, robbing nests and relentlessly slaughtering the birds, an 'evil business' deplored by Audubon in 1833.[12]

There were other problems as well. Spring shooting for some species of waterfowl was prohibited in Ontario as early as 1873[13] and most provinces eventually abolished the practice, but there were frequent abuses and restrictions were not effectively enforced by provincial game guardians. The spring shooting issue was hotly debated by the North American Fish and Game Protective Association at its first annual meeting in 1902. The Association, composed of Americans and Canadians, was large and influential. The Honourable S.N. Parent, Quebec Premier and Minister of Lands, Mines and Fisheries, was its first president, and officers with the Grand Trunk and Canadian Pacific railways sat on its executive boards. During the 1902 meeting,

Edwin Tinsley, Ontario's Chief Game Warden, declared that he knew of no action so urgently needed as the uniform and general prohibition of spring shooting.

It has long been a mystery to me that you, our American friends, follow business principles in your Trades and Professions and then act so inconsistently in the matter of spring shooting. There is not one redeeming feature or valid excuse for otherwise intelligent people acting so foolishly as to shoot birds when full of eggs en route to the nesting grounds. [14]

Tinsley's remarks sparked a lively discussion on the subject of spring shooting and the Association passed a resolution strongly urging the legislatures of New York state and the province of Ontario to enact measures prohibiting spring shooting of all wildfowl species.

But in contrast to the protectionist movement well underway in the United States during the early 1900s, few Canadian organizations were concerned about migratory bird protection. The subject was a relatively new one and although a few individuals understood it and spoke out, their voices seldom carried far. The North American Fish and Game Association might well debate the issue and propose protective measures, but most Canadian field naturalists' clubs confined their studies and activities to more local, regional concerns. One exception to the rule was the South Essex County Conservation Club, founded by Jack Miner of Kingsville, Ontario. Miner came to Ontario as a boy in 1878 and with his two older brothers engaged in market hunting, selling their booty in Detroit and Windsor markets. A hunting accident claimed the life of one of Jack's brothers in 1898. Six years later Jack gave up hunting and established a wild bird sanctuary on the family farm in Kingsville. Each year after that, he succeeded in attracting wild geese during their spring and fall migrations. Miner believed that if there was to be any bird life left for future generations, a conservation movement had to be started and, with four other members, he founded the Essex Conservation Club to spread the gospel of conservation.[15] But it was another fifteen years before Miner's experiences with migratory geese and the fame of the Kingsville sanctuary became known around the world. Canadians, in 1904, were still a long way from initiating a movement for migratory bird protection.

Meanwhile, the campaign for bird protection continued unabated in the United States. Another federal migratory bird bill, the Weeks Maclean bill, was attached as a rider to the Agricultural Appropriations bill and introduced to Congress in 1913. It passed both Congress and the Senate and became law on 4 March. Howevver, it did little more than place migratory birds under custody of the United States federal government and authorize the Department of Agriculture to provide for protective regulations. The Department was given no powers of arrest or seizure and only a very small sum of money was provided for enforcement of the new law. Moreover, many doubted that the federal government had either the authority or the constitutional power to pass such legislation over state legislatures. President Taft declared that the bill was unconstitutional in its legal form and that if presented to him he would be compelled to veto it. Nevertheless, he did not veto the bill in 1913. Woodrow Wilson was waiting to become the new Democratic president and Taft later claimed he 'didn't have time' to read the bill fully before he left office.[16]

The law was far from secure and encountered enemies both in and out of the House. Representative Frank Mondell of Wyoming was bitterly opposed to it, dramatically declaring himself against it in 1913 and later introducing a motion for its repeal:

If this Bill should become law no man who voted for it would ever be justified in raising his voice against any extension, no matter how extreme, of the police authority and control of the federal government ... Pass this bill and every barrier standing against the assertion of Federal police force in every line and with regard to every act and activity of the American people is broken down, and we no longer have a government of self-governing States but are well on the way to an empire governed from this Capital.[17]

A District Court Judge in Arkansas dismissed a case against one Harvey Shauver for illegal possession of ducks shot out of season in 1914 on the grounds that the federal migratory bird law was unconstitutional. The case was later appealed to the United States Supreme Court, but a decision was never handed down.

Although the federal bird law encountered many enemies, it also had a growing number of friends who were determined to safeguard its object and principle. The American Game Protective and Propagation Association was formed in 1911 with the sole object of securing migratory bird protection. Its President, John Burnham, led an active campaign in the United States and later in Canada to further the objects of the Association. It was Burnham who thought of attaching the 1913 bill to the Agricultural Appropriations bill, and after its passage the Association filed countless legal briefs in support of the bill's constitutionality.[18]

But by far the most significant event of 1913 was a resolution to the

Senate by Elihu Root suggesting that a treaty be concluded with Great Britain (representing Canada) for migratory bird protection. There were good reasons for the Americans to conceive of an international treaty. Their own federal bird law, passed in 1913, went before the Supreme Court that same year for a judgement on its constitutionality, but a decision was never handed down. The hearing was postponed twice and the case dragged on, unresolved, for the next three years. All the evidence indicated, however, that the Court might well have declared the law unconstitutional. (Indeed, Judge Van Valkenburg stated in 1919 that each state controlled its own wildlife resources and, in the absence of any treaty, there was no delegation of that state authority to the federal government. In principle, therefore, the 1913 federal act had exceeded the legitimate power of Congress.) Aware of the possibility that the federal law could be declared unconstitutional, the supporters of bird protection became convinced of the urgent necessity for a treaty. Such a treaty, they believed, would supersede the federal law and render all opposition and arguments to the question of federal jurisdiction purely academic. It was at this juncture that American advocates of bird protection began to turn their attention to Ottawa.

The dominion government seldom discussed wildlife conservation policies with the provincial governments and only occasionally advised or interfered in provincial game administration matters. The establishment of the federal Commission of Conservation in 1909, however, set up an appropriate and valuable forum for informal discussions between members of the federal and provincial governments covering the full range of natural resource questions and issues. Moreover, it provided an opportunity to raise some of the jurisdictional problems that wildlife conservation presented. At the Commission's annual meeting in January 1913, J. Walter Jones, appointed by the Commission to report on fur farming in Canada, pointed out that the changed conditions of modern life, the newer methods of hunting, and the increased value of fur pelts focused on new and difficult problems which the framers of the British North America Act had not foreseen when they placed natural resources under provincial jurisdiction. 'For example,' he said, 'what legislative body should have charge of migratory birds?' The matter was of immediate concern since the Weeks-Maclean bill was before the American Congress. A copy of the bill was presented at the Commission's meeting and published as an Appendix to the 1913 Report. It was Jones's conviction that migratory birds would ultimately have to come under Canadian, and American, federal government jurisdiction:

Of what use would provincial authority be when one hundred and fifty-four species of insect-eating game birds are being legally slaughtered, and when most of these nest in Canadian territory, and winter in the United States, Mexico, and other parts of America?

Jones told the Commission that the robin was killed as a game bird in Louisiana, Tennessee, Mississippi, Maryland, North Carolina, Virginia, and Florida; that the bobolink, protected by provincial legislation in Canada, was slaughtered in most southern American states. Birds were vitally important to Canadian agriculture and Jones quoted Professor E.H. Forbush, State Ornithologist of Massachusetts, who estimated American annual agricultural losses through insect damage to crops at $800,000,000. Based on this figure, Jones guessed that Canada's crop loss would amount to one-tenth that of the American, and concluded that the decline of insectivorous bird populations was responsible for that loss. Given the tremendous importance of agriculture and the economic value of bird life, Jones contended that only federal jurisdiction would secure uniform game laws and intelligent, scientific protection on the continent. 'Migratory birds,' he said, 'should come under the jurisdiction of the Federal authority for the same reasons that foreign commerce is administered by the Federal Government.'[19] There was no debate among members following his address, however, and no resolutions embodying the major principles of his talk were presented to the government.

Members of the Parks Branch followed the activities of the Commission very closely. Both James Harkin and Maxwell Graham were fully aware, not only of the United States federal bird law currently before Congress, but also of all the facts that Jones had presented to the Commission. Two months after its meeting, Graham sent a memo to Harkin regarding migratory birds. 'The time would appear propitious,' he informed the Parks Commissioner, 'for the enactment of suitable legislation by which these birds could be efficiently protected.' Graham quoted Jones's facts: that there were 154 known species of insect-eating birds being legally slaughtered in the United States, that most of these birds nested on Canadian territory and wintered in the United States and South America, and that Canadian agricultural losses due to insect damage were estimated at $80,000,000 a year. He enclosed a copy of the United States federal migratory bird bill for the Commissioner and suggested to Harkin that a similar bill be drafted by the Parks Branch and introduced to the House of Commons. Graham admitted that the whole subject required 'extensive study' but was quick to point out that it 'already justifies this Branch in bringing before the Dominion Government the expediency of its administering the protection of migratory birds, and thus co-operating with the United States Government which passed the Weeks-Maclean Bill.'[20]

Two days later, Graham checked out his facts more thoroughly with James Macoun, a naturalist-botanist with the Geological Survey, asking him to substantiate the facts he had sent off so hurriedly to Harkin. 'If you concur,' he wrote, 'the work of supplying the necessary arguments [for protection] will be much simplified.' Macoun was unable to confirm Graham's figures, but believed that many of the arguments used in the United States would be equally valid for Canada. He did not have specific provincial regulations at hand regarding insectivorous birds, but told Graham that 'from my own experience throughout Canada, practically no attempt is made to enforce [provincial] regulations.' Hoping to assist Graham further, however, Macoun passed the request for information to Percy Taverner, staff ornithologist with the National Museum of Canada and consultant to the Geological Survey.[21]

Taverner was one of the early pioneers in North American bird banding. He was born in 1875 in Guelph, Ontario, and educated at Ann Arbor, Michigan, where his interest in bird life developed. In 1905, he organized the first systematic method of bird banding, making his own bands and supplying them to other ornithologists in the United States and Canada. Jack Miner used Taverner's bands when he first began banding Canada geese at Kingsville, Ontario. Eventually, Taverner returned to Canada and joined the National Museum as staff ornithologist in 1910. In later years, he established his reputation both nationally and internationally. His major books, *The Birds of Eastern Canada* (1919), *Birds of Western Canada* (1926), and *The Birds of Canada* (1937) became standard ornithological works.

Taverner had long recognized that migrating birds could be protected only through some sort of international agreement. Spring shooting was not allowed on the Ontario side of the border, he informed Graham, but was 'much indulged' in in Michigan. Regarding Graham's estimate for Canadian agricultural losses, Taverner judged that ten per cent would not be 'far out of the way,' but he advised Graham to check more thoroughly with the United States Biological

Survey, a government body that had collected biological data over the previous fifteen years.[22] It is questionable today whether the decline of bird life was, in fact, responsible for agricultural losses on the scale many believed. Taverner himself admitted in 1916 that while birds were an important influence in the reduction of insects, they were only one of many influences, and not a major one. He told James Fleming, a Toronto ornithologist, that the real reason for protecting birds was purely aesthetic, for the sheer pleasure of 'having them around and becoming acquainted with them either individually or specifically':

I think there is a place for wholesome sentiment. Sentiment is not sentimentality and true sentiment is not slush. The more we can connect birds with other interests, literature, poetry, music etc. the better. Wordsworth's Cuckoo and Ode to a Waterfowl, Shakespeare's Hark, Hark, the Lark, Bryant's Bobolink, and even Who Killed Cock Robin and the Babes in the Wood are all legitimate methods of awakening interest in their originals. It connects the species with something familiar even if it does no more than to show that some of the greatest minds have not felt it beneath them to notice common every day birds ...[23]

While Graham was busily seeking authoritative support to back up his estimates, Harkin conducted some research on his own. Late in March, he wrote to the Secretary of the American Game Protective and Propagation Association, advising him that passage of the Weeks-Maclean bill had been watched with considerable interest by members of the Parks Branch. Now, Harkin stated, 'it is felt that some action should be taken in order that this country may co-operate with your government in protecting these migratory species which divide their life between our two countries.' Harkin knew that John Burnham, the Association's President, had filed numerous arguments and briefs on behalf of the constitutionality of the American bill and asked the Secretary to send copies of the briefs together with 'cogent reasons' the Association had collected for supporting the bill.[24]

Shortly after Harkin contacted the Game Association, a dispatch arrived in Ottawa from the British ambassador in Washington, stating that the United States government was interested in investigating the possibility of an international convention to protect migratory birds. Harkin seized the opportunity and immediately sent off a memo to the Deputy Minister, William Cory. There was no reason to doubt the desirability of such an agreement, he wrote, from both aesthetic and commercial viewpoints. He told Cory that the American law was under severe attack as being outside the jurisdiction of Congress, but that an international treaty would make the United States federal law 'automatically valid and immune from attack in the Courts.' Harkin realized the implications of federal action in the matter and warned that it was imperative that the provincial governments be contacted and their approval secured before any action was taken between the two governments. He suggested that copies of the British ambassador's communiqué be circulated to the various provincial governments and then, when their approval was given, a conference held and the matter fully discussed between dominion and provincial representatives.[25]

Having set the wheels in motion, Harkin continued his investigations. He wrote to James Fleming, asking if there was any need in Canada to protect migratory birds along the lines of the Weeks-Maclean bill. Fleming replied that concurrent legislation was essential if either country was to benefit. Uniformity of protection was vital but 'it is impossible so long as the various provinces and states have no Federal laws to strengthen their legislation.' A general law in Canada to protect migrating birds, he concluded, would strengthen the provincial laws by 'closing the loopholes we know exist.' Furthermore, Fleming argued that the federal government had a clear responsibility to act. By far the greatest number of North American waterfowl nested on Crown lands west of the Great Lakes that were under federal jurisdiction, a fact that made federal responsibility even greater. The government could do a great deal, he suggested, to 'restore the balance that has been so greatly disturbed' by establishing sanctuaries to protect wildfowl on their western breeding grounds and by regulating the sale and interprovincial transit of game.[26] Fleming's colleague, William Saunders, added his support. While the Territories and western provinces had experienced a serious decline in bird life, the American bald eagle and great blue heron were nearly extinct in Ontario. 'It would seem a great pity,' he wrote to Harkin, 'to allow the extermination of any species of our native fauna to be accomplished for lack of protection.'[27] Harkin replied to both Fleming and Saunders, thanking the latter for the 'valuable suggestions' contained in his letter and promising that they would be filed away and used later when the whole question of proposed legislation was submitted to the Minister of the Interior.[28]

Events speed up by the end of 1913. The North American Fish and Game Protective Association held its annual meeting in Ottawa in early December and H.R. Charlton, a member of the Association and also Advertising Manager of the Grand Trunk and Grand Trunk Pacific railways, moved an important resolution:

Resolved, that the executive committee communicate with the provincial governments of Canada to urge them of the importance of soliciting the good offices of the Dominion Government in obtaining the negotiation of a convention or treaty between Great Britain and the United States looking to the more efficient protection of migratory birds, now threatened with extinction.[29]

Although moved by Charlton, the resolution had been drafted by Edward Chambers, secretary to the Fish and Game Association, and a member of the Fisheries Branch in the Quebec provincial government. Chambers, a strong believer in federal intervention on the question of bird protection, was aware that the provinces retained jurisdiction over their natural resources. He was highly sensitive to the 'delicacy' with which the subject would have to be handled and thought it best to phrase the resolution in such a manner as to persuade the provincial governments, instead of the Dominion, to take the initiative. Because he was a member of the Quebec government, he declined to put forward the resolution himself.[30]

Graham was pleased with the work of the Association and told Harkin that 'other influential bodies and individuals' were trying to bring the matter before both governments. By this time, a list of regulations under the Weeks-Maclean bill had been drawn up by the United States Department of Agriculture and Graham noted that all the birds listed in the regulations nested and bred in Canada, a fact 'which makes our country even more vitally concerned in their preservation.' With his characteristic eagerness to have the Parks Branch administer all areas of wildlife protection in Canada, Graham suggested to Harkin that the matter of protection be submitted to the Minister of the Interior and that the Parks Branch be authorized to draw up suitable regulations for Canada. He proposed gathering information from ornithologists and other government members familiar with the problem in order to decide what bird species needed protection, how best to regulate open seasons across the country, where protected migratory flight paths should be proclaimed, and how to establish uniformity of protection across the land. So anxious was Graham to secure migratory bird protection for the Parks Branch that he seemed to overlook the fact, under the BNA Act, provincial governments were responsible for natural resource administration.[31] Migratory birds were designated neither a provincial nor a federal responsibility in 1913, yet 'provincial consultation' was not an item that appeared high on Graham's list of priorities.

Harkin, however, was far more aware of the necessity for close dominion/provincial co-operation and consultation. As a result of Graham's memo, he wrote directly to Chambers in Quebec, seeking his advice on the proposal for a federal/provincial conference to discuss the migratory bird legislation. Outlining the topics for debate as suggested by Graham, Harkin told Chambers that any proposed legislation arising from the convention would not be intended to affect or interfere with local provincial laws already in force. He insisted that the main purpose of the convention was consultation and reminded Chambers that, 'as secretary of the North American Fish and Game Protective Association, it is felt that you can materially help this branch in its efforts to bring about concerted inter-provincial action so that necessary legislation, uniformly protecting all migratory and insectivorous birds everywhere in this Dominion, may be secured.'

After some consideration, Chambers replied, promising to do what he could to aid the Parks Branch. While the idea of a convention was sound, Chambers warned Harkin of the 'jealous care' with which the provinces held on to their constitutional rights. 'This rather causes me to fear for the success of any movement seeming to curtail provincial rights and apparently emanating from Ottawa,' he concluded. Harkin believed the chief purpose of the proposed convention was to further interprovincial co-operation and arouse public opinion in support of international action. He was as aware as Chambers of provincial 'jealousies,' and later decided that should a convention be held in the near future, one of the prairie provinces would make a more appropriate setting for migratory bird discussions than Ottawa. 'It is not even suggested,' he told Chambers, 'that Dominion Government members should necessarily attend such a conference, unless their presence is deemed necessary for purposes of furnishing information. This Branch is only anxious to do whatever possible to bring about a healthy public opinion on the question of migratory bird protection.'[33]

The subject continued to draw attention in the months that followed. William Haskell, legal counsel for the American Game Association, came to Ottawa in January and addressed the Conservation Commission's Fifth Annual meeting. He had planned to give a short paper on the wildlife conservation movement in the United States, but Dr Cecil Jones, Chairman of the Commission's Game Committee, asked him to preface his talk with a few remarks on the American federal Bird Law. The latter agreed and outlined the history of legislative attempts for bird protection in the United States that had culminated in the 1913 bill, emphasizing the growing importance of international protection. He argued that Canadians would benefit as much from bird protection as the Americans, and told Commission members that although the fate of the American law was undecided, should a treaty be concluded, 'the question of whether or not the federal government has any power to make such a law will be forever settled, because a Treaty is the supreme law of the land and no State or Federal Court can attack it.' He concluded his remarks by asking Commission members to use their influence in helping Canada join with the United States in securing the international agreement.[34]

The Commission added its weight to the proposal, calling upon the provinces 'to solicit the good offices of the Dominion Government in obtaining the negotiation of a convention for a treaty between Great Britain and the United States for the purpose of securing more effective protection for the birds which pass from one country to the other.'[35] In a letter to Prime Minister Robert Borden, James White, the Commission's Secretary, enclosed the resolution and added that protection could be effective only if it were international and that without protection many species in Canada would be 'annihilated or reduced to a mere fraction of their former numbers.' White came from the prairies and told Borden that from his own experience in the west over the previous thirty years, 'the decrease [in bird life] is almost incredible.'[36]

A month after Haskell's Ottawa address, the United States government submitted a draft treaty for the protection of migratory birds to the Canadian government. It was drawn up by members of the United States Biological Survey, and Graham noted that its terms covered all the general requirements, but told Harkin that the Americans would consider any amendments, alterations, or additions that Canada proposed. Graham was pleased with the draft proposal. 'A treaty is much more effective than a statute,' he wrote to Harkin. 'It is a guarantee of the law.'[37] Plans for a federal/provincial conference were postponed indefinitely and the draft, approved by the Parks Branch and the departments of Agriculture and Interior, was sent off to the provincial governments on 20 March. Graham and Harkin settled down to await the provincial responses. Through an unfortunate oversight at the time, however, copies of the draft proposal were not sent to the Yukon and Northwest Territorial governments, nor were Indian and Inuit peoples consulted on the issue.

Over the next two months, provincial replies gradually filtered into Ottawa. Nearly all the provincial governments approved the draft and the principle of bird protection. Most claimed that few new restrictions were needed under the treaty since provincial regulations were already in harmony with the proposed legislation. Lieutenant-Governor

François Langelier of Quebec told the Secretary of State that his province's sportsmen unanimously voted their approval of a convention at the annual meeting of the North American Fish and Game Protective Association in 1913 and stated that the treaty would be of great value to Quebec, particularly as it prohibited the illegal shipment of game. 'This provision will put an end to the ruthless destruction of our grouse and partridge,' Langelier pointed out. Spring shooting was already abolished by the Quebec provincial government, but the Lieutenant-Governor warned that notwithstanding the desirability of game protection, 'the restrictions that may or may not be placed upon the killing or sale of game in the Province of Quebec are its own prerogative and cannot be delegated to others.'[38] The governments of Prince Edward Island, Ontario, Manitoba and Saskatchewan were in full agreement with the proposed international convention, but the New Brunswick government was more hesitant in its support. Its provincial laws conformed with the treaty, but Lieutenant-Governor Josiah Wood knew that the constitutionality of the American Bird Law was still to be tested in the Supreme Court. He advised the Canadian Secretary of State that 'a similar difficulty will be found in legislating for Canada' as 'the laws upon this subject come within the jurisdiction of the different provinces.'[39]

British Columbia and Nova Scotia were the only two provinces to express opposition to the terms of the treaty. Under the draft regulations, the international open hunting season for both countries was set between 1 September and 1 February. The latter date was chosen to abolish the practice of spring shooting in North America, for the open season was to end a good month before birds began their spring migration north. Within the general open period specified under the treaty, each state and provincial government could select its own local hunting season. But no open hunting season was to exceed three and one-half months in duration. Nova Scotia was quick to point out, however, that by 1 September most shore-birds had left the province on their southward migration and the provincial government requested that the general open season under the treaty begin earlier, so as to cover the latter half of August. Other changes would be necessary to bring Nova Scotia's legislation into accord with the treaty provisions; the province had no closed season at all for wild geese, sea ducks, gulls, loons, bitterns, or brant, but the provincial government conceded that there was no serious objection to modifying provincial laws to conform with the new regulations.[40]

The objections of British Columbia were to prove far more difficult

to overcome than those of Nova Scotia. The Lieutenant-Governor of
the province wrote that while his government was in accord with the
basic principles of the convention, 'it feels that it cannot become a party
to the treaty as it stands at present.' He declined to state the province's
specific objections to the draft proposal, but referred only to the
'different conditions' existing in British Columbia and stated that 'it
would not be advisable to consent to any arrangement which would
interfere with the Government's own local authority to grant open
seasons for birds in the province.'[41] It was later learned that British
Columbia was unwilling to accept either the specified closed season on
ducks, geese, and other game birds or the restrictions against killing
cranes, swans, curlews, and wood ducks (wood ducks, seriously endangered, would be given a five-year closed season under the proposed
treaty while swans, cranes, and curlews were to have full protection for
ten years). Sportsmen in British Columbia were accustomed to spring
shooting and a five and one-half month open hunting season,
privileges the provincial government was unwilling to surrender
lightly to federal authorities.[42]

Harkin was not disheartened by the provincial responses. He was
certain that British Columbia and Nova Scotia could be dealt with on an
individual basis, and was anxious to begin negotiations as soon as
possible. However, World War I intervened and it was not until the
spring of 1915 that an order-in-council, agreeing to the principle of
international protection for migratory birds, was passed. The Privy
Councillors recognized the objections of Nova Scotia and British Columbia, but stated that those objections should not present 'insuperable
difficulties.' His Majesty the King was therefore requested to inform
the British ambassador in Washington that Canada 'was favourably
disposed towards conclusion of the proposed Treaty.' The ambassador
was instructed to so advise the American government. On 7 June,
1915, the order-in-council was sent to Washington.[43] All, it seemed,
was in readiness, but the hard part was just beginning.

Unknown to either Graham or Harkin, another Canadian senior civil
servant was preparing to work actively for migratory bird protection.
Gordon Hewitt was born near Macclesfield, Cheshire, England, in
1885. His interest in the natural world developed at an early age and at
Manchester University he studied zoology, receiving his B.Sc. in 1902,
an M.Sc. in 1903, and his PH D in 1909. Described as a 'prize man and
university scholar,' Hewitt was soon appointed Assistant Lecturer and

then Lecturer in Economic Zoology by the university. While lecturing there in 1909, he was offered the position of Dominion Entomologist with the Canadian Department of Agriculture. The previous entomologist, James Fletcher, had died suddenly and Arthur Gibson, who had been Fletcher's assistant, was appointed temporarily until Hewitt's arrival.

Hewitt was a young man when he came to Canada in 1909 and the values that he placed on wildlife were not moulded by the North American experience, but rather shaped in the British and European traditions. As Dominion Entomologist, he was to be concerned with the economic value of birds and their importance to agriculture; but as a keen student of nature and lifelong crusader for wildlife protection, he was also aware of the aesthetic and sentimental value of bird life. Two years after his arrival in Canada, he married Elizabeth Borden, the daughter of Sir Frederick Borden and the niece of Prime Minister Robert Borden. Elizabeth recalled in 1920 how her husband's love of nature was infinitely practical as well as theoretical and sentimental:

He liked to dig in the soil and to spread manure. He planted with the skill and precision of an artist; he sowed seeds with equal zest; and, after a rain, he loved to fork around, and thus make each bulb, perennial, or vegetable "comfortable." Morning and evening – before his office hours and after – he walked around the garden, bathing himself in greenness, and in the odour of lilacs, roses, and newmown grass. Then it was he spoke to every flower and bird, no matter how small or how shy, and held converse with the chipmunks and squirrels, who held a safe tenure within the garden precincts. [44]

It has been said that Hewitt's appointment marked a new era in entomology, the end of the 'naturalists and hobbyists' and the coming of the professional scientists.[45] It might also be said that Hewitt's arrival marked a new era in conservation, for the preservation movement could not have found a more energetic or dedicated wildlife defender.

In the middle of February 1913, one full month before members of the Parks Branch first took notice of the migratory bird question, Hewitt wrote to Henry Henshaw, Chief of the United States Biological Survey. He did not write in his official capacity but simply as a private citizen interested in bird protection and wanting to know more about the bill for federal protection in the United States. Hewitt agreed that migratory bird protection was an important matter and suggested that 'we should co-operate if the means can be found.'[46] In reply, he was told that the bill was presently before the Senate and had a good chance of passing. Henshaw sent Hewitt copies of the Senate hearings, a report by the Investigating Committee, and a speech by Senator Mac-lean, co-author of the bill.

The following spring, Hewitt made a private trip to Washington, where he met informally with members of the Biological Survey and discussed with them the possibility of some kind of international ag-reement to protect migratory birds. This was the beginning of his close relationship with members of the American government that was to prove of great value in the months ahead. Hewitt was made aware of the broadly based movement for bird protection well under way in the United States and, bolstered in his own convictions by the Washington talks, returned to Ottawa convinced that greater information and publicizing of the issue was needed if Canadian support for an interna-tional treaty was ever to be won.[47]

He was provided with an opportunity to air his views when he addressed the Conservation Commission's annual meeting in 1915. As a professional entomologist, his concern was with insect damage to agricultural crops and he spoke at length to Commission members on the importance of native insectivorous birds; their protection consti-tuted an important part of the Department of Agriculture's work in controlling insects. All the provinces had protective legislation for birds, but Hewitt called such legislation 'practically a dead letter' and believed public education on the subject was needed urgently. He described how members of his department had joined with the Ottawa Improvement Commission in establishing bird sanctuaries in the heart of Ottawa, one encompassing the entire Central Experimental Farm and the other comprising a wooded section in the Rockcliffe district. Two hundred and fifty bird nesting boxes were put up throughout the sanctuaries and Hewitt took satisfaction in knowing that most of them were occupied the first spring. The Department was trying to get Ottawa farmers to follow similar practices by encouraging birds to nest around their homesteads and in close proximity to field crops and orchards. By educating the public and demonstrating the value of insectivorous birds, Hewitt hoped people would understand better the importance of bird protection. The Conservation Commission, he believed, had a vital and important role to play in educating the Canadian public and the various provincial governments, which 'did not fully appreciate the importance of bird protection.' He urged the Commission to take up the question of protection as it related to all native birds and to press the government for the establishment of bird sanctuaries on both the Atlantic and Pacific coasts. Hewitt pointed out that, in contrast to the work of the Americans, the Canadian government had not established a single bird sanctuary. 'We are falling far behind in our co-operation with them [the Americans] in the protection of our native birds. Unless we co-operate in this matter, I think we are not nearly doing our duty as inhabitants of, and as trustees for, this enormous northern portion of the continent, so wealthy in bird life.'[48] Although he said nothing to the Commission of his private discussions with the Americans, he confided to Theodore S. Palmer, a member of the Biological Survey, at the end of 1915, that 'I am still doing what I can to keep the matter warm.'[49]

International co-operation moved closer to reality during the next few months. In early January 1916, Hewitt was directed by the Minister of Agriculture to pursue negotiations on behalf of the Canadian government with the Americans and to work out possible compromises to cover the objections of British Columbia and Nova Scotia.[50] As the decline in bird life was related to agricultural losses to the Dominion, it was only natural that this branch of government should play a prominent role in migratory bird protection. Hewitt also had a large personal interest in the subject of bird protection and probably his relationship through marriage to Robert Borden put him in a highly favourable position for the job. No sooner did he begin, however, than he met with a temporary setback. On arriving in Washington, he learned that few government members were even aware that Canada had consented to the agreement. The Order-in-Council sent to Washington in 1915 apparently had been misplaced, and then lost, in the British Embassy. After much searching, Hewitt finally located the document and, putting its loss down to the 'pressures of war,' sent it on through official channels to the American government.[51]

Compromise and concession formed the fabric and substance of Hewitt's Washington talks as both sides sought solutions to meet Nova Scotian and British Columbian demands. The Americans readily agreed to permit the Maritime provinces to take shorebirds during the latter half of August instead of after 1 September as outlined in the draft proposal. Several Atlantic seaboard states had raised similar objections under the 1913 federal bill and had been specially exempted from the law's provisions in that one instance. There was no reason why the Canadian Maritime provinces should not receive similar concessions under the treaty.

The concessions made for British Columbia were far more substantial. The provincial government protested a provision whereby 1 February would mark the end of the open period during which ducks and geese could be legally shot. The province's open season did not end until 31 March, a date that permitted spring shooting, and the government was adamant in maintaining this right for provincial sportsmen. It was up to Hewitt and the Americans to find a compromise. The result was a special article written into the treaty permitting wildfowl to be killed – under permit – if they were 'injurious to agriculture.' Hewitt admitted that BC crops were largely unaffected by birds but that geese 'could be considered' injurious during the early spring months.[52] Clearly, the inclusion of the article was intended to appease the provincial government by permitting west coast sportsmen to indulge in their springtime hunts.

Another clause to which British Columbia objected called for a five-year closed season on wood duck, a popular game bird on the west coast, and it was up to the Washington negotiators to find another solution. This was reached by a clause decreeing that states and provinces could protect wood ducks either by establishing the five-year closed season or by other accepted conservation measures such as creating sanctuaries or erecting wood duck nesting boxes. This new clause was designed to permit BC sportsmen to continue wood duck hunting so long as the provincial government instituted other methods of preservation for the endangered species.

There was still another objection to be dealt with – British Columbia's opposition to the ten-year closed season on swans, cranes, and curlews. There is no record of the Washington talks and no knowledge of the method by which Hewitt and members of the Biological Survey arrived at their compromise, but, under yet another special clause written into the treaty, British Columbia was fully exempted from the ten-year restriction. It thus became the only single province or state named in the treaty and granted such a sweeping exemption under its provisions. No doubt the Americans were displeased, and for bird lovers and preservationists in both countries, the concessions made for British Columbia must have been bitter pills to swallow. But its support was absolutely necessary for the success of the treaty, and on 11 April 1916, Hewitt informed Harkin that agreement had been reached and all the provincial objections but one overcome. British Columbia still argued for a five and one-half month open season, but the Americans were unwilling to grant any more concessions to the Canadians.[53]

While Hewitt was in Washington, Maxwell Graham was keeping a careful eye on the developments in the capital. Shortly after Hewitt returned, Graham sent a long, plaintive memo to Harkin citing the extensive and painstaking work done by members of the Parks Branch since 1913 on behalf of migratory bird protection. He reviewed the contents of all the memoranda he had sent the Commissioner and reminded Harkin that he, Graham, had originally recommended that the Parks Branch take responsibility for migratory birds. Graham was upset that Hewitt was now directing the course of events. 'Even if this Branch is not to have the gratification of bringing this very important question to a successful conclusion,' Graham wrote, 'it is at least a matter of record that its efforts in behalf of much needed legislation have not been fruitless.'[54] It was up to Hewitt to unruffle the feathers of his concerned colleague before interdepartmental jealousy upset the course of the negotiations. He regretted the false impression Graham had drawn and told the Commissioner he deeply appreciated the 'large amount of valuable work your Branch has accomplished' since passage of the 1913 Bird Law in the United States. He denied that the whole question of migratory bird protection had been turned over to him. In future, he told the Commissioner, he would like to see migratory bird administration handled by a small interdepartmental body of qualified men, not more than four or five at most and drawn from each of the government departments most concerned in the matter – Agriculture, Interior, Mines (Geological Survey), and the Conservation Commission. In the meantime, however, Hewitt hoped that Graham would continue his 'enthusiastic work,' and concluded that 'only through co-operation can we secure best results.'[55]

Having soothed Graham's sensibilities as best he could, Hewitt returned to Washington for final negotiations on the revised treaty draft. But it was soon apparent that the situation on the American side had changed drastically in his absence. He was informed by Edward Nelson, Acting Chief of the US Biological Survey, that the general open season under the treaty was to be extended from 1 February to 10 March.[56] Hewitt was appalled. The very principle of spring shooting that Canada opposed was to be clearly embodied in the international agreement. He was told by Nelson that heavy lobbying by Congressmen from states along the Mississippi Valley (a major migratory flyway) had forced the American government to change the treaty terms in their favour.[57] Nelson was as concerned as Hewitt over the change. He had long been opposed to shooting birds in the mating season and to have to yield on this point was, reportedly, 'wormwood to his soul.' But fifty-two Congressmen persuaded him to permit spring shooting and he was afraid that, if refused, they would use their considerable influence in Congress to block the appropriations bill for the Biological Survey. He told Hewitt that attempts to curtail the activities of the branch had been tried in the past and he had little doubt that the current threat was real and intended.[58]

Hewitt was bitter over the proposed alteration to the treaty and told Harkin that the reasons for the change were purely political, a fact that was freely admitted to him in Washington. Canada's attitude towards spring shooting was clear; it was to be eliminated completely by establishing 1 February as the end of the continental open season. Hewitt reminded Harkin that, with the exception of British Columbia, all the provinces had abolished spring shooting and Canadian protective associations were opposed to the principle. Therefore, 'we cannot subscribe to the surrender of so important a principle or agree to the unconditional adoption in an international convention, particularly as spring shooting in the states of the Mississippi Valley, which is one of the main migration routes north, involves the killing of birds travelling to Canada to breed.' There was no room to negotiate on the American demand and no chance of compromise. It was up to Hewitt to surrender gracefully. In his final summation to Harkin, he stated that the American government should be told Canada opposed the spring shooting principle and would only agree to the treaty change if every effort was made to bring the midwestern states gradually into line through regulation of the us federal migratory bird law. 'If the United States Government will give us assurance,' he concluded, 'arrangements could be made for signing the Treaty.'[59]

Hewitt might well have imagined his job was finished when the revised treaty was drafted and submitted once again to the Canadian government. He was wrong. British Columbia was still 'resolutely opposed' to the three and one-half month open season and Hewitt was hastily despatched to Victoria in one last attempt to reach a compromise with the provincial government, an attempt, it was hoped, that would not require any more concessions.

Once in Victoria, Hewitt found himself faced with yet more demands by the provincial government. Besides two minor changes,[60] the government now demanded a five-month open season for ducks and more than a six-month season on geese. Hewitt desperately cabled Henshaw in Washington, telling him that the dominion government had to have the 'unqualified support' of British Columbia, but that all arguments with the government were unavailing. Hewitt asked the American if yet another exception could be made under the agreement for British Columbia. Henshaw replied that should such a concession be granted, ratification of the treaty would be blocked in Washington. He could only suggest varying the three and one-half month open season for separate districts within the province as a possible solution in order that sportsmen could travel around from district to district and enjoy a longer open season overall.[61]

Discouraged, and facing apparent failure, Hewitt returned to Ottawa. But he had reckoned without the concerted movement under way in the United States for bird protection. John Burnham of the American Game Protective Association happened to be in Ottawa when Hewitt's train pulled in from the west coast, and called his office soon after Hewitt arrived. Burnham was at the forefront of the campaign to secure international protection and had followed developments closely as they transpired both in Washington and Ottawa. Certainly he was not prepared to see the treaty fail because of any one province or state. According to Burnham's recollections, Hewitt told him he was en route to see Martin Burrell, the Minister of Agriculture, to report that his west coast mission was an utter failure and that British Columbia was opposed to any further restrictions under the International Treaty. Burnham apparently instructed Hewitt not to tell the Minister that the mission had failed, but that 'while British Columbia has not acceded, the action of one province should not be allowed to thwart the desires of two great nations.'

Hewitt went off to see the Minister and during their discussions Burrell expressed an interest in talking directly with Burnham. The American was summoned to the Parliament buildings, where he talked at length with the Minister, telling him of the strong sentiment in both countries for migratory bird protection. When Burrell questioned whether there was much support for the treaty in Canada, Burnham cited prominent members of the Canadian Pacific and Grand Trunk railways who favoured the agreement (and who were also members of the North American Fish and Game Protective Association). The Minister then asked Burnham: 'But what has Canada to gain when you already, under your federal migratory bird bill, are protecting birds on your side of the line?' Burnham then told Burrell the story and uncertain fate of the American Bird Law. There was a distinct possibility the bill would 'be lost' through Supreme Court action, or be repealed by Congress. Should this be the case, countless birds breeding in Canada would be annihilated south of the border 'to the detriment of Canada.' The American emphasized that only an international treaty, concluded at once, would ensure continuation of North American wild birdlife. Burnham's account of the conversation was published in 1918, but, while corroborated by at least two American writers in later years, it is found nowhere among Canadian manuscript collections or government documents. Nor did Hewitt make any reference to this reported exchange between the Canadian Minister and the President of the Game Association in *The Conservation of Wild Life in Canada* (1921).[62]

There were no further concessions granted to British Columbia and the treaty was concluded shortly thereafter. This leaves the impression that someone in government persuaded the government of British Columbia to renounce its demands and abide by the internationally agreed upon three and one-half month open season. Perhaps it was Martin Burrell. He was, after all, British Columbia's representative in the Conservative cabinet, and this put him in a strong position to exert influence on the provincial legislature. According to an American author who wrote about the incident in 1934, Burrell told Burnham he would 'give the matter very close attention and probably recommend that the Dominion Government take action without the approval of British Columbia.' This author also remembers Burnham saying on his return to the United States, 'I had received no definite promise but had every reason to believe that Sir [sic] Martin would take favourable action.'[63]

After years of talk and planning, and months of negotiations, the order-in-council giving Canada's full consent to the conclusion of the treaty as revised was proclaimed. The King was requested to instruct the British Ambassador in Washington that Canada was now ready to agree to the international convention. On 16 August 1916, the Treaty for International Protection of Migratory Birds was signed in Washington by Sir Cecil Rice Spring, the British Ambassador signing on behalf of Canada, and by Robert Lansing, the United States Secretary of State. (See appendix.) 'We can now congratulate each other,' Hewitt cabled Nelson the next day, 'on the successful conclusion of the international migratory bird treaty.'[64]

All that remained after the treaty had been signed was formal ratification by both the American and Canadian governments. This was to be effected by passage of an Enabling Act in the American Congress and a Migratory Birds Convention Act in the Canadian Parliament. The Convention Act was to contain regulations carrying out the provisions of the international treaty for migratory bird protection. Unfortunately, there were still more delays.

The first problem arose immediately after the treaty was signed. William Hornaday told Hewitt that he had been advised by the British

Embassy in Washington that the King's signature was needed to complete the treaty.[65] 'In spite of my recent experiences in diplomacy,' Hewitt admitted to Henshaw, 'my education is evidently not complete and this was news to me.'[66] Hewitt telegraphed Hornaday to find out if some 'special arrangements' could be taken by the Embassy in view of the matter's great urgency. But there were no special arrangements and early in September, almost a month after the agreement had been signed in Washington, the Treaty was sent off to London. No further action could be taken either by Congress or Parliament until the King signed the document. Hewitt deeply regretted the delay. He also feared that, once in London, the Treaty would be set aside, for in 1916 war concerns were taking top priority in Britain. It was not until 2 December that the Treaty was returned to Washington. Nelson was 'greatly relieved,' and told Hewitt that the American bill ratifying the Treaty would be introduced to Congress at the next session in early 1917. He asked Hewitt to keep him closely informed on Canada's progress and promised to send up copies of the American bill and Congressional debates as they came up.[67]

The Canadian Migratory Birds Convention Act to ratify the international agreement was introduced to Parliament in June 1917. The Convention Act was designed to sanction and formally execute the provisions and articles of the Treaty. Under the Act, the Governor-General-in-Council was given authority to make all regulations 'deemed expedient' to protect migratory game, migratory insectivorous, and migratory non-game birds that inhabited Canada during the whole or any part of the year. The Minister of the Interior was authorized to appoint game officers to carry out the regulations under the Convention Act that had been drawn up by Hewitt. These regulations defined the different migratory bird species; set forth various open and closed hunting seasons in each of the provinces; designated certain bird species to be permanently protected and those to be protected for a specified number of years; regulated the issuing of special permits to kill migratory game birds, and prohibited the shipment (interprovincial and international) of migratory birds during closed seasons.[68]

The bill met with little opposition during the course of its passage through the House and Senate. Members were concerned only that the bill might have an adverse effect on provincial legislation, but Dr William Roche, the Minister of the Interior, informed them that the provincial governments fully agreed to the principle and that few changes in provincial regulations would be required under the Convention Act regulations. Roche conceded that special permits would be given to kill some migratory birds causing crop damage – cranes in Saskatchewan; geese, pigeons, and robins in British Columbia, and mergansers in Quebec – but there was no opposition to this policy expressed in the House.[69] There was one query regarding the limits of the general open hunting season under the treaty,[70] but obviously few members were aware of the significance of the 10 March date as it related to spring shooting, and none had been a party to the Washington negotiations. Once members of Parliament were assured that the provincial governments were in full agreement, the bill passed the House and Senate by mid-summer and received royal assent on 29 August. Edward Nelson of the Biological Survey was pleased to learn of Canada's success in passing the necessary legislation and wrote to Hewitt of the 'cordial spirit of co-operation' that existed between the Canadian authorities and the Americans in the handling of the bird question. 'We shall undoubtedly do great things in the way of conserving the wildlife through this treaty,' he concluded.[71] The American bill, however, was delayed throughout 1917 and 1918 as more pressing problems connected with the United States's entry into World War I came before Congress. 'It is not so simple a matter to put an administrative measure through as it appears to be with you,' Nelson admitted to Hewitt as 1918 wore on. The American bill finally passed Congress and the Senate, and on 3 July 1918, President Woodrow Wilson signed the Migratory Bird Treaty Act into law.[72]

Both the American and Canadian Migratory Bird acts established federal control over a natural resource that hitherto had been considered under state and provincial jurisdictions. The US federal Bird Law of 1913 was before the Supreme Court from 1913 to 1916 in a test case of its constitutionality, but a decision was never handed down. As its supporters had hoped, the International Treaty of 1916 superseded the federal law. In 1919, a District Court Judge upheld the constitutionality of the American Enabling Act in a historic case, the State of Missouri *v* Ray P. Holland, a federal game warden attempting to enforce the migratory bird regulations. The case was appealed by the state to the United States Supreme Court a year later, but Chief Justice Holmes ruled that both the Treaty and the Enabling Act were valid exercises of federal authority under the Constitution. He further ruled that migratory birds belonged not to any one state, but to the nation as a whole and that they could be protected by the federal government through national action in concert with that of another power:

But for the treaty and the statute there soon might be no birds for any powers to deal with. We see nothing in the Constitution that compels the Government to sit by while a food supply is cut off and the protectors of our forests and our crops are destroyed. It is not sufficient to rely upon the States. The reliance is vain, and were it otherwise, the question is whether the United States is forbidden to act. We are of opinion that the treaty and statute must be upheld.[73]

A similar test case was argued in Canada before the Supreme Court of Prince Edward Island in 1920. Russell C. Clarke shot fourteen Canada geese in violation of Convention Act regulations. The case was dismissed by a PEI Magistrates Court but the Department of the Interior appealed it to the PEI Supreme Court. During the trial the defence claimed that the Migratory Birds Convention Act was beyond the jurisdiction of the federal government as birds within the province of PEI were the property of that province. But it was the judgement of the Court that the system of protection designed to save birds from 'indiscriminate slaughter' was not within the power of provincial legislatures to enforce. The presiding judge quoted Judge Holmes's decision and ruled that the Canadian Parliament also had the right to protect migratory birds on behalf of the Canadian people.[74] Both the International Treaty and the Convention Act were found to be within the jurisdiction of the dominion Parliament.

Recognition of the dominion government's responsibility for migratory bird protection carried far-reaching implications. Following Hewitt's suggestion to Harkin, an interdepartmental body of officials concerned with bird protection was created in late December 1916 to administer the international agreement. Far from administering only migratory bird legislation, this Advisory Board on Wild Life Protection was given responsibility for framing policies to cover all aspects of wildlife protection in Canada. A Dominion Ornithologist was recruited to the civil service to administer the Migratory Bird Regulations under the Parks Branch, and a new NorthWest Game Act was passed in 1917 to reflect the changed wildlife conditions in the Canadian north. In many ways, protection of migratory birds became a catalyst for government action. Areas of responsibility were clearly defined and administrative machinery and policies designed to handle the government's new role in wildlife conservation.

For all of the civil servants who had worked in the movement for migratory bird protection, the passage of the Convention Act was a momentous occasion. Hewitt, particularly, had worked long and hard towards the goal. The full burden of negotiations, the working out of compromises, the agreement on concessions, and the drafting of the

Convention Act had been his responsibility. Migratory bird protection underscored Harkin's commitment to wildlife protection as a definite government policy. 'I am convinced,' he wrote to Nelson soon after the American Enabling bill had passed, 'that the Treaty will prove itself the most important step taken for the protection of birds on this continent.'[75]

The Migratory Bird Treaty was much more than an important step. As a continental protection policy designed for continental travellers, its significance and value are as important today as they were in 1916, perhaps even more so, for North America is the only continent in the world whose bird populations are covered by an international agreement of such magnitude. Today, we recognize that the treaty itself is not perfect. The Yukon Territory is at a distinct disadvantage under its terms, for by the time the hunting season opens there on 1 September, most waterfowl species have already left on their southward migrations. And hawks, eagles, and owls, species that we now know have an important place in the environment, were never included under the treaty's protective provisions. But in spite of these and other slight imperfections, the international agreement stands as a landmark in Canadian wildlife conservation history and as a tribute to the men who dedicated themselves to securing its passage.

The soft, shaggy coat of the muskox was as popular in the early twentieth century as the buffalo robes had been in the mid-nineteenth. *Canadian Wildlife Service*

ABOVE Dr Rudolph Anderson, one of the leaders of the Canadian Arctic Expedition, 1913–15. *National Museum of Canada*

LEFT Vilhjalmur Stefansson, the internationally renowned explorer and author, on the same expedition, 1913. *National Museum of Canada*

Hoyes Lloyd, Canada's first Dominion Ornithologist, camped at Oak Lake, Manitoba, 1921. LEFT TO RIGHT Hoyes Lloyd, Percy Taverner, Sampson, Hamilton Laing. *National Museum of Canada*

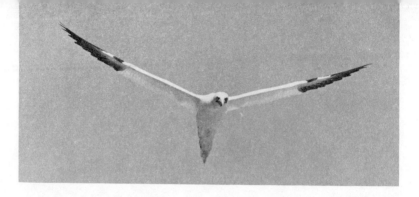

ABOVE Gannet in flight, Bonaventure Island, Quebec. *Janet Foster*

BELOW Seabird colonies on the cliffs of Bonaventure Island. *Janet Foster*

ABOVE 'The Shack' at Point Pelee, built by a group of naturalist-collectors. LEFT TO RIGHT James Wallace, Bradshaw Swales, William E. Saunders, James Fleming, Percy Taverner (front). *National Museum of Canada*

BELOW Bryant Walker and Percy Taverner cataloguing specimens inside 'The Shack,' 1909. *Detroit News, courtesy Royal Ontario Museum*

The results of a twenty-minute shoot at Point Pelee in 1911 – six whistling
swans and six good reasons for the establishment of the area as a national park
in 1918. *From the William E. Saunders collection, courtesy Royal Ontario Museum*

7
New Responsibilities

The job of protecting migratory birds was by no means finished once the Convention Act passed Parliament and the Regulations under the Act were drawn up. It soon became evident that even greater federal intervention was needed to ensure migratory bird protection under the international treaty. Throughout the months of negotiation on the bird protection issue, both Gordon Hewitt and James Harkin had hoped that the various provincial governments would bring their game legislation into harmony with provisions under the Bird Act. With the exception of British Columbia, all the provincial governments had responded favourably to the proposal for bird protection in 1915, and most saw little conflict, if any, with their own game laws. Once the Act passed Parliament in 1917, the western provinces quickly brought their game regulations into accord with the Convention Act requirements. But difficulties soon arose with the three Maritime Provinces.

Support for migratory bird protection had never been widespread in the Maritimes and after the Convention Act passed it was clear that none of the Maritime provincial governments was going to enforce the federal regulations. New Brunswick promptly repealed all its provincial waterfowl legislation, taking the position that as Ottawa had legislated for bird protection it could take full responsibility for carrying it out.[1] Nova Scotia did not go to the same extreme, but the provincial legislature felt that, as the Dominion had made the Convention, it should 'bear the burden.'[2] And Prince Edward Island was quick to complain that the province did not have the necessary warden service to provide for enforcement of the new regulations.[3] Thus, none of the Maritime provinces amended their game legislation to comply with either the letter or the spirit of the Migratory Birds Convention Act.

Maritime opposition was directed primarily at the prohibition of spring shooting. All three provinces were located in the path of the Atlantic flyway, one of the major continental migratory bird routes, and spring shooting was both a traditional sport and a dependable means for remote coastal communities to secure a fresh meat supply. Under the international treaty, however, spring shooting was effectively abolished in the Maritimes by establishing 1 March as the end of the open season. By 1 March, many bird species were still on their wintering grounds in the south. East coast sportsmen, deprived of spring hunting opportunities, brought strong pressure on their provincial governments.

Gordon Hewitt was disappointed by the Maritime opposition, particularly with New Brunswick's actions in repealing its game legislation. He had hoped all the provinces would continue to protect migratory birds under provincial regulations and he personally conferred with the provincial authorities in the eastern provinces soon after the Convention Act passed. But it was evident that the federal government was going to have to appoint officers to enforce migratory bird regulations in the Maritimes.[4] Even Harkin had no luck in persuading the provincial governments to comply with the treaty terms.[5] The attitude of the New Brunswick government troubled Hewitt the most. He was aware that restrictions under the Act were far from popular on the coast, but confided to Edward Nelson at the Biological Survey in Washington that he hoped New Brunswick's opposition would soon die away, and that the provincial government would assume its fair share of enforcement. Until then, he assured the American, the dominion government would honour the international agreement and see to it that migratory birds in New Brunswick received full protection.[6]

Resentment against the migratory bird regulations did not fade away as quickly as Hewitt hoped. In 1922, Alfred Maclean, the Liberal member for Prince, PEI, declared in the House of Commons that the Migratory Bird Treaty benefitted all the provinces in Canada except Prince Edward Island, Nova Scotia, and New Brunswick. East coast fishermen complained that they were unable to shoot any birds in the spring and Maclean read a resolution passed by the provincial government formally requesting that spring shooting be permitted in the province. He stated that a similar resolution had been passed by the Nova Scotia legislature.[7]

The eastern provinces were not alone in voicing dissatisfaction with the Act. Through an unfortunate oversight, the original draft treaty had never been submitted to the Yukon Territory. The open season under the Treaty was to begin 1 September, but by that time most of the ducks, geese, and shorebirds had left the Yukon on their southward migrations. Finding themselves thus placed at an obvious disadvantage compared with other provinces and states, members of the territorial government asked that the start of their open season be moved back to 15 August.

Hewitt regretted that a copy of the draft treaty had not been sent to the Territories.[8] During the Washington negotiations, the early departure of birds from the Yukon had been overlooked and he felt that the Territory's claim for special consideration was well founded. He thought that a slight revision could be made in the treaty to accommodate the Yukon request, and told Nelson it was obvious the treaty should go through an initial trial period first before taking on a 'cast iron rigidity.' Nelson agreed. Both the Yukon and Alaska, he believed, had been dealt with unfairly and an open season commencing 15 August would be an equitable arrangement for both. But Nelson warned that any attempt to revise the treaty might well be 'a long winded and cumbersome undertaking.' Hints for a treaty change or modification had been made in Washington and Nelson was persuaded that it would be dangerous to attempt any change, no matter how slight, for fear that 'the whole structure of bird conservation as we now have it might be wrecked.' Harkin adopted a similar view. He informed Nelson that the treaty as it stood was accepted generally throughout Canada. Any proposed changes would only cause 'certain elements' in the Dominion who were dissatisfied with the arrangement to seek even larger changes. It was the opinion of the Canadian government, the Commissioner told Nelson, that any change in the treaty 'would have a bad effect on the situation here.'[9] Thus there were no changes made to accommodate the Yukon or Alaska requests.

Not all the news was bad, however. Alberta, Saskatchewan, Manitoba, Ontario, and Quebec quickly brought their legislation into accordance with the new federal regulations. British Columbia had been the biggest stumbling block to agreement throughout the protracted negotiations, demanding and receiving special exemptions under the treaty provisions. Yet, after the Act passed Parliament, there was no evidence that the province took advantage of the privileges awarded to it. Harkin told Nelson four years later, with some satisfaction, that the British Columbia legislature was currently changing provincial migratory bird regulations to omit all special privileges granted to the province under the international agreement.[10] Hewitt must have been highly pleased.

The movement for migratory bird protection produced a number of results but none so significant as the heightened interest in bird life and bird conservation that was stimulated among the Canadian public. Ontario's Ministry of Education published 15,000 copies of British author James Buckland's report on 'The Value of Birds to Man' in 1915, which enjoyed a wide circulation. That same year, when a Canadian Society for the Protection of Birds was incorporated in Toronto, 162 citizens promptly enrolled as life members.[11] A similar society, the Province of Quebec Society for the Protection of Birds, was founded in Montreal in 1917. Gordon Hewitt delivered the society's first public lecture and chose as his subject the value of wildlife sanctuaries.[12] Local clubs and wildlife organizations began to display far greater interest in animal life and game protection than ever before. The Essex County Wild Life Association of Ontario proposed to the provincial government that Jack Miner's farm in Kingsville be declared a wildlife sanctuary for migratory birds, and that the federal government be asked to provide Miner with an annual grant for his 'good works' on behalf of Canada geese. Hewitt was invited to address the Essex club in 1917 on the bird treaty and afterwards he was taken on a tour of nearby Point Pelee, an area of federal land the club wanted set aside as a government bird and game sanctuary.[13] A year later, the president of the Essex club demanded that the Ontario government institute even more stringent protective regulations under the provincial Game Protection Act.

Most natural history clubs also enjoyed expanding memberships. The Ottawa Field-Naturalists' Club, for example, counted a growing roster of affiliated societies. By 1919, the Alberta Natural History Society, the Vancouver Natural History Society, and the McIlwraith Ornithological Club of London, Ontario, had linked up with the Ottawa based organization. The club had followed the migratory bird issue as it developed between the two countries, and once the bird regulations were out it published lists in its monthly reports of all the fines and convictions, province by province, for infractions committed under the Act.

Sportsmen's and outdoor magazines also began to devote more space to wildlife conservation matters. A 1916 editorial in *Rod and Gun in Canada* cited the 'enormous destruction' to wild game caused by automobiles and irresponsible hunters, and recommended that the government set aside more federal wildlife sanctuaries. The editorial also urged Canadians to organize more local game protective associations and set a goal for the establishment of one hundred of them by 1 January 1917.[14]

Confronted by a concerned public, the federal government took steps to deal with the problems and issues of wildlife protection. Responsibility for administering the Convention Act was given to the Parks Branch, and thereafter anything relating to or concerning wildlife automatically came under Harkin's jurisdiction. Thirty years later, in 1947, this section of the Parks Branch became the Canadian Wildlife Service which, today, is a department in the Ministry of the Environment. The Parks Branch was not enlarged, nor were its appropriations increased, but the scope of its activities was considerably broadened.

New responsibilities also produced new demands. Ornithology was not a well understood branch of the zoological sciences by government in 1918. There were no formal courses in ornithology offered by Canadian universities, few 'life scientists' existed in government, and even men with limited practical experience in wildlife were, reportedly, 'scarce as hen's teeth.' Although provincial governments gave official recognition to the field of ornithology, the federal civil service did not have even an accepted definition of what an ornithologist was.[15] Nevertheless, Hoyes Lloyd was hired on 11 December 1918, as 'Ornithologist' with the Parks Branch and given authority to administer the Migratory Bird Regulations under the Convention Act.

Lloyd had specialized in chemistry at the University of Toronto and was appointed Assistant to the Head of the Chemistry Department in 1910. Two years later, he became Chemist to the City of Toronto Health Laboratories, with special duties to help improve Ontario's milk supply. Bovine tuberculosis was communicable to man through cow's milk and Lloyd worked with a team of veterinarians and milk inspectors to eradicate the problem of tubercular cattle. In the course of his duties, he delivered numerous lectures to the Biological Club of the university, the Public Health Officers of Ontario, and to the Academy of Medicine. But while Lloyd's formal training was in chemistry, his lifetime interest was ornithology. He was an avid bird-watcher and collector in his youth and later became a member, and one-time President, of the American Ornithologists' Union. When the position of Ornithologist with the Parks Branch was advertised in 1918, Lloyd, recommended as the University of Toronto's official candidate, applied with eight or ten other applicants for the job. In Ottawa, he was interviewed by Harkin, Hewitt, and Rudolph Anderson, a zoologist with the Canadian Geological Survey. All three were obviously impressed with his credentials and offered him the position. His appointment in 1918 was significant because it was the first government position to be filled from 'outside': the job was advertised to the general public and openly competed for.

Lloyd was appointed game officer by the Justice Department and given the powers of Justice of the Peace throughout the Dominion. Enforcement of the Migratory Birds Convention Act was the biggest problem and Lloyd wasted little time in contacting the wildlife departments of each provincial government. Many years later, Lloyd recalled how well he got along with the provincial officials and claimed he had little trouble dealing with provincial governments that were, at least, nominally favourable to the treaty. He noted that he had, of course, 'been dealing with wildlife officials and not with politicians'! He admitted that there were the usual 'sore heads and troublemakers' to be dealt with, but that by and large, the groundwork for future dominion/provincial co-operation was laid in these initial months.[16]

Lloyd's duties were taken up in the Maritimes and the west for much of the first year. He had no more luck than Hewitt or Harkin in negotiating with New Brunswick, and due to the non-compliance of the three Maritime Provinces in carrying out the Treaty provisions, Lloyd appointed temporary federal officers to enforce migratory bird regulations. In the west, he inspected lands set aside as potential bird reservations. The prairies were major breeding grounds for North American ducks, particularly mallards and pintails, and western sanctuaries were a vital component of any program for migratory bird protection on the continent. Lloyd decided where the sanctuaries were needed, and, either directly or through the province, had them set aside by order-in-council. Seven such reserves were established in Alberta before 1920. A number of farmers were against setting aside prairie lands for birds but Lloyd pointed out that sanctuaries would not only attract people to the area but would also improve fall duck hunting by increasing game bird populations.[17]

The biggest problem Lloyd faced in these early years was a constant lack of money for conservation programs. In 1918 there was little to be had for wildlife outside Dominion Park Appropriations. The Animal Division was 'always pinched' and Migratory Bird Appropriations were not large. After World War I Lloyd recalled that things eased up somewhat and the increase in public interest made it possible to coax more funds from a 'reluctant Parliament.' But it was not until the end of the 1940s, after Lloyd left government service and the Canadian

Wildlife Service was established, that the purse strings loosened up and more money was made available. In the meantime, the Parks Branch used whatever means it could to educate the public on the growing importance of wildlife conservation.

Government officials began to make themselves far more visible than ever before to the general public. Both Harkin and Hewitt were frequent speakers to game organizations in Canada and the United States, while Lloyd became President of the Ottawa Field-Naturalists' Club in 1923. All three spoke extensively on the need for wildlife protection whenever given the opportunity. The Parks Branch published a number of pamphlets (in French and English) on the importance of migratory birds; 'Canada's Feathered Friends,' 'No Shooting Means More Migratory Game,' and 'Protection of Bird Neighbours.' Most of the pamphlets were written by Lloyd, but other articles were prepared for the government by the internationally recognized ornithologist, Percy Taverner. Newspaper articles, radio interviews, and public lectures were also used by the Parks Branch to publicize the importance of bird conservation to the Canadian people.

Lloyd was hired to look after migratory birds, but his responsibilities were soon expanded to include all the wildlife in dominion parks, and later he was responsible for administering the Northwest Game Act. Just one year after he joined the Parks Branch, his official title of Ornithologist was changed to Supervisor of Wild Life Protection in Canada – a substantial change indeed, and one that clearly revealed the government's intention to pursue a more active role in wildlife conservation.

Beyond doubt, the most significant development within the government service was the creation of the interdepartmental Advisory Board on Wild Life Protection in 1916.[18] Hewitt had recognized the need for such a body ever since the misunderstanding arose between himself and Maxwell Graham over which department was to conduct the migratory bird negotiations. With the government embarking on new fields of responsibility, Hewitt recognized the necessity of framing definite policies for the protection and use of wildlife in Canada. As questions of wildlife touched many departments, he contended that an interdepartmental committee, charged with establishing government policy, was indispensable to what he hoped would be a continuing government program of wildlife conservation.[19]

The Advisory Board constituted by order-in-council in December 1916 was composed of five members, all key men and senior members of those departments most concerned with wildlife. James Harkin, as

Parks Commissioner, was an obvious choice. So too were Gordon Hewitt and James White, secretary of the Conservation Commission. Both Harkin and Hewitt were aware that better game protection was needed in the Northwest Territories – the Unorganized Territories Game Preservation Act had been allowed to lapse in 1912 – and on their recommendation, Dr Rudolph Anderson, a zoologist with the Geological Survey, and Duncan Campbell Scott, Superintendent-General of Indian Affairs, were invited to join the Board. Anderson had led the Canadian Arctic Expedition with Vilhjalmur Stefansson in 1908 and 1913 and thus could provide the Board with firsthand information on the conditions of wildlife in the north. And, as Canada's native Indian and Innuit people would be directly affected by any legislation covering game conservation in the north, it was only logical that the Department of Indian Affairs be represented on the Board.

The Advisory Board was given no administrative or legislative powers. Its job was to investigate, gather information, formulate policy and then advise the government, presenting it with well-considered, well-balanced opinions and recommendations on all wildlife matters referred to it.[20] But the strength of the Board lay in its composition. All its members were top administrators who could pool their resources, knowledge, experience, and opinion. Although the Board was small, its voice was effective; and because of the stature of its individual members, Board recommendations carried considerable weight and commanded much respect. These five original Board members, particularly Gordon Hewitt, cared deeply about Canada's wildlife from both professional and personal points of view. As Board members, they were in a strong position to influence government policy on many aspects of wildlife conservation over the next few years.

Both Harkin and Hewitt had great aspirations for the Board's effectiveness. Hewitt believed that its establishment was a decided step forward for wildlife conservation in Canada, and told the Conservation Commission in 1918 that 'the usefulness of the Board will continue as time goes on. It will ensure the carrying out of well considered policies in respect to all matters affecting the conservation of wild life.' Hewitt also hoped the Board would be able to help the provinces carry out conservation programs, for 'these problems are national in character and there cannot be too great a spirit of co-operation ... to secure the necessary protection that the continued welfare of our wild life requires.'[21] Harkin entertained similar hopes, particularly regarding provincial co-operation. He told Deputy Minister William Cory that while game matters in the provinces came under their respective governments, there were many questions that could be solved by federal and provincial authorities working together. He hoped that Board members, by sharing their information with the provincial governments, could do much towards securing that co-operation.[22]

The Advisory Board met a total of eight times in 1917, holding meetings in the board room of the Conservation Commission. Advising on the administration of the Migratory Bird Act was one of the chief reasons for the Board's establishment, and the early meetings dealt at length with the provisions and regulations for bird protection. Hewitt had drafted the Convention Act Regulations and the Board recommended that the Act be administered by the Parks Branch, with the Board to continue supervising general policy. Also discussed at these early meetings was the preservation of wapiti and antelope in Alberta, the question of higher bounties on wolves, and the possibility of using barren ground caribou as a meat supply.[23] Another topic for debate among Board members was the proposal to relax the various provincial game laws so that wild game could be used to augment food supplies throughout Canada, particularly in regions where wartime shortages had resulted in increasing hardship. But after extensive investigations, the Board rejected the proposals outright. Protection of wildlife had been an 'up hill battle,' Hewitt told the Conservation Commission in 1918, and to relax the laws would 'undo the results of the hard work and efforts of years.' It was the Board's opinion that the amount of wild meat obtained would be comparatively small, but the destruction involved in obtaining it would 'affect in the most serious manner possible the future of our game animals.'[24]

Hewitt took a similar stand regarding the suggestion to use barren ground caribou as a meat supply for domestic markets. He told Commission members that the proposal came up because so many northern travellers in the past (among them, Ernest Thompson Seton) had reported great herds of caribou numbering anywhere from 10 to 30 million animals moving southwards on their annual migrations. But Hewitt suspected that these estimates were mere guesswork and he doubted that such numbers existed any longer, if, indeed, they ever had. The animals were almost gone from Alaska and nearly extinct along the Alaskan arctic coast. In Canada's Mackenzie Delta region, caribou had been killed off to such an extent, Hewitt claimed, that the Eskimo there were forced to import Alaskan domestic reindeer skins for their clothing. Even if the caribou herds could be harvested, he argued, the lack of labour, transportation lines, and cold storage facilities would make the whole project uneconomic. The Board was more convinced that a program for using domesticated, or semi-domesticated caribou, already experimented with in Alaska, would be far more successful as a means of securing adequate food supplies for the north.[25]

The future of wildlife in the Northwest Territories, however, was becoming increasingly critical. Harkin warned the Deputy Minister in 1916 that the combined impact of opening the Canadian north to railways and settlement and the subsequent invasion by American hunters and free traders were having an adverse effect on the wildlife resources of the north.[26] It was imperative that action be taken quickly to secure adequate wildlife protection. A much-needed revision of the Unorganized Territories Game Preservation Act thus became the focus of the Advisory Board's attention in 1917.

Conditions in the Northwest had changed considerably after 1900 as settlement pushed steadily northward beyond the fertile belt and into the Mackenzie Basin, Peace River, and Athabasca districts. A Senate Investigating Committee heard evidence in 1907 that the northern regions were far more valuable than had ever been supposed and were capable of supporting a large population in agriculture, as well as in mining, industry, and forestry. Committee members were told there was as much good agricultural land for settlement in the Peace River region as there was already settled in Alberta, Saskatchewan, and Manitoba combined. It was reported that at Fort Providence, 400 miles north of Edmonton, 'splendid' crops of wheat, barley, oats, and peas were grown, while at Fort Good Hope, just fourteen miles south of the Arctic Circle, cabbage, onions, and garden vegetables could be raised without difficulty. Geologists had determined that the shortness of the northern summer growing season was more than compensated for by the length of the summer days and the extreme heat of the sun at higher latitudes. Farming was thus as productive as it was profitable. W.F. Bredin, a resident at Lesser Slave Lake, estimated that there were one hundred million acres of available agricultural land north of Edmonton and in the Mackenzie District, certainly enough to make the north Canada's 'Second Best West.'[27] Agriculture provided the key incentive for northward expansion in the early twentieth century, but there were other inducements as well. The resource potential of the north was extolled at length during the Senate hearings. Alfred von Hammerstein, a pioneer in the Athabasca, had found seams of coal, iron, silver, and copper as well as pockets of natural gas. He told members about the Athabasca tar sands – beds of petroleum welling up and 'soaking the ground for miles around' – and predicted that these beds of 'asphaltum,' as he called it, would become commercially valuable once transportation lines to the north were improved.[28] The heavily timbered banks of the Peace and Athabasca rivers, capable of producing 'millions of cords of spruce for pulp wood,' were described by Henry Conroy, Inspector for the Department of Indian Affairs, who was also convinced that water power could be developed on the Peace and Athabasca.[29] The resource potential of the north seemed limitless, and later government publications such as 'Canada's Fertile Northland' (1907), 'The Great Mackenzie Basin' (1910), and 'The Unexploited North' (1914) echoed and enhanced the optimistic findings of the Senate Committee.

Northern railway expansion also continued unabated throughout the first decade of the century, luring settlers into the north. The Grand Trunk Railway announced in 1902 that it was building a line from Gravenhurst through northern Ontario, across the Assiniboia district, Alberta, and Saskatchewan, and out to the Pacific; while the Grand Trunk Pacific, a subsidiary of the Grand Trunk, began a line through the Peace River valley. By 1912, the Canadian Northern Railway reached Athabasca Landing, and a branch line was soon completed to the shores of Lesser Slave Lake, 160 miles north of Edmonton. Water transportation also improved and steamboats easily plied the waters of the Mackenzie, Peace, and Athabasca rivers.[30]

The coming of railways, permanent settlement, and modern industries all had a decisive impact on native peoples and wildlife resources in the north. Railways brought with them a growing number of full-time white free traders and migratory trappers bent on taking advantage of the abundant game resources which reportedly awaited the physically hardy and commercially adventurous. They had a devastating effect. Unlike the natives, who trapped primarily for food, clothing, and shelter, they hunted for game and trapped fur species to the limit, competing among themselves for the maximum return. Conservation did not concern them and when one area was depleted of its wildlife inhabitants, the trappers merely moved on to another. Ernest Thompson Seton wrote in 1912 that 'it was the worst thing that ever happened to the region when the irresponsible free-traders with their demoralizing methods were allowed to enter and to traffic where and how they pleased.'[31] A more recent author recognized that increased man-made forest fires, modern weapons, and competition between migratory trappers and free traders 'encouraged a race to destruction' for many northern wildlife mammals.[32]

The coming of trappers, and of traders eager to buy furs and hides, carried far greater implications, for they brought with them new and improved firearms which made their impact on the northern environment more immediate. Indians and Eskimo in the past had hunted only what they needed for survival, using traditional hunting methods and tools, none of which seriously affected or endangered wildlife numbers. But given a new technology and a new incentive for killing by white traders, natives killed for a commercial purpose and the populations of some wildlife species in the north began to decline dramatically. A similar situation had occurred in Alaska during the latter half of the nineteenth century. Firearms were unknown to the natives when the United States purchased the territory in 1867, but traders soon moved in searching for easy profits and supplying the Indians with guns and ammunition. Thereafter, natives reportedly began to slaughter hundreds of caribou for their skins alone, while 'nearly as many more were shot down and left untouched, merely for the pleasure of killing.'[33] Once the caribou resources were depleted in Alaska by the end of the century, American traders began to move into the Yukon and across the Canadian northwest.

Writers, explorers, members of government, and politicians were all aware of what was happening in the north. British naturalist Warburton Pike explored the region northeast of Great Slave Lake as early as 1892, publishing his findings in *The Barren Grounds of Northern Canada* that same year. Guns were supplied to the Indians, and Pike recalled that they made a 'stupid slaughter' of the caribou herds, recklessly killing the females and young as the animals passed in great numbers on their annual migrations. Pike was appalled by such 'indiscriminate slaughter' in a land where ammunition was scarce.[34] Frank Russell, another explorer-naturalist, travelled north of Great Slave Lake two years later. At Fort Rae, on the north arm of Great Slave, he was told how, fifteen years before, observers had watched an unbroken line of caribou moving north that took fourteen days to pass the fort, moving in such a mass that daylight could not be seen through the herd. 'Now,' Russell recorded in 1894, 'they are seldom seen within miles of Fort Rae.'[35]

The muskox suffered an even greater decline than the caribou. An arctic animal that inhabited the vast regions of the Northwest Territories, the muskox bore a slight resemblance to the buffalo, although the two species were not related. There was a strong similarity, however, in their shaggy, long-haired hides, and muskox robes proved to be as popular and as valuable in the early twentieth century as the buffalo had been in the nineteenth. Between 1862 and 1900, 12,365 muskox skins were traded by the Hudson's Bay Company, a figure that did not include the great numbers taken by native peoples for their own needs or those killed by many an arctic expedition that relied on the animals for their basic food supply. Large herds of muskox were found on Melville and Ellesmere islands and in the areas of Great Slave and Great Bear lakes. From the latter two regions, close to nine thousand skins were traded by the Hudson's Bay Company between 1862 and 1885.[36]

While the number of muskox skins traded annually did not represent an overharvesting of the species, the demand for live muskox calves by European zoos in the late nineteenth century and the methods used to capture them contributed greatly to the decline of the species. Northern whalers and hunters frequently killed off whole herds of adults in their efforts to capture the young, a practice that critically reduced the breeding population. The behaviour and natural characteristics of the muskox only contributed to their rapid destruction. When danger threatened, the animals formed a circle or 'fan' around the calves and stood their ground to face any attacker. In the nineteenth and early twentieth centuries, such heroic stands were nothing short of disastrous. 'To kill them was simple butchery,' Frank Russell acknowledged in 1894, and he advised hunters that it would be less expensive and a lot easier to spend an afternoon shooting sheep in a farmer's pasture.[37] But there was good money to be made in capturing muskox calves; the Duke of Bedford reportedly paid $2500 for the first two successfully shipped to Europe. The Swedish, Norwegian, and Danish governments all sent expeditions into the Canadian north solely for the purpose of getting muskox calves. Julius Schiott, Director of the Zoological Gardens of Copenhagen in 1914, described the early methods used by some of the hunters as 'wantonly, wickedly, and cruelly wasteful.'[38] In 1898, C.J. Jones ('Buffalo Jones') led a small party into the barren lands and succeeded in capturing five calves, which he and his white companions proceeded to drive south. But on the fourth morning they awoke to discover that a small band of Indians had killed all their calves during the night. The Indians believed that if the living calves were taken away, all the muskox would leave the country.[39] There was a good deal more truth than superstition in the Indians' belief.

Concern over the decline of muskox found expression by the turn of the century. In 1902, Madison Grant, Director of the New York Zoological Society, wrote to Clifford Sifton, Minister of the Interior, and deplored the wholesale slaughter taking place in the Barren Grounds. He told Sifton that there was great zoological interest in the species that had once abounded on the Asiatic steppes and in regions of the Old World before the ice ages. It was Grant's understanding that, as muskox had been exterminated in most regions of Alaska, the barren grounds of central Canada was the species' sole remaining range on the North American continent, but there they were threatened by whalers advancing down from the north and hunters moving in from the south and west in large numbers. Grant warned Sifton that unless something was done, muskox would go the way of the buffalo. Their disappearance, he wrote, would be a 'source of unending regret to all public minded men.' He asked Sifton to use what influence he had to bring the facts before the proper authorities and to secure effective protective laws for the north.[40]

No record survives of Sifton's reply to Grant. Three years later, he resigned as Minister of the Interior and the Act to amend the 1894 Game Preservation Act, passed the following year in 1906, contained no new measures for muskox protection in the Northwest Territories. Frederick White, Commissioner for the Territories, tried to take up where Grant left off, appealing in 1907 to Frank Oliver, the new Minister of the Interior, for a closed season on muskox for a period of ten years. White realized that there would be protests from the Hudson's Bay Company and others trading in the far north, but told Oliver that it would be in the interests of the Canadian fur traders to prohibit the killing of muskox until the species had had time to recover its former numbers.[41]

These appeals seemed to fall on deaf ears. Seton explored the region north of Edmonton to Aylmer Lake, NWT, in 1907 but found only one muskox where ten years before Buffalo Jones had found them plentiful and common.[42] Seton's concern, however, moved at least one prominent public official. On his return from the north, he was a guest of the Governor-General, Lord Grey, who later wrote to Laurier that Seton urged the establishment of national parks and game sanctuaries in the northwest. 'Do you not think it would be a good plan,' Grey asked the Prime Minister, 'to ask him to make a report to the government on the whole question of national parks suggesting the localities (in the north) with estimates of the cost?'[43] Perhaps Laurier disagreed with the Governor-General, for no such request was made to Seton. But if appeals for protection fell on deaf ears in 1907, the plight of northern wildlife could no longer be ignored five years later. The Stefansson-Anderson Arctic Expedition of 1908–12 revealed to a far greater extent, and publicized in a more effective manner, the results of settlement and exploitation on the wildlife resources of the north. Financed by New York's Museum of Natural History, the expedition was chiefly an ethnological study of the arctic. Explorer-scientist Vilhjalmur Stefansson, leader of the expedition, was to examine the Eskimo culture, while Rudolph Anderson, second in command, was to observe and record arctic fauna and collect specimens for the museum. The two men had been classmates at the University of Iowa, where Anderson received his doctorate in zoology. Anderson had written learned papers on birds and mammals and was, according to Stefansson, 'a crack shot and experienced in roughing it.' When Anderson wrote to Stefansson in 1908 that he was 'tired of civilization' and eager to go north, Stefansson quickly invited his old friend to join the Arctic Expedition.[44]

The Expedition covered the coastal regions of Alaska east of Colville River, and the barren grounds of the Yukon and Mackenzie districts west of Coronation Gulf. Anderson quickly discovered that while moose numbers were increasing all through the Mackenzie District, barren ground caribou were steadily declining. In nearly every region where thousands had roamed a few years earlier, he reported that only a few caribou remained and 'many a former feeding-ground now sees the animals no more.' Anderson recalled that not many years before, the coastal plain from Alaska to the Mackenzie was a pasture land for vast herds of caribou, but now only an occasional scattered herd was seen. At the mouth of the Mackenzie River on the arctic shore, the animals had all but disappeared. They were still fairly plentiful on Victoria Island and around the Coppermine River, he found, but only because the Eskimo in those regions possessed no firearms. Caribou was the single most important wildlife resource in the arctic for Eskimo survival, but Anderson feared that with the advent of guns, there would be a 'speedy diminution' of caribou in the Canadian arctic, as in Alaska.[45]

He published his first report in the *American Museum Journal* in 1913, charging that whalers were hastening the extermination of caribou just as they had hastened the extermination of muskox in the far north. Eskimos, persuaded to hunt for the whalers, had killed the last muskox around Franklin Bay on the arctic shore fourteen years earlier, while Indians were currently killing off the remaining herds around Great

Bear Lake. 'Muskox are seldom if ever seen near the mainland coast less than seventy-five miles east of the mouth of the Coppermine,' Anderson wrote, 'The muskox are so readily killed, often to the last animal in the herd, that the species cannot hold its own against even the most primitive weapons, and the advent of the modern rifle means speedy extermination.'[46]

Stefansson was also concerned about the wildlife decline in the north. In his popular narrative of the expedition, *My Life with the Eskimo*, Stefansson blamed the decline of the caribou in arctic Alaska on the 'let-alone policy of government, the cupidity of traders, and the ignorance of Eskimos themselves.'[47] These same factors, he believed, were now threatening wildlife in the Mackenzie District. Caribou, which fifty years earlier had passed in great numbers on their seasonal migrations between Fort Norman and Bear Lake in the NWT, were now 'seen no more.'

Stefansson waited until he and Anderson were on their second Canadian Arctic Expedition to voice his opinions more formally. The second Stefansson-Anderson Arctic Expedition, 1913–15, was financed completely by the Canadian government. It was to have been jointly financed by the New York Museum and the National Geographic Society, but Prime Minister Borden informed the president of the Museum that the Canadian government felt 'it would be more suitable if the expenses are borne by the government more immediately interested and if the expedition sails under the flag of the country which is to be explored.' Accordingly, the Museum and the National Geographic Society relinquished all claim on the expedition so as to allow the Canadian government complete control.

In 1914 Stefansson wrote to Clifford Sifton, Chairman of the Conservation Commission, from the Mounted Police barracks at Fort Macpherson in the Mackenzie District. Stefansson confessed that he was ignorant of politics and of the nature of government machinery and procedure, but felt that because Sifton headed a commission titled 'Conservation,' and because he was prominently connected with the conservation movement, he would be interested in what the explorer had to report. He chronicled for Sifton the decline of wildlife throughout the northern regions. He described how, twenty years previously, the western Canadian arctic north of the Arctic Circle had been occupied by hundreds of thousands of caribou. But whaling vessels had penetrated the arctic coast after 1889, bringing the most efficient firearms of the time to the natives and giving them a profitable market for large quantities of meat and skins.

Eskimos, and even white men, would frequently shoot a whole herd when they knew that they would have to abandon everything to the wolves but for a single carcass or portion of one. At other times bands of Eskimos would shoot down hundreds from the large herds they met, and never touched a single animal after it fell. At other times they would go so far from their homes to hunt caribou that it was impossible for them to bring back anything but the skins ... and the meat was abandoned as too heavy to carry.

The result of such indiscriminate slaughter, he told Sifton, was the near extinction of caribou north of the Arctic Circle and 'many an Eskimo either starved to death or was forced to abandon the interior for the coast, there to subsist on fish and seal.' There were still a few large herds located further east near the Coppermine River and around the Great Bear Lake district. The number killed there by Eskimos was limited by the 'comparative inefficiency of their bows and arrows against so wary an animal.' But new white hunters were pouring into the north and upsetting the natural balance between Eskimo and wildlife numbers. Like Anderson, Stefansson feared that once modern firearms were introduced to the natives, the caribou would disappear forever.

In Stefansson's opinion, rigid controls were needed to remedy a worsening situation. Caribou should be killed only during the summer months, he argued, and no one should be permitted to sell caribou skins outside the district in which the animals were killed; this would limit the competitive hunting for pelts. He also proposed that a licensing system be instituted for the NWT, similar to that for Alaska, where licence fees in the state were as high as $400 for killing two animals. 'We should have not only a direct source of revenue in the license fees,' he noted, 'but also indirect sources of profit through employment furnished by wealthy sportsmen to licensed guides, either native or white.' He also recommended that muskox be protected under a permanently closed hunting season. At stake, he pointed out, was the traditional way of life for the Eskimo people. For three thousand Eskimo in the northern regions, the barren ground caribou was their only source of wealth and of suitable food and clothing supply for summer and winter. 'It is for their future I am really pleading,' he told Sifton, 'although I present the case as one of conservation of natural resources through which the people of the whole land and of all races will profit.'[48]

Stefansson was an internationally recognized explorer, scientist, and author, and his report to Sifton in 1914 brought an immediate response from within government. The Minister of the Interior informed Prime Minister Borden that Stefansson's recommendations would be of considerable value. 'Our Dominion Parks Branch is making a study of these animals,' he told the Prime Minister, 'and is prepared, if necessary, to submit an exhaustive report on the subject suggesting regulations for protection.'[49] James White of the Conservation Commission also wrote to Borden, suggesting that the Royal Northwest Mounted Police extend their law enforcement patrols further into the north, where 'much could be done to protect these valuable animals,'[50] and Inspector Jennings of the RNWMP examined Stefansson's report and concluded that he too was in favour of restricting entry into the Northwest Territories. All whalers and legitimate traders, he believed, should be inspected at Herschel Island in the Yukon before entering the territories and he recommended that all individuals entering from Alaska be prohibited from passing Herschel Island. Jennings went even further and suggested to the Minister that all traders be kept out of Eskimo country for 'the less the Eskimo have to do with the white man, the better.' He agreed with Stefansson's contention that exports of caribou skins should be prohibited and that musk-ox and arctic fox should be permanently protected.[51] Concern for northern wildlife resources was at last being listened to. But it was not until the end of 1914 that any appreciable steps were taken to cope with the problem.

The Game Preservation Act for the Unorganized Territories passed in 1894 had been designed to protect a number of specific northern wildlife species, particularly the wood buffalo, by establishing a system of annual closed hunting seasons. Members of the RNWMP were empowered as game officers and given authority to carry out and enforce provisions under the Act. Amendments extending the protected period for wood buffalo had been enacted in 1902 and 1906, but no new provisions had been added to provide for the changed conditions in the north that had occurred since 1894. It was only after the provisions of the Act once again expired in 1912 that the necessary moves were made to extend protection to other wildlife species. In a letter to Sifton in 1914, Hewitt maintained that Stefansson had 'most convincingly demonstrated the importance of caribou conservation in the north.' Hewitt noted that there was a law already in existence prohibiting the export of deer, but felt that in any new Act this provision could easily be extended to cover caribou as well. The export of muskox could be stopped through a simple order-in-council and Hewitt believed it would be a wise step to declare Victoria Island – or an even larger area on which there were muskox herds – a permanent wildlife reserve. He promised Sifton he would explore the matter and write again if 'it is desirable that your Commission [Conservation] should take any further steps in the way of advising the government.'[52]

Hewitt also corresponded extensively with Henry Henshaw, Chief of the United States Biological Survey, who impressed upon Hewitt the importance of preservation measures. Both muskox and caribou were declining as the areas they inhabited were becoming more restricted. With the advance of settlement and the introduction of modern firearms, this process of extermination, Henshaw believed, was 'certain to continue and even to be hastened.' He urged Hewitt to draw up regulations that would permanently protect all female and yearling caribou, but warned that unless the greatest care was taken of all caribou, they would be exterminated 'in the not too distant future.'[53] Hewitt, more convinced than ever that new preservation measures were needed in the north, advised Sifton in July that the Conservation Commission should submit a formal recommendation to the government for northern wildlife protection.[54]

Hewitt took the first step himself in an address to the Conservation Commission's Game Committee at the end of the year. Emphasizing the points Stefansson had made in his reporting and citing all the reasons for greater wildlife protection in the northern territories, Hewitt spoke eloquently on the need to educate the general public who, as products of a material age, viewed things only from a materialistic point of view, questioning why money should be spent or land set aside just for 'a lot of wild animals.' Hewitt told the Committee that it had to 'set its face' against such an attitude and make people aware that Canadians had a duty towards future generations 'who would blame us if they found we had allowed this fauna to become extinct and to disappear forever when it was in our power to preserve it.'

We cannot speak once and then be silent. We must continue to preach this gospel and impress upon the people of Canada that, once an animal is exterminated, it cannot be regained and the nation is the poorer in those resources which increase our happiness, improve our health and add to our material prosperity.[55]

Three months after his address to the Game Committee, Hewitt went before the Conservation Commission as a whole and stated unequivocally that the 1906 Game Act had to be amended to meet the changed conditions of the north and to prevent the rapid extermination of certain economically important animals. He had drafted a proposed revision to the Game Act for the Parks Branch and sketched some of its broader outlines for the Commission. Under his proposed regulations, wood buffalo protection would be continued indefinitely, the killing of female and yearling caribou strictly prohibited, and a licensing system initiated for the whole of the Northwest Territories, limiting the number of muskox killed and regulating the export of caribou skins from the north. Hewitt further stated that, should his proposals be adopted, Victoria, Banks, and Melville islands in the Arctic would be declared permanent muskox reserves and the Arctic fox, not mentioned in the 1906 Act, would receive protection through regulated closed hunting seasons. Competent game guardians would be appointed by the Minister of the Interior to carry out, with officers of the RNWMP, all the provisions of the proposed Act. Hewitt believed it was desirable that the Dominion Parks Commissioner administer the new Act. The present Act already in existence came under the Department of the Interior, but was not administered by any special officer. Hewitt recognized that in order to carry out 'this very vigorous and much needed policy of game protection in the Northwest,' the Act should be administered by the Commissioner, who already had control over game in the national parks and whose branch had 'the basis of the necessary machinery.' Hewitt concluded his talk by drawing attention to the economic aspects of preservation. In a very short time the north would be settled, he said, and wildlife would constitute a very great and important resource for people living and working in the territory: 'These are valuable natural resources and can be protected for the future. For that reason I think we should take very energetic action now and leave no stone unturned to secure proper and adequate protection for these animals.'[56]

The members' response to Hewitt's address was immediate and favourable. Dr George Bryce, a Commission member from the University of Manitoba, recalled buying three buffalo hides for $14 from a Hudson's Bay store at Winnipeg in 1880. There were 1000 skins in stock then, but 'you can see the change now,' he said, 'and realize the tremendous loss that has occurred.' Bryce told Hewitt he could count on the support of western people generally and on the four provincial governments in particular that were greatly interested in the question. 'I believe the feeling is very strong to co-operate with the Dominion in this matter,' he said, 'I think we can count on the local governments to do their very best.' Dr C.W. Wilson, Assistant Surgeon with the RNWMP, maintained that there was no law operating at all above Fort Smith and Indians killed all they liked. And he agreed emphatically with all the provisions laid out in Hewitt's proposed regulations for a new Northwest Game Act. At the close of the Commission's meeting, a strongly worded resolution was passed unanimously recommending that the 1906 Game Act be immediately revised. Not surprisingly, the resolution contained, almost word for word, the provisions outlined in Hewitt's address, including the proposal to turn administration of the new Act over to the Dominion Parks Commissioner. Undoubtedly, Hewitt had a large hand in composing the resolution.

The Department of Indian Affairs was also involved in the discussions for northern wildlife protection. Inspector Henry Bury made an independent study for the Department that bore out most of Stefansson's findings and substantiated Hewitt's conclusions and recommendations. He added pelicans to the list of endangered species and suggested making it a criminal offense for anyone to have unprime furs in his possession.[57] Copies of Bury's report were sent to both Hewitt and Harkin in 1916 and Hewitt, considering it advisable to bring the matter to the Conservation Commission's attention, sent his copy to James White. He told White that Bury apparently possessed 'indisputable evidence' that American fur traders had opened posts in the Canadian north, and it was rumoured they intended to import aliens, coloured and white, to hunt the Canadian territories as far north as the arctic shores. Evidence had already been gathered, he said, that one Captain Lane, an American, had trapped 1600 foxes on Herschel Island alone, of which 1200 were white Arctic foxes, currently unprotected under the 1906 Act. Hewitt urged White to see that the Commission took 'immediate action' in advising the government of the 'real state of affairs' and speed up the implementation of a new Game Act.[58]

The seriousness of the matter was brought to Sifton's attention, and he forwarded Hewitt's letter directly to the Prime Minister. 'If you read Hewitt's letter,' he pointed out to Borden, 'you will appreciate the urgency of the case.'[59] Borden, clearly impressed, told his Minister of the Interior, William Roche, that 'it is a case in which circumstances disclosed indicate the necessity of immediate and vigorous action.' Roche replied that it was his intention to introduce legislation to Parliament for a revision of the Northwest Game Act 'along the lines indicated in Hewitt's letter.'[60] Responsibility for drafting the revised Northwest Game Act was turned over to the newly established Advisory Board on Wild Life Protection, whose members were all the leading government spokesmen for wildlife protection in the north. By this time Anderson had returned from leading the southern party of the second Canadian Arctic Expedition, 1913–16, and wrote in the 1916 Summary Report of the Geological Survey that muskox were no longer found on the arctic coast east of the Coppermine River, that they were extinct around Great Bear Lake and the lower reaches of the Coppermine, and that only skeletal remains were found on Banks Island, an area of former abundance.

The revised Northwest Game Act drawn up by members of the Advisory Board included most of the recommendations Hewitt had made to the Conservation Commission. A licensing system was instituted for the territories and the Governor-General-in-Council given authority to issue licences and permits, control the possession of firearms, appoint game guardians, and determine the number of birds and mammals that could be killed in any single year. The Governor-General-in-Council could also regulate the possession and transportation of game throughout the territories. Muskox, wood buffalo, elk, and white pelicans were all permanently protected under the Act, as Hewitt had recommended. Wild swans and eider ducks were given a permanent closed season until 1928, and the Arctic fox, not mentioned in the 1906 Act, was protected through annual closed hunting seasons.[61]

There are no records of the Advisory Board debates during the drafting of the new Act, but there were numerous compromises made by the five members of the Board. An earlier suggestion that caribou should be permanently protected for a specific number of years was not adopted and under the bill's provisions, protection was to be achieved only by shortening the hunting season by two weeks. And there was no mention of prohibiting the killing of female and yearling caribou that Hewitt had urged; nor were Victoria, Banks, and Melville islands in the Arctic set aside as permanent muskox preserves. Possibly board members believed the closed annual hunting seasons were enough protection and that the licensing system would curb the customary caribou slaughters. Indians and Eskimos continued to be exempt from most of the new restrictions (except those applying to wood buffalo, muskox, and white pelicans) so long as they were bona fide residents of the territories. Duncan Campbell Scott, as the Board's representative of the Department of Indian Affairs, was concerned about protecting the welfare of Canada's northern native peoples. One important clause in the Act, however, specified that no one was permitted to enter into agreement with any Eskimo or Indian for the purpose of trapping, trading, or trafficking wildlife in the northwest. It was hoped that this restriction would curb the commercial exploitation of wildlife resources in the north.

The long awaited Bill 100 to revise the original Game Preservation Act was introduced to Parliament by the Minister of the Interior on 7 July 1917. House debate was short, with most members either realizing the importance of the proposed legislation or simply not caring about the issue. On 23 July, the bill passed final reading, and in September the new Northwest Game Act became law. As Hewitt had recommended, it was to be administered by the Parks Commissioner but under the supervision of the Advisory Board. In 1918, Hoyes Lloyd as Supervisor of Wild Life Protection, was given the responsibility of administering the Northwest Game Act under the Parks Branch.

On the whole, Hewitt was pleased with what had been achieved and told the Conservation Commission that 'with adequate machinery we may now confidently look forward to maintaining a policy that will ensure the conservation of this valuable natural resource of our northern regions.'[62] Thus, the federal government did acquire new administrative machinery for handling wildlife conservation in 1917, but more important, it was fortunate in having Gordon Hewitt and James Harkin on the government payroll. The success of the Advisory Board and the successful framing of government wildlife policies can be directly attributed to their professional efforts and personal concerns.

8
The Sanctuary Idea Broadened

The International Migratory Bird Treaty went a long way towards giving a measure of protection to birds that travelled thousands of miles on their spring and fall migrations. But in both Canada and the United States certain species required greater and more specific protection, and the sanctuary idea that had been of growing interest even while the migratory bird treaty was under negotiation continued to develop.

The sanctuary idea was not new. Ever since the establishment of national parks in the nineteenth century, the beneficial effects of protection for bird and mammal species had become increasingly apparent. Howard Douglas, as Rocky Mountains Park Superintendent in the early 1900s, had been among the first to comprehend the value of national parks as wildlife sanctuaries. His recommendations and arguments for park expansion had been based on the firm understanding that parks helped not only to preserve but also to increase wildlife numbers. His successor, James Harkin, shared this belief. His annual departmental reports to the Minister of the Interior contained glowing descriptions of the natural increase of wildlife in all the dominion parks. Park wildlife protection proved so successful by 1913 that Harkin anticipated the establishment of more parks and wildlife refuges throughout the Dominion and called for an extension of the 'preserve idea.'[1] (There were few known alternatives at that time for protecting wildlife species and increasing their numbers other than the establishment of sanctuaries and the control of hunting. These reserves were, in fact, simply protecting habitat and it would be many years before scientific management techniques were developed that would adequately protect wildlife within and beyond the borders of parks and refuges.)

The justification for wildlife reserves and sanctuaries was based on both aesthetic and economic considerations. Prime fur pelts were bringing high prices in the second decade of the twentieth century and, as most of the pelts came from the high north, Harkin suggested that breeding preserves be established in the northern regions, the home of the 'best fur bearing animals.'[2] But he also recognized the need for bird sanctuaries to protect Canada's wildfowl. Even before the Migratory Bird Treaty was signed, Harkin reported to the Minister that songbird sanctuaries were being established throughout the United States with 'encouraging results':

There is no doubt that these reserves are doing much to repair the waste to bird-life which is proving so costly to agriculture, through the consequent increase to insect life. The creation of song-bird sanctuaries in Canada in those parts of the country which suffer most from the depredations of insects might well be considered.[3]

Harkin told the Minister that he hoped sanctuaries would be created also for gulls, terns, and gannets on the seacoasts, and for wild geese, ducks, and plover on the western prairies.[4]

Few individuals at the time, either in government or among the public, recalled that the first bird sanctuary in North America had been created in the Northwest Territories (present-day Saskatchewan) in 1887. The islands and eleven miles of shoreline around the north end of Last Mountain Lake, fifty miles northwest of Regina, were withdrawn from settlement and set apart as a breeding ground for waterfowl. This was the first sanctuary reserved solely for wildlife by the federal government. After the Migratory Birds Convention Act passed in 1917, the reserve was formally designated Last Mountain Lake Bird Sanctuary. The reservation of the sanctuary in 1887, however, did not signify a popular movement for bird protection among the Canadian public, nor did it represent the beginning of a wildlife reserve policy on the part of the government. Rather, it was the result of one prominent individual's concern. Edgar Dewdney, then the Lieutenant-Governor of the Northwest Territories, feared that the extension of Last Mountain Lake Railway would bring in settlement and development that would destroy the area's natural wildlife habitat. He wrote to Thomas White, Minister of the Interior in 1887, telling him that the islands of

Last Mountain Lake were the favourite breeding grounds for nearly all the different species of wildfowl in the Northwest Territories. Snipe and rare pelicans nested in the region and, during breeding season, the shorelines of the islands were 'literally covered with eggs.'[5] Dewdney recommended that the area be withdrawn immediately and reserved as a wildfowl sanctuary. Accordingly, on 8 June 1887, the islands and shoreline of Last Mountain Lake were set aside by order-in-council. But once reserved, the sanctuary was promptly forgotten. Throughout the discussions on the migratory bird question between 1913 and 1916, no mention was made of the sanctuary already in existence. Even Gordon Hewitt, addressing the Conservation Commission in 1915 on bird protection, declared that, in contrast to the United States, Canada did not have 'a single government bird sanctuary.'[6]

Although Last Mountain Lake was the only federal sanctuary established before the Migratory Birds Convention Act passed in 1917, the idea of sanctuaries was becoming more widespread. Jack Miner's experience with Canada geese on his Kingsville farm after 1908 prompted a number of game organizations to request government support for his work. In 1917, the Miner farm was declared a provincial crown game preserve, the first for Ontario, and after 1919 Miner was awarded annual grants from the federal government for maintenance of the Jack Miner Bird Sanctuary, a practice that has continued down to the present day.

Private individuals also promoted the sanctuary idea. Lieutenant-Colonel William Wood, a military historian and native of Quebec, was passionately concerned about the decline of wildlife in the St Lawrence Gulf and along the coast of Labrador. He published numerous articles, books, and pamphlets on the subject and in 1912 he spoke to the Canadian Club of Ottawa. In an address titled 'Our Kindred of the Wild and How We are Losing Them in Labrador,' he told how birds and mammals were being destroyed faster than they could breed back. Using the buffalo, passenger pigeon, and great auk as examples, he pointed out that a large population of any species did not necessarily guarantee its survival:

I have seen an old fisherman down in Gaspe who remembered the great auk being slaughtered by the thousands. There once were so many auks that nobody thought of saving them. Yet no great auk has been seen alive since seventy years ago.

Wood believed too many Canadians and Americans were imbued with the mistaken belief that no matter how many wildlife numbers were killed, there would always be more. He remembered one member of a hunting party, a 'gentleman of large means and good education,' who shot six caribou in the hills near Quebec City just to see how well a particular sight was working on his new rifle. The animals were merely living targets and the sportsman claimed neither the meat nor the antlers, taking the attitude that it really did not matter for there were plenty more caribou where those six came from. 'But there is not plenty more,' Wood warned, 'not anywhere, not even in the Arctic, not even in Labrador.'[7]

The Canadian Labrador coast, running 200 miles from the Strait of Belle Isle between Bradore and Kagashka, was an area of Wood's special concern. The 30,000 islands dotting the coastline should have been a paradise for wildlife, yet bird life was being 'absolutely wiped out.' The Canadian coastal population was small and Wood blamed wildlife predation on Newfoundland fishermen. He told Canadian Club members how bands of Newfoundlanders destroyed a dozen eider duck eggs just to get one guaranteed fresh egg:

They will simply go round and gather up all the eggs they want, no matter whether it is the first laying, the second or the last. Then, to find out which are fresh, they throw them all into a barrel of water. Those few that are fresh will sink. The many that are about to hatch out will float. These are simply pitched into the sea. In this way the men throw out ten eggs overboard, perhaps, and only keep one.

Sportsmen, Wood charged, were as guilty as fishermen. He recalled seeing motorboats endlessly circling off Esquimaulx Point in the St Lawrence. Thinking perhaps a man had fallen overboard, Wood went to their assistance but found instead that the waters the boats passed over were covered with dead and dying birds, divers of all species. In a 'brutal travesty of sport,' the boats had cut circles around the terrified birds that kept diving and diving until all drowned from fear and exhaustion. Then, the motor boats left, having provided their masters with 'an enjoyable morning's sport.' Such evil practices had to stop and Wood appealed to his Canadian Club listeners to give thought to wildlife preservation measures. 'We have the wildlife still,' he concluded, 'but it is vanishing fast, and chiefly because most of us are quite indifferent, and some of us are recklessly ignorant, greedy or wanton.'[8]

Wood followed up his Canadian Club address with a formal recommendation to the Conservation Commission in 1913 that it take over protection of the seabirds along the Labrador coast for a period of five years. In a paper subsequently published and circulated privately, Wood outlined for the Commission a detailed program for wildfowl conservation. He advised that closed 'egging' and hunting seasons be instituted immediately for the Labrador coast and recommended that the Conservation Commission establish island bird sanctuaries in the St Lawrence. The Commission should then charter a number of vessels, as many as five, to patrol the shorelines and enforce protective measures. He estimated the total expenditure for seabird conservation over a five-year period would be $30,000, a sum Wood considered a small price to pay for wildfowl protection. Certain parts of Labrador were bound to become ideal public playgrounds as time went on, Wood believed, but only if their wildlife was saved in time. 'The time has come when the seabird life must be either made or marred forever':

We still have far too much wanton destruction of wild life in Canada, not only among those who have ignorantly grown up to it, but among the well-to-do and presumably well educated sham sportsmen who go into any unprotected wilds simply to indulge their lust of slaughter to the full. Both these classes will be stopped in their abominations and shown a better way; for whenever man is taught a lesson in conservation, he rises to a higher plane in his attitude towards all his humbler fellow-beings and eventually becomes a sportsman-naturalist and true lover of the wilds. [9]

Wood's ideas were discussed by Commission members and although the matter was submitted to its executive committee for further discussion, no action was taken.[10] Members supported the proposal for seabird conservation in the St Lawrence, but the cost of implementing Wood's program might well have been prohibitive. Wood decided to spread his appeal for protection further afield.

He published his Commission address and sent it to prominent individuals in both Canada and the United States for their comment and opinion.[11] After reading Wood's recommendations for the Labrador coast, the Duke of Connaught, Canada's Governor-General, replied that from his own personal experience he knew what the game preserve principle had accomplished in East Africa. The same could be applied to Canada, since there was 'so much land which is favourable for birds and beasts, though unfavourable to the settler, that it would seem to be no hardship to give up a suitable area or areas for the purpose of a reserve.'[12] Ernest Thompson Seton declared that Wood had 'hit the nail on the head' for it was already proved that the only sure way to preserve wild animals was by giving them well placed, well selected sanctuaries where they would be permanently protected.[13] And President Roosevelt wrote that Canada could teach no more important lesson to other nations than by 'resolutely setting to work to preserve her forests, and the strange and beautiful wild creatures, both beasts and birds, of her forests and sea coasts.'[14]

One of the most significant replies Wood received came from Dr John M. Clarke, Director of the New York State Museum. Clarke had been a frequent visitor to the Gaspé over the previous fifteen years, studying and writing extensively on the local and natural history of the St Lawrence Gulf region. He was greatly concerned about the destruction of bird life taking place on the Magdalen Islands and Bird Rocks in the Gulf, and in the bird colony of Bonaventure Island. The Magdalens were rich in shorebird populations, their island lagoons providing ideal breeding conditions, but Clarke warned that hunting laws were not observed. Birds were shot out of the provincial hunting season and student ornithologists collecting bird skins and eggs subjected the shorebirds to a 'ruthless slaughter.' On Bird Rocks, just off the Magdalens, these same students conducted 'fearful attacks' on the bird colonies. Clarke told Wood he encountered one student on Bird Rocks who took 369 clutches of eggs from each of the seven or more species that bred on the island, thus destroying 2000 potential birds at one swoop. 'It is a severe indictment of the ornithologist,' confessed Clarke, 'that such statements as the foregoing happen to be true.' The gannet colonies on the rock faces of Bonaventure Island were fortunately not so readily accessible as the Magdalens, but even here, Clarke wrote, there was a reckless shooting of the birds 'simply for the sake of stirring them up.' Bonaventure was not a protected reserve but Clarke hoped that it could be made a sanctuary by placing the matter in the hands of 'some responsible citizen.'[15]

The bird colonies of the St Lawrence had long been well known. Writing in 1534, Jacques Cartier, one of the first white men to see Bonaventure Island, wrote that the island was 'as full of birds as any meadow is of grass.'[16] The island was indeed full of birds – gannets, double-crested cormorants, great black-backed gulls, herring gulls, kittiwakes, black guillemots, razorbill auks, common murres, common puffins, and Leach's petrels. The presence of large bird colonies had been a blessing for early settlers. The birds were used as bait by Norman and Breton fishermen in the sixteenth century, and after the arrival of permanent French settlement to the region they provided fresh meat and eggs for pioneer settlers and sailors. But the excessive and often needless exploitation of this abundant natural resource had brought about a rapid decline in the seabird populations by the nineteenth century.

John James Audubon was the first to publicize the decline of bird life in the St Lawrence. Voyaging into the Gulf and along the Labrador coast in 1833, he deplored the reckless slaughter of bird life he witnessed there. On Bird Rocks, where gannets were so great in numbers that Audubon thought at first they were snow, he found parties of fishermen had climbed into the colonies and clubbed the birds to death for use as cod bait:

The birds, alarmed, rise with a noise like thunder and fly off in such hurried, fearful fashion as to throw each other down, often falling on each other till there is a bank of them many feet high. The men strike them down and kill them until fatigued or satisfied. Five hundred and forty have thus been murdered in one hour by six men. [17]

Egging had gone on since the first white men appeared in the Gulf of St Lawrence. It is likely that coastal communities along Labrador and the Gaspé Peninsula, as well as Newfoundlanders, participated in the activity. Its greatest impact was on the seabird colonies. Audubon described how commercial eggers destroyed all the eggs that were incubated, forcing the birds to lay fresh, and 'by robbing them regularly compel them to lay until nature is exhausted, but so few young are raised.'[18] Egging was a profitable business in the nineteenth century and Audubon learned how one party of four men took 400,000 eggs in a two-month period, and sold them in Halifax for twenty-five cents a dozen. 'These wonderful nurseries must be finally destroyed,' he wrote in 1833, 'unless some kind government interpose to put a stop to all this shameful destruction.'[19]

Commercial egging could be objected to on moral grounds alone, but the practice had a devastating effect on the gannet populations. Gannets are beautiful white birds with distinctive cheek markings, blue-rimmed eyes, and a wing span that measures easily over six feet. They winter along the Atlantic coast from Virginia to Florida and return each April to their breeding grounds along the North Atlantic coast from Nova Scotia to Newfoundland. The birds require isolation during the nesting season and their breeding colonies are usually found at the top of steep, highly inaccessible cliffs, or on small offshore islands where they feel safe from predators. Each mated pair returns to the same location, and frequently to the same nest, as the previous year. In all of North America, there are only six known gannetries, three in

Newfoundland, and three in Quebec, the largest of which is on Bonaventure Island.[20] Perched high above the sea and the cliff face of Bonaventure, the birds crowd closely together in the colony, shrieking their raucous calls and loudly defending their nesting sites, usually defined by the distance each bird can peck while sitting on the nest. There, each female gannet lays just one single egg. If any disturbance occurs during the incubation period to prevent the egg from hatching, or if, later, the young dies or is killed, the female will not renest that year. Of all the seabird species that nested in the coastal regions of Atlantic Canada in the nineteenth century, the gannets were the most vulnerable to the egging and killing that was taking place. From an estimated 200,000 gannets in 1830, the population declined to 8000 by 1880, and of these it was believed that a mere 3000 birds remained on Bonaventure Island.[21] The end of a truly magnificent wildlife resource was in sight, but it was to take many more years before the 'responsible citizens' and 'kind governments' that Audubon appealed to came forward to stem the tide of destruction.

Just one year after William Wood addressed the Conservation Commission, an order was issued to the Chief Game Inspector in the Gulf of the St Lawrence to destroy all the double-crested cormorants nesting on Percé Rock. The order came from the Department of Marine and Fisheries in response to complaints that the birds were destroying young salmon fry in nearby fish hatcheries.[22] Both Gordon Hewitt and Percy Taverner learned of the plan from Commander Wakeham, the Game Inspector, who was opposed to the measure and doubted that the cormorants were responsible for salmon predation.[23] Taverner protested vigorously to the Department of Marine and Fisheries, but with little effect. Members of the Department answered only that the cormorants were 'of little value, either directly or indirectly.'[24]

Undeterred, Taverner wrote immediately to Theodore Palmer of the United States Biological Survey in Washington, telling him of the plans. He admitted that his protests thus far were based on sentimental rather than practical grounds. 'All I can bring before them is the danger of making any disturbance in the balance of nature,' he wrote, 'but that is such a vague generalization as to have little or no weight with them against the demands of the fishing industry, which claims protection.' He told Palmer that the Department of Marine and Fisheries intended to destroy, and keep on destroying, all the birds and eggs on Percé Rock until the birds were forced to nest elsewhere. But Taverner feared such a program would merely result in the local extermination of cormorants without making any significant difference to the fishing industries. He pleaded with Palmer to furnish him with any arguments that would reach 'practical and hard headed businessmen and politicians' and help save the seabirds of Percé from extermination. Taverner added that he was appealing in a personal, not official, capacity. 'Some of our departments, probably like some of yours,' he confided, 'are jealous of interdepartmental interference and a little care must be exercised in dealing with them,' and he instructed Palmer to be sure and write 'personal' on the envelope of his reply.[25] Hewitt also wrote to Palmer a few days after Taverner, asking whether cormorant protection was justified. Hewitt knew it was a debatable question in Europe (the British fishery boards were launching a movement to put bounties on cormorants), but personally did not believe any special protection was needed. 'On the other hand,' he admitted, 'I do not think their destruction is called for.'[26]

Palmer replied speedily to both Taverner and Hewitt, pointing out that Canadians might be interested in knowing that the United States was currently protecting cormorants on all National Bird Reservations where they nested, not because the birds were useful but because it was not American policy to destroy any species until it was shown 'beyond question' to be injurious. Although cormorants subsisted largely on fish with great commerical value, it had yet to be proved the birds were critically affecting fishing interests. Both China and Japan used semi-domesticated cormorants as fishing partners and considered the birds of great value. 'The mere fact that we have not yet learned to utilize these birds,' wrote Palmer to Taverner, 'is no reason why we should hasten their destruction.'[27] The Percé Rock rookery was famous throughout the world and Palmer told Hewitt that the colony should not be disturbed in any way. It was one of the most important breeding grounds on the continent and Palmer believed it would be a 'most unwise policy' to authorize the birds' destruction.[28]

This information was communicated to Harkin, and in June he sent off a formal note to the Private Secretary to the Honourable John Hazen, Minister of Marine and Fisheries. Harkin by this time had been told that the gannets on Bird Rocks were also to be destroyed for the same reason as the cormorants on Percé and he stated in his memo that Bonaventure and Bird Rocks were the only known nesting colonies of gannets in the Gulf. He reminded the Secretary that the Parks Branch was interested in the preservation of bird life and that the United States and Great Britain were contemplating a proposed treaty for migratory birds, to which class the gannets belonged. Harkin also pointedly reminded the Secretary that the Minister of Marine and Fisheries had an affiliation with, and great interest in, the North American Fish and Game Protective Association and 'I venture to think this matter should be brought before him so that the facts of the case from this Branch's viewpoint may be fairly presented.' (In point of fact, John Hazen was the 1913 President of the North American Fish and Game Protective Association and had presided over the annual meeting held that year in Ottawa.) Not unexpectedly, the gannets and cormorants won a reprieve, and that summer Taverner was sent down to the Gulf to investigate personally the charges against the defendants.

From his own observations and through talking with local fishermen, Taverner found that the effects of cormorants on commercial fishing interests in the St Lawrence Gulf were practically nil and that there was no data whatever to substantiate the charges against the species. He estimated the number of gannets on Bonaventure around 8000 and although the birds were of no economic value, he noted that they were a magnificent spectacle and the presence of the great rookery 'makes a sight that should prove a constant asset in attracting visitors to the neighbourhood.' Contrary to popular belief, Taverner found that local fishermen valued the gannets and could tell by the birds' behaviour when schools of squid and herring came in and where they were located (herring was popular as fish bait). And in foggy weather, Taverner was told, the chorus issuing from the colony acted as a natural fog horn warning mariners away from the dangerous rocks and shoals of the island.[30] On his return to Ottawa, Taverner, having found no evidence of salmon fry predation by cormorants or gannets, acquitted both species.[31]

But if Taverner found the birds innocent of all charges by man, he found man guilty of a 'most shameful persecution' of the birds. He described how boatloads of supposed sportsmen shot up the island rookeries, littering Bonaventure's rocky base with the bodies of dead and wounded birds, their 'sodden remains washed back and forth in the adjoining seas.' Saddest of all, Taverner reported, was the scene on the lower ledges where pot shots had been aimed into the sitting birds:

Here for some distance lay a trail of dead birds still on the nests where they had been shot with the young pinned beneath the cold bodies of their parents. Other young stood disconsolately about until a humane heel or blow of a gunstock put an end to their hunger and cold. Below, on rocks just above the swirl of the sea

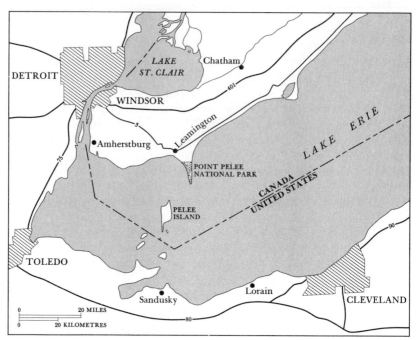

Point Pelee National Park

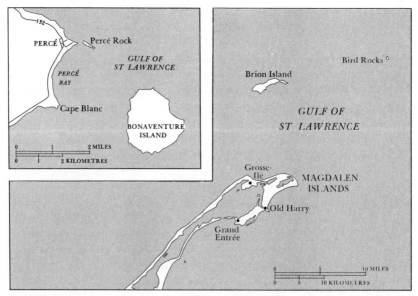

Bird sanctuaries in the Gulf of St Lawrence – Bonaventure Island, Percé Rock, and Bird Rocks

where they had managed to clamber, were numerous wounded adults patiently awaiting death that lingered in its coming.[32]

Such destruction was evident on Percé Rock and Bonaventure Island and Taverner informed Harkin that both areas should be preserved either as national parks or bird sanctuaries.[33] He also made the same suggestion to James White, for the question of national parks and wildlife conservation was 'of as much interest to your Conservation Commission as it is to the Dominion Parks Branch.'[34] Hewitt agreed with Taverner and admitted to Harkin that the Conservation Commission's influence could be helpful to the Branch in securing the reservations.[35]

Early in 1915, Taverner, Hewitt, and John Clarke presented papers to the Conservation Commission's annual meeting in Ottawa. All three recommended the reservation of Bonaventure Island, Percé Rock, and Bird Rocks as federal bird sanctuaries. Clarke described the colonies in detail, noting that as Bird and Percé Rocks were already Crown lands, there would be little trouble in declaring them sanctuaries. Bonaventure Island, however, was private property, its area of roughly six square miles held in fee simple by its present occupants. The gannets nested on top of the vertical eastern ledges of the island, which rose to a height of 300 feet and stretched over an approximate distance of $1\frac{1}{4}$ miles. Protection of the colony thus presented a few 'provisional obstacles' in the way of reservation. Clarke had investigated already the possibility of reserving Bonaventure and told the Commission that he had secured a tentative promise from the property owners to deed the back ends of their lots that adjoined the bird colony to the federal government in exchange for construction of a fence near the cliff edges. Such a fence would prevent farm cattle and sheep from falling over the cliffs. This was one of the hazards of island farming and the idea of a fence was popular among Bonaventure's farmers. Clarke felt that this was a reasonable exchange and suggested that the Parks Branch reserve just the bird ledges, which would not infringe upon the property rights of the islanders. This would be a simple solution, Clarke believed, to what could be a complicated problem.[36]

Hewitt did not anticipate any difficulty in reserving the sanctuaries. He revealed to Commission members that only a few days previously, in Washington, Dr Palmer had said to him that he wished Canadians would declare Percé Rock a bird sanctuary, for it was 'the greatest breeding place of one species of cormorant on the whole Atlantic coast.'[37] In view of the current seabird slaughter in the Gulf, there was an urgent need to establish the sanctuaries. Hewitt thought the Conservation Commission might well take up the question. It would not only bring 'great credit' to the Commission, but would also help create the public sentiment needed in Canada for bird protection. Taverner underlined the importance of these concerns and put forward a formal recommendation to establish Bonaventure Island and Percé Rock as national parks.[38]

Shortly after the Commission meeting, William Wood wrote to Harkin, asking what the Parks Branch intended to do with the reserve recommendations. He told Harkin he had recently met with Quebec's premier, Sir Lomer Gouin, who was favourable to the idea and who had, in turn, commended Wood to Honoré Mercier, Minister of Colonization, Mines and Fisheries, and another supporter of the reserve idea.[39] Harkin replied that the Parks Branch was authorized to open negotiations with the Quebec government, but explained that before any park could be established, the land in question had to belong to the Crown in the right of the Dominion. He told Wood that Professor Frank Adams, Dean of the Faculty of Applied Science at McGill University and a member of the Conservation Commission, and James White, the Commission's secretary, were currently in Quebec to investigate the transfer of land. No further action would be taken by the Parks Branch until their reports were received.[40] He added that he was glad both Gouin and Mercier approved of the proposed sanctuaries. Clarke also wrote to Harkin, reiterating the arguments in favour of reserving Bonaventure Island and Percé Rock and telling the Commissioner about his own negotiations with Bonaventure's residents. The island, unfortunately, was under Quebec provincial jurisdiction, and even if a fence was to be erected and the cliffs reserved, the problem of conflicting federal and provincial jurisdiction would still remain.[41] Taverner had warned Clarke earlier that the Quebec government was 'jealous of federal interference' and that its attitude might well hold up the entire scheme.[42] But the Quebec government was not prepared to put any obstacle in the way of reserving Bonaventure Island and Percé Rock. Mercier himself was as anxious to establish wildlife reserves as were members of the Parks Branch. The Minister took a keen interest in wildlife conservation and later frequently addressed the International Association of Game and Fish Commissioners. However, the 'simple solution' Clarke had proposed to the Conservation Commission and Harkin in 1915 – of reserving only the cliff faces – turned out to be not so simple after all.

Not all the residents of Bonaventure Island were in favour of deeding any portion of their lands to the government, federal or provincial. Even Mercier recognized that if either government formally stepped in, the owners might well block the scheme indefinitely. He advised Harkin that Clarke should be authorized to conduct the necessary and sensitive negotiations. Clarke was familiar with the island and, more importantly, knew the various owners well and 'would be in their confidence.'[43] Harkin agreed. It would be best to use someone without 'official connection' and the fact that Clarke was an American presented no great problems because he was interested in the sanctuaries from the point of view of a scientist and a 'friend of wildlife.'[44] Once the necessary land releases were obtained for the government, Harkin confided, the Parks Branch would be happy to withdraw all claims to the land so that the Quebec government could administer the area as sanctuaries. The Parks Commissioner wisely added that when Clarke acquired the releases, he should put someone else's name on them, preferably Professor Adams or 'some other Canadian.'[45] Indeed, during the next two months both Adams and Clarke were warned by members of the Parks Branch to maintain an element of secrecy, for it was feared that if the islanders learned of the government's interest in the land, concessions would be more difficult to secure. Taverner had looked forward to seeing his recommendations for the sanctuaries published in the Conservation Commission's Annual Report for 1915, but the Parks Branch instructed the Commission to delay publication until after the negotiations for land acquisition were completed.[46]

John Clarke and Frank Adams proceeded with the private negotiations throughout the early spring and summer. By June, it was learned that all the island residents except two were in favour of deeding their lands for reserve purposes. Taverner reported to Harkin that one of the owners could be reached 'through public influence and opinion,' but the other was the island postmaster, who was reportedly holding out for the position of game guardian on the new reserves. 'If the Post Office has any humanitarian principles,' Taverner suggested to the Commissioner, 'a slight manifestation of them to him would probably cause him to reconsider his decision.'[47] During the negotiations, Clarke found that the major objections to deeding land came not from the island residents but from a commercial fishing company that owned one of the larger properties. The company had operated a fishing station on the island since the seventeenth century and the company manager – 'an obtuse fellow with no sentiment' – opposed the entire project. Clarke also discovered that the company had considerable influence with the people and was regarded by them 'somewhat in the light of the seigneur of the island.' The result was that the private owners had become 'terrorized' by the company and were afraid to sign the deeds. Clarke did not name the company but claimed that control of the company stock was held by a Senator Turner of Quebec, an elderly gentleman who was also opposed to creation of the sanctuaries. Hewitt, Adams, and James White paid repeated visits to the senator but, according to Clarke, it was of no avail. 'Senator Turner was a man of peculiarities,' he recalled in 1920, 'and the interviews were not successful, not always amicable.' Nothing was accomplished by the end of 1915 towards acquiring the sanctuaries. Nor was any substantial progress made over the next two years.[48]

The climate became more favourable by 1917. The Migratory Bird Treaty had been signed, providing a basis for establishing the sanctuaries, and the Migratory Birds Convention Act was being drawn up. Mercier met formally with Hewitt early in 1917 and suggested reserving the cliffs of Bonaventure, Percé Rock, and Bird Rocks as federal bird sanctuaries under the Convention Act. The Quebec minister expressed a willingness to pass concurrent legislation with the Dominion in establishing the reserves and asked that a copy of the federal regulations be sent to the provincial government so that similar regulations could be drawn up by the province.[49]

Everything seemed in readiness, but there were further delays. The issue came up in the House of Commons in 1918 and Arthur Meighen, Minister of the Interior, replied to a question by Liberal member Rodolphe Lemieux that the delay was due to the 'difficulties of securing titles' and that the Conservation Commission was having trouble dealing with the Quebec government,[50] presumably regarding administrative details. Taverner, particularly, was becoming impatient with the prolonged negotiations. He published an article in the May 1918 *Ottawa Naturalist* in which he blamed the delay on the 'conservativeness' of the island's local population. 'After three years of effort,' he wrote, 'it is still doubtful whether the plan will succeed or not. Until some light breaks upon the community, and awakens public opinion and a spirit of protection, the senseless destruction will proceed.'[51] He also prepared a report for Hewitt for presentation to the Advisory Board on the urgent necessity of reserving Bonaventure and Bird Rocks as sanctuaries. He stressed that the region was a decided tourist attraction and that a large tourist revenue could be anticipated from the proposed reserves because they were a national as well as a local asset.[52] Taverner no doubt hoped that economic considerations rather than sentimental persuasions would help speed up the laboured process.

The efforts of Clarke and Adams in securing land titles finally met with success, a success that Clarke attributed to the death of Senator Turner. He deemed Turner's death fortuitous, for land deeds passed to Turner's heirs, who were not opposed to creation of the sanctuaries, and to the provincial government, where it was taken up by Mercier and Edward Chambers, both of whom had long supported the proposed reservations.[53] With the deeds secured, Harkin sent the Deputy Minister a draft memorandum for the Privy Council recommending that the Bonaventure cliffs, Bird Rocks, and Percé Rock be declared sanctuaries under the Migratory Birds Convention Act.[54] A few days later, a similar draft was sent to Mercier in Quebec. The following year, on 7 March 1919, the Quebec bill establishing the designated areas as provincial bird sanctuaries received assent from the Lieutenant-Governor. Twelve days later, the same designated areas were declared federal migratory bird sanctuaries by the Dominion government.

The wisdom of the government's efforts can only be seen in retrospect. Taverner had estimated in 1914 that the Percé Rock and Bonaventure Island bird colonies would become a major attraction in the Gulf, while ornithologist Charles Townsend had argued that visiting scientists and bird-watchers would spend large sums of money to the benefit of all the St Lawrence coastal communities. Both of their predictions proved correct. Today, the colonies have been described as one of the most splendid and spectacular ornithological sights on the North American continent. The number of gannets on Bonaventure Island has been estimated at 60,000 and it was recently reported that the birds produce $100,000 a year in tourist revenues for the town of Percé alone.[56] Harkin was right when he predicted that protective policies for wildlife would pay for themselves 'many times over.'[57] Just in economic terms, the fame of the colonies and the increasing tourist revenues more than justified to the government the preservation of the bird species and the establishment of their major breeding grounds in North America as federal bird sanctuaries.

The establishment of Point Pelee National Park in 1918 did not take nearly so long as the reservation of the St Lawrence colonies. As the federal government owned a substantial portion of the area in question, land acquisition did not present a troublesome obstacle.[58] Large portions of the Point had been in the possession of the Crown since the war of 1812, but other areas had been alienated from government control by squatters' claims. The Point was six miles across at its base and jutted nine miles out into Lake Erie, making it the most southerly point of mainland Canada. It was unique in botanical and zoological life and straddled one of the major migratory bird flyways on the North American continent. Pelee had long been a gathering place for amateur bird-watchers and professional ornithologists. Percy Taverner, James Fleming, and William Saunders were all regular visitors and members of the 'Pelee Club,' a group of naturalist-collectors. In the very early years of the century, they built a small cabin – 'The Shack,' as they called it – on the point and used it as a base for their bird collecting activities. They took advantage of the unique opportunity Pelee offered for natural history observations and scientific ornithological studies.

Taverner was the first to recommend reservation of Point Pelee to the federal government. He did so through an address to the Conservation Commission in 1915. He had inspected Pelee with this purpose in mind the same summer that he investigated Bonaventure and Percé, and found the point admirably suited for a park reservation. He told the Commission that the biggest threat facing Pelee was the annual permits granted to take sand from the lake bottom offshore. The sand was used as a building material and, while the business appeared harmless enough, Taverner pointed out to the Commission that Pelee itself was sandy in composition and the practice of removing sand from the lake bottom was steadily eroding the shoreline. The very existence of the park was threatened, for the point had been reduced by at least half a mile since 1905. The Dominion did not profit from the sand's removal, he said, for practically all of it went to the United States to be used in the construction of American ports on the south shore of Lake Erie.[59]

Taverner was not the only one concerned about Point Pelee. The Essex County Wild Life Conservation Association, organized by Jack Miner, was largely responsible for having the park set aside in 1918. They were determined to protect not only the unique and fragile habitat of the point with its rich marshlands, but also to stem the flow of Americans from Detroit taking up summer residence on Pelee.[60] But there was another reason why the club was so anxious to have the park reserved. All the members were game hunters, and Point Pelee, because of its strategic location on the migratory bird flypath, was a choice location for the fall duck hunt. Surprisingly, when the park was set aside in 1918, the practice of fall duck hunting was allowed to continue under special permit in the new park. It was this privilege, seemingly granted to the Essex Club members in recognition of their efforts in helping establish Point Pelee National Park, that became the root of all the park's problems during the first year of its administration.

Trouble began in Pelee shortly after the park was proclaimed. Farmers on the point and in the nearby towns of Mersea and Leamington were long accustomed to muskrat trapping in the Pelee marshes. It was a profitable business and one the farmers were not prepared to give up after the area became a national park. Early in 1919, a lengthy petition was sent to the Advisory Board by the ratepayers of both towns requesting that their trapping privileges continue.[61]

Muskrat trapping and fall duck hunting soon became emotionally charged issues. The Essex Club, whose members continued to enjoy their special duck hunting privileges, had little use for what they termed the 'bar-room, whiskey soaked classification of sportsmen' that wanted to trap muskrats in the park.[62] The Association's Secretary, Edward Kerr, wrote to Harkin that he fully anticipated that the 'enemies of wildlife' (trappers) would try to upset conservation plans, and told the Parks Commissioner that muskrats were vital to the maintenance of a rich marshland waterfowl habitat.[63] Forest Conover, another club member, added his appeal to Kerr's, pointing out that muskrats were helpful allies of waterfowl in the preparation and recuperation of rice beds and that a loss of the animals on even a normal basis alone would cause 'the ruin of waterfowl.' He begged Harkin to turn down the farmers' petition with the 'strongest contempt.'[64]

Harkin did turn down the request for trapping privileges in Point Pelee, but not for the reasons Conover stated. The Commissioner informed the trappers that parks were established game sanctuaries where all forms of life could increase under natural conditions. There was no law against trapping muskrats in the areas adjacent to the park and Harkin saw no justifiable reason to extend the principle into the sanctuary.[65] (Oddly enough, Harkin did not seem to find fall duck hunting incompatible with the sanctuary ideal.) But the argument did not stop there. A delegation of farmers travelled to Ottawa in 1919 to lay their case for muskrat trapping before the government and Harkin was compelled to send Dr Rudolph Anderson, a fellow member of the Advisory Board, to Point Pelee to investigate both sides of the dispute.

Anderson met with Essex Club representatives and local farmers in Leamington, where he quickly discovered that the dispute was many-sided. Club members, who opposed all trapping, claimed muskrat numbers were declining in the marsh and that the animals needed protection and time to recover their former populations. They pointed out that muskrats helped clear cat-tails from the marshes and stirred up the muddy bottoms so that wild rice, a great attraction for ducks, had a better chance of growing. All parties to the dispute conceded that wild rice crops were diminished, but while club members believed it was because of the muskrat decline, the trappers argued that it was because the marsh waters were becoming stagnant from other causes.

Contrary to farmers' claims, Anderson found little evidence that muskrats were damaging the diking system that protected low-lying fields from Lake Erie's waters, but admitted that the animals could cause local crop damage if they increased in numbers significantly. One farmer on the point complained loudly to Anderson that muskrats were menacing his ditches, rabbits threatened his trees, pheasants ruined his corn crops, crows destroyed all his other crops, and hawks killed his chickens. 'He wants to shoot all these birds and animals,' Anderson told Harkin, 'and is sore-headed about everything connected with the park.'

Anderson suspected the real basis of the farmers' complaints lay in the fact that members of the Essex Club were permitted fall duck hunting in the sanctuary while the farmers were deprived of their former trapping privileges in the same area. The trappers considered they had equal rights in the new park and felt the prohibition a 'rank injustice and undemocratic proceeding.' Anderson told the Parks Commissioner that these duck hunting privileges, besides being contrary to the very principle of a national park, were having a divisive effect among park inhabitants and creating dissatisfaction with the park reservation. He told Harkin that some of the Essex Club members considered themselves entitled to the shooting privileges as a 'reward of merit for being instrumental in having the park reserve established,' but it was Anderson's firm belief that the park principle was compromised. The fact that fall hunting was permitted in a sanctuary could be used by park opponents, he believed, to charge the department with 'unjust discrimination, special privileges to wealthy sportsmen and general undemocratic administration.' At the conclusion of his report, Anderson strongly advised the Parks Commissioner to withdraw this shooting privilege and place Point Pelee on the same basis as all the other national parks.[66]

There is no explanation why Harkin permitted duck hunting under special permit in Point Pelee National Park. Certainly it was against the wildlife sanctuary principle and ran counter to Harkin's stated intention in 1913 to extend the preserve idea. He told Deputy Minister Cory that only residents of Pelee would be given the special hunting privilege and, unquestionably, this concession was granted as a means of making the park reservation popular and possible in 1918. Members of the Essex Club were influential in helping establish the reserve and formed an effective lobby to press for the continuation of their hunting privileges after the park was established. Those privileges were never withdrawn despite Anderson's strong recommendation in 1919. Today, Point Pelee and Wood Buffalo are the only two national parks in which hunting and trapping are allowed.*

With the reservation of Percé Rock, Bird Rocks, the cliffs of Bonaventure, and Point Pelee, the sanctuary idea was considerably broadened and became a formal aspect of wildlife policy on the part of the federal government. Hewitt, Taverner, Wood, and Clarke, collectively and individually, had contributed much. The movement for bird reservations really began in 1912 with William Wood's address to the Canadian Club on the need for wildlife protection along the north shore of the St Lawrence and the Labrador coast. Eight years later, in 1920, Harrison Lewis, Federal Migratory Bird Officer for Ontario and Quebec, investigated potential sites for bird reservations along the North Shore. He identified a number of locations that were ideally suited for reservations and, in 1925 ten islands were set aside as federal bird sanctuaries under the Migratory Birds Convention Act.[67] Lewis also discussed the full range of migratory bird protection issues with Maritime officials, explained the new regulations under the treaty with Newfoundland fishermen (Newfoundland was not a party to the agreement), and enforced provisions of the Convention Act throughout the St Lawrence Gulf and Labrador regions.[68]

Local natural history clubs had all played prominent roles in the bird reservation movement. At various times the Province of Quebec Society for the Protection of Birds, the Canadian Society for the Protection of Birds, the Essex County Wild Life Conservation Association, and a number of field naturalists' organizations had supported the protection of Bonaventure, Percé, and Point Pelee.[69] The Conservation Commission once again played an important part, providing a public forum to publicize the need for bird protection and framing resolu-

---

* Native hunting rights are recognized and permitted today in the three northern national parks – Aujuittuq and Nahanni in the Northwest Territories and Kluane in the Yukon Territory. But rights have been given only to those native peoples who traditionally hunted for subsistence in the general park areas (Section 11, National Parks Act).

tions in favour of the proposed new reserves for the federal government. There was now a far greater interest in wildlife and bird protection among Canadians generally, an interest largely stimulated by the ever widening measures of protective legislation adopted by the federal government.

Each new reservation came under the administration of the Parks Branch and James Harkin, as Commissioner, became even more convinced of the value of wildlife sanctuaries. He believed that they afforded the most effective method of wildlife conservation, and told William Hornaday in 1919 that 'so far as my wild life work is concerned, I certainly intend to strenuously work for more and still more sanctuaries.'[70] Given the past record of efforts made on behalf of wildlife preservation by the Parks Branch there was little doubt that Harkin's actions would prove as good as his words in the years ahead.

9
Wildlife Conservation Comes of Age

Early in the negotiations between Canada and the United States for migratory bird protection, James Harkin had suggested to the Deputy Minister of the Interior that the government call a convention with the provincial governments to discuss fully the proposed international treaty. Harkin knew provincial approval had to be secured before any treaty was passed, and he told William Cory in 1913 that an informal, round-table discussion between federal and provincial officials would be the best means of achieving agreement.[1] But the convention was never held. The American draft proposal arrived in Ottawa before Harkin's suggestion could be explored further and was simply submitted to the various provincial governments for their approval. The treaty was subsequently signed in 1916 and the Migratory Birds Convention Act, formally ratifying the treaty, passed by Parliament in 1917. The suggestion of a dominion-provincial convention did not come up again.

By 1919 the situation had changed. The federal government had assumed far-reaching responsibilities for wildlife protection under the Migratory Birds and Northwest Game Acts and both Harkin and Gordon Hewitt felt that the time was ripe for calling a national conference on wildlife protection. It would give government members a chance to meet provincial delegates for the first time and to discuss informally with them the regulations under the Migratory Birds Convention Act as well as other wildlife matters. The conference was set for 18 and 19 February. (Two highly significant events occurred shortly before the Conference. Theodore Roosevelt died on 6 January and Wilfrid Laurier on 17 February. The former American president had initiated the crusade for conservation in the early 1900s, convened the North

American Conservation Conference in 1909, and created America's National Conservation Commission. Laurier followed Roosevelt's lead and established Canada's Conservation Commission the same year. Both men helped lay the foundation for the movement of natural resource conservation on the North American continent.)

The Advisory Board and Commission of Conservation were co-hosts of the convention, and with the exception of Harkin, who was ill, all members of the Board were present. The fact that the Advisory Board was co-host symbolized both the federal government's expanded role in wildlife protection and the realization, by government members, of the need for a broad citizens' effort and dominion-provincial co-operation in all phases of wildlife conservation. It was an impressive group of delegates that assembled in Ottawa. Eleven representatives of the Commission of Conservation attended, including ex-officio members Arthur Meighen, Minister of the Interior; Martin Burrell, now Secretary of State; Aubin Arsenault, Premier of Prince Edward Island, and Orlando Daniels, Attorney-General of Nova Scotia. Clifford Sifton was absent, having resigned the chairmanship of the Commission the previous year. From the various provincial governments came all the senior officials in charge of provincial game and wildlife administration – game commissioners, provincial foresters, inspectors-general and superintendents of game and fisheries, and provincial game guardians. Local game protective associations were also represented, with delegates attending from the Vancouver Angling and Game Association, the Vancouver Game Club, the Essex Wild Life Conservation Association, the Sudbury District Game and Fish Protective Association, the Petawawa Camp Fish and Game Club, and the Province of Quebec Society for the Protection of Birds. The three most prominent and influential members of the American wildlife movement were also present as special representatives of the United States: John Burnham, President of the American Game Protection Association (remembered in Ottawa for his role in the migratory bird negotiations); William Hornaday, Director of the New York Zoological Society; and Edward Nelson, Chief of the United States Biological Survey, Department of Agriculture.

It was, indeed, a most prestigious gathering. For most of the delegates, the conference provided the first opportunity to meet face-to-face with their counterparts in other departments and governments. Arthur Meighen, who opened the conference, admitted that the Dominion had learned only 'very late' the importance of wildlife conservation, but that wildlife was as economically valuable as any other

Canadian natural resource. Meighen hoped that the informal exchange of opinion brought about by the conference would lead to greater uniformity in wildlife administration and in all the laws relating to wildlife.[2]

Although Senator William Edwards, Acting Chairman of the Conservation Commission, introduced the various speakers throughout the conference, it was Gordon Hewitt who led and directed most of the important debates. He opened his address by declaring that the conference marked 'an epoch' in the history of the movement for wildlife conservation in Canada, for it was the first time that the Dominion had made an effort to bring together all public officials and private citizens concerned with matters of wildlife protection. He recognized that there had been a slow awakening in Canada over the previous ten years to the fact that wildlife, more than any other natural resource, was the most sensitive to human interference. He told the conference that this awakening had resulted both in a significant change of attitude towards wildlife by Canadians, and in the realization that they bore a responsibility to future generations for the nation's wildlife. In the past, he pointed out, game laws had been framed more for human enjoyment and advantage than wildlife benefit, and game itself had been regarded simply as a 'convenient and easy source of revenue.' The same was true of Canada's forests, which once were viewed only as sources of public revenue in the form of timber licences and stumpage fees and not as 'an economic asset requiring wise conservation.' Fortunately, the limits of 'inexhaustible' resources were recognized before it was too late, he declared, and the contemporary game officer was 'more concerned in protecting game than in issuing licenses for its destruction.'

Hewitt stressed three points in his address that were to form the basis and set the tone of the conference: the need for foresight in wildlife preservation, the need for a national effort in wildlife conservation and, most important, the need for close dominion-provincial co-operation. The need for foresight was vital; once wildlife species were destroyed they could never be replaced. He explained that Canada was more fortunate in this regard than the United States, for while 'wanton destruction and excessive killing' had taken place throughout Canada, most of the original wildlife stock was not depleted. But better and more efficient measures for its preservation were needed to ensure the future of the country's wildlife resources.

In the past it has been almost an invariable rule to wait until serious depletion of game animals has taken place before instituting protective measures ... Why

*should we continue to be lacking in foresight and of those attributes that make a
nation progressive, as to be unwilling to provide against contingencies that we
know from experience will occur?*
  Conservation is practical foresight.[3]

The need for co-operation had never been greater, Hewitt contended. Wildlife conservation was no longer a matter that any one
province, state, or territory could handle alone, since most forms of
bird and mammal life were migratory and recognized neither provincial nor national boundaries. What good would it be, he asked, if
Saskatchewan or New Brunswick prohibited the sale of game when an
adjacent province permitted it? The chief object of the conference, in
Hewitt's view, was to secure as great a degree of co-operation as
possible so that such problems need never arise. He praised the Conservation Commission for taking the lead in educating public opinion
on the importance of conserving wildlife resources and for promoting
effective preservation measures. But the assistance of all organizations
concerned with wildlife protection was urgently needed. More
sportsmen's associations should be organized as active centres for
'wildlife conservation propaganda,' more naturalists' clubs were
needed to assist provincial governments in law enforcement, and game
associations and provincial governments needed to co-operate in a
nation-wide effort at wildlife conservation. 'We shall never again have
such an excellent opportunity,' he concluded, 'of attaining, by mutual
efforts, the ends for which we are individually striving, as we have now.'
  With the intentions and goals of the conference clearly stated, Hewitt
led a general discussion into the Migratory Bird Treaty and Convention Act. This was the chief reason most provincial delegates attended
the conference and while Hewitt admitted that no amendments could
be made to the Convention, he hoped the discussion would revolve
around questions of administration generally. To Hewitt, the treaty
was not a 'scrap of paper,' but the most far-reaching measure ever put
into operation for bird preservation. He hoped discussions between
government representatives would lead to a better understanding of
the treaty's provisions and their significance, and to a better enforcement of migratory bird regulations.
  Opinions on the Convention Act were freely expressed.[4] As expected, representatives from the western provinces, Ontario, and
Quebec, were in hearty agreement with the protective principle and
the new regulations. Benjamin Lawton, Alberta's Provincial Game
Guardian, praised the Migratory Bird Treaty as the 'greatest move

towards game conservation that has ever been made on the North American continent,' while Fred Bradshaw, Saskatchewan's Game Guardian, deemed it the best legislation ever enacted for game conservation. The Chairman of British Columbia's Game Conservation Board, Dr A.R. Baker, remembered the strong initial opposition in his province to the shortened hunting season under the treaty, and admitted taking the platform in opposition. But since then, he said, there had been 'an entire change of heart' in British Columbia and sportsmen realized that reducing the open season from $5\frac{1}{2}$ to $3\frac{1}{2}$ months was 'the best thing that could have happened to British Columbia.' Baker claimed that he personally had fought to win support for the treaty, and read out resolutions passed by two prominent game associations in his province strongly endorsing the Migratory Birds Convention Act and its regulations. Manitoba's representative was 'gratified' to see the results of the treaty already evident in his province; Ontario's Superintendent of Game and Fisheries declared his province was in accord with the treaty and would do 'all in its power' to enforce the regulations; and Edward Chambers, Special Officer in Quebec's Department of Colonization, Mines, and Fisheries, claimed that his province's legislation was already in harmony with the treaty terms and that almost no amendments were needed to comply with the Convention Act Regulations.

Only delegates from the Maritime Provinces and the Yukon Territory expressed dissatisfaction with the Convention Act. New Brunswick's Minister of Lands and Mines, the Honourable Ernest Smith, told how the province's coastal fishermen were suffering through the ban on spring shooting. Mergansers and coots were considered edible by many people, he said, and for New Brunswick settlers, the birds were an important food source. 'These men do not see meat every day, as many people do,' Smith declared, 'they do not see meat oftener than once a month, perhaps.' The Minister also explained that his government did not have the necessary money to support a large warden service along the coast to prohibit spring shooting and to enforce the Convention Act regulations. It would cost the province many thousands of dollars and 'I don't want to undertake anything I cannot carry through,' he concluded.

Nova Scotia's Chief Game Commissioner echoed Smith's reservations. Fishermen were in the habit of shooting wild geese along Nova Scotia's southern coast in the spring and the cost of providing an effective warden service to patrol the region would be high. And Aubin Arsenault, Premier of Prince Edward Island, admitted that his government had not even tried to pass legislation bringing provincial game laws into harmony with the federal regulations because the opposition to it was so great on both sides of the House. Spring shooting had long provided recreation and food supplies for the island's coastal communities and its prohibition was causing both hardship and resentment among the islanders. 'The expressions that I have heard,' Premier Arsenault declared, 'have been to the effect that the legislation was designed for the benefit of the southern portion of North America.'

The MP for the Yukon Territory, Colonel Alfred Thompson, strongly sympathized with Premier Arsenault and the people of Prince Edward Island who felt discriminated against by the treaty terms. In the Yukon, Thompson pointed out, by the time the hunting season opened on 1 September most of the migratory birds were long gone. 'We are in the peculiar position in the Yukon of breeding these birds, and, because of the Migratory Bird Treaty, seeing them fly gracefully along the valley of the Yukon over our heads to our southern neighbours, who take them when they arrive in their districts. We can't take them without breaking the law.' Thompson argued that his constituents, far removed from world markets, had to import all their beef, mutton, and fowl. Wild game was thus an important factor in their daily menus and spring and fall hunting had always augmented their food supplies. But 'this Migratory Bird Treaty hits us very hard.' He had no criticism of regulations prohibiting spring shooting – he personally opposed it – but did ask that a 'little leniency' be shown the Yukon with respect to fall hunting.

Many provincial complaints were legitimate. The cost of enforcing Migratory Bird Regulations along vast stretches of Maritime coastline was going to be very high.[5] The Yukon case was unfortunate but, as Hewitt stated in his opening address, no amendments could be made to the Treaty or Convention Act to allow the Yukon an earlier hunting season. Nor could spring shooting be allowed for the Maritime provinces. The public would have to learn to accept the new regulations in the interests of better wildlife protection. Premier Arsenault later admitted that the principle and intention of the Treaty might well be explained more fully to his fellow islanders and that with a 'little education' and some 'pioneer work,' support could be won for the restrictive regulations on Prince Edward Island.

Hewitt was familiar with all the complaints against the Treaty and Convention Act – he had tried to work out compromises to meet them three years earlier – but the arguments were new for other delegates attending the conference. For the first time, provincial members had an opportunity to learn of the difficulties, and advantages, that were common to all. Premier Arsenault quickly discovered that on the question of hunting seasons he was voicing arguments on behalf of Prince Edward Island that were similar to those Colonel Thompson was presenting for the Yukon Territory. He proposed to Thompson that they get together to discuss their mutual problems, whereupon another delegate suggested that, as Dr Baker had helped bring about an 'entire change of heart' in British Columbia towards the regulations, he join Arsenault and Thompson and 'make a trio of it.'[6] The spirit of co-operation that Hewitt had hoped to see was becoming evident throughout the debates.

Many other aspects of the Convention Act were dealt with and discussed at length: the procedure for securing permits from Ottawa to kill migratory birds under special Treaty clauses; the position of provincial game officers in enforcing Convention Act regulations, and the constitutional standing of provincial laws under the federal act. Hewitt explained that the Dominion was responsible for carrying out legislation putting the treaty into effect, and in that regard federal power was supreme to provincial. But to avoid any conflict of jurisdiction, he said, the Dominion hoped provincial governments would bring their own game legislation into line with the federal regulations. That way, both sets of laws would be identical and legislation could be carried out and enforced on a co-operative basis. Benjamin Lawton of Alberta was concerned, for example, that a conviction secured by his province for a Migratory Bird offence might be overturned in the Supreme Court. But he was assured by Hewitt and James White that provincial governments had the power defined by the British North America Act to pass such legislation under a federal act and any conviction would, unquestionably, be ruled *intra vires*.

There were no major disagreements between dominion and provincial representatives over the principle of migratory bird protection and it is debatable whether such a round-table conference would have altered the treaty terms had it been held in 1913 when Harkin first proposed such a conference. Certainly Hewitt and his American counterparts who hammered out the international agreement would have been more aware of the special Yukon situation and might have allowed the annual fall hunting season to begin earlier in the northern territories. But representatives to the 1919 conference generally accepted the larger principles of bird protection and most delegates seemed more inclined to discuss the administrative mechanics of enforcing the new regulations than any other aspect of the Convention Act.

Numerous papers were presented to the conference dealing with all aspects of wildlife preservation and discussed at length. The federal government had gained considerable experience with wildlife sanctuaries through the establishment of Dominion Parks and a paper prepared by James Harkin chronicled the success of those parks as wildlife preserves. The Parks Commissioner told the Rocky Mountains Park story, noting that regulations within the park were so successful in benefitting wildlife species that all the provinces should be surveyed for potential sanctuaries. The delegates were quick to agree. New Brunswick's Minister of Lands and Mines pointed out that the Maritime Provinces were the only regions of the country that did not have wildlife preserves, and he urged the dominion government to create sanctuaries in both New Brunswick and Nova Scotia.[8]

The sanctuary idea sparked a great deal of interest among the delegates. Western members explained the best methods of game protection in Dominion Parks to their eastern counterparts; Jack Miner related his experiences in attracting wildfowl to his Kingsville sanctuary; and Edith Marsh told how the owners of Peasemarsh Farm on Georgian Bay had succeeded in getting the Ontario government to declare their 300 acres of land a wildlife preserve in 1917. Maritime members, particularly, were interested to learn that a sanctuary only ten acres in size could be an effective wildlife preserve.

The conference also explored new areas of concern that clearly demanded dominion-provincial and interprovincial co-operation. There was a necessity to regulate the fur trade and to control the number of hunting and fishing licences issued; a need to prevent illegal, interprovincial shipment of game skins; and a need for uniformity in all provincial game laws affecting the fur trade. There was also a demand for more accurate dominion fur statistics. This could only be achieved through a reliable exchange of information between federal and provincial authorities, and Hewitt suggested that the matter be submitted to the Advisory Board for such a body 'desires to serve as an intermediary.'[9] Provincial representatives also agreed that 'pump' or repeating shotguns, because of their rapid-fire capability, were the most deadly to wildlife numbers, and they passed a resolution recommending that all firearms with magazines capable of holding more than one cartridge be prohibited by law.

There was by no means agreement on all topics discussed at the conference. Duncan Campbell Scott, Deputy Superintendent General of Indian Affairs, delivered a paper on the Indians' relationship to wildlife and pleaded for sympathy and understanding for Indians, the 'original fur hunters.' So many companies and individuals were competing for furs, Scott said, and there were so many game hunting restrictions throughout the country, that the Indians were finding it increasingly difficult to support themselves. His department was endeavouring to control Indian tribes and bring them under provincial game laws and Scott believed it had finally succeeded.

This declaration brought sharp disagreement. Fred Bradshaw of Saskatchewan claimed that the Indians in his province ignored the game laws and that there were frequent complaints about their 'wanton slaughter' of big game animals:

The Provincial Government has repeatedly sought assistance from the Department of Indian Affairs, but there has been little response. Our correspondence has always been courteously acknowledged, and promises of co-operation were repeatedly given. I regret to say, however, that there is little or no evidence of any improvement.

'I may be wrong,' Bradshaw concluded, 'but the attitude of the Indian Department seems to be, that, while they are extremely sorry that such things are happening – the poor Indian must be fed, and presumably in the cheapest possible manner.' The Department of Indian Affairs was responsible for the various tribes, but Bradshaw accused the average government Indian agent of encouraging, rather than discouraging, the illegal killing of game in order to keep departmental costs down, and he believed such a practice was, indeed, expected by the Department's headquarters at Ottawa. 'Is the Indian Department in sympathy with the enforcement of our Provincial Laws?', he asked Scott. Scott replied that the policy of his department was to assist provincial officials in any way it could, but that the lawmaking power and the enforcement of the law was in the hands of the provinces. 'If the provincial delegates can make any suggestion at any time as to action that might be taken by the Indian Department,' he answered, 'we shall be delighted to co-operate.'[10]

The discussions following the papers were the most important aspect of the 1919 conference. Members confronted each other for the first time in a friendly, round-table atmosphere, and had a chance to air grievances, exchange valuable insights and information, and, in some cases, to reach agreement on many aspects of wildlife protection. The three visiting Americans opened up a number of avenues for discus-

sion. William Hornaday denounced the commercial sale of game
species for food purposes, a practice permitted in Alaska and a few
Canadian provinces (notably Nova Scotia, New Brunswick, British
Columbia, and the Yukon and Northwest Territories where the sale of
moose and bear was legal); Edward Nelson warned that the need to
maintain and increase prairie wildfowl habitat was becoming crucial in
both countries, and John Burnham stressed the continued and pressing need for more public education on the importance of wildlife
conservation.[11]

At the conclusion of the conference, Hewitt expressed a keen desire
to hold similar meetings every one or two years. He foresaw a convention, not just of dominion and provincial game officials, but of
sportsmen, conservationists, and all those interested in wildlife preservation. He believed a great deal could be accomplished in discussing
mutual problems together and endeavouring to co-operate in every
way. 'The idea appeals to us in Ottawa,' he said, 'who are concerned in
the matter and anxious to bring about greater Dominion-Provincial
co-operation.'[12] Most of the delegates applauded the suggestion. Jack
Miner claimed provincial members could only benefit through yearly
meetings with dominion officials, and Dr Baker of British Columbia
declared the idea 'the best thing suggested' at the conference, although
he did caution that his province would strongly object if the Dominion
tried to take over any aspect of BC's game administration. The proposal
to hold annual wildlife conventions was put into a formal resolution
and referred to the Conservation Commission for further action.

The conference was a great success. Private citizens and government
officials from all across the country had come together to help publicize
and advance the cause of wildlife preservation. Provincial delegates
had been given the opportunity for the first time to discuss the regulations and implications of the Migratory Birds Convention Act. Although no amendments could be made to the Act, a better understanding was reached regarding the necessity of protection and the nature of
the regulations under the Act. Each year these regulations would be
drawn up by members of the Parks Branch, specifying the length of
open and closed hunting seasons for each province and decreeing bag
limits on various wildlife species. It was thus necessary and invaluable
for federal officials to gain first-hand information from provincial
delegates about wildlife conditions in the different regions of the
country. The suggestion to hold continuing wildlife conventions must
have delighted Harkin. He was not present at the conference but
followed its development closely. In his 1919 report to the Minister of

the Interior, he wrote: 'Important points were discussed and the foundation laid for better co-operation and understanding between Provincial and Dominion Governments.'[13]

The annual wildlife conventions that were recommended at the 1919 National Conference did not begin the following year, nor the year after that. Two unfortunate events occurred that explain why – the death of Gordon Hewitt, who died at the age of thirty-six in 1920, and the abolition of the Commission of Conservation.

Hewitt's death was a blow to the wildlife protection movement, which was just beginning to gain momentum in Canada. Ever since his arrival in Ottawa in 1909, his influence within government had been substantial. His diplomacy and untiring labours had been in large part responsible for the securing of the Migratory Bird Treaty, and he had been awarded the gold medal in recognition of his work in furthering the Treaty by the Royal British Society for the Protection of Birds. It was Hewitt who worked out the various compromises that won provincial approval for the Treaty, drafted the Convention Act Regulations, and later prepared the Northwest Game Act, which brought increased protection to northern wildlife resources, a measure Hewitt had long advocated.

As Consulting Zoologist to the dominion government and Conservation Commission, and as Secretary to the Advisory Board on Wild Life Protection, he had been in a strong position to influence and guide government policy towards his own wildlife goals. Frequently, he had used the Conservation Commission as a public platform to air his views on the importance of wildlife conservation and to advance measures for greater protection. He had attended the last meeting held by the Commission in Montreal on 18 and 19 February 1920, and delivered a paper there on 'Fur Bearing Animals, Their Economic Importance and Future.' On his return to Ottawa, he became seriously ill and ten days later died of pleural pneumonia.[14] For some reason, probably political, the report of the last Conservation Commission meeting was never published by the government and no copy of Hewitt's final address survives.

During the last years of his life, Hewitt was working to complete a manuscript titled 'The Conservation of the Wild Life of Canada.' The book, published in 1921 after his death, contained a biological and economic description of many bird and mammal species, a narrative of dominion/provincial legislation enacted for wildlife preservation, a

survey of provincial game laws, and a description of all parks and
sanctuaries, both federal and provincial, that had been set aside for
wildlife protection. Today, Hewitt's book remains the only detailed
work written on the early legislative history of wildlife conservation in
Canada. He was a man of exceptional talent and ability. The Dominion
Entomological Service was a small division of the Experimental Farm at
Ottawa when Hewitt came to Canada in 1909, but under his leadership
and guidance the service became an important branch of the Department of Agriculture, with four divisions in Ottawa and twelve
laboratories throughout the country. He is also credited with initiating
the important Dangerous Insects and Pests Act passed by Parliament in
1910.

Had Hewitt lived, there is no telling what he might have accomplished. Many more national parks and wildlife sanctuaries might
well have been established much earlier than they were, particularly in
the far north, where Hewitt had envisioned them. At the time of his
death, many new reservations were recommended and he had written
in his book that 'there is every reason to believe that a policy that is sure
to have so important an effect on the conservation of our wild life will
be continued by both the Dominion and by the Provincial Governments.'[15] In the words of his colleague, Duncan Campbell Scott: 'His
death was tragic in its suddenness. ... He seemed to be on the threshold
of a long career, in which added years would bring even greater
success, and would fulfil all that he was destined to accomplish ...'[16]

Today, the name Gordon Hewitt is scarcely known. His story and
achievements lie buried in departmental records and scattered among
dusty manuscript collections in the National Parks Archives and Canadian Wildlife Service in Ottawa, and in the records of the United States
Biological Survey in Washington DC. Only in the Agricultural Research
Building of the Department of Agriculture in Ottawa does a more solid
memory remain. In the entrance hall to the departmental library, the
visitor encounters a bronze bust of Hewitt mounted on a white pedes-
tal. The most fitting tribute to Hewitt's life and ability comes not from
present-day government members or wildlife conservationists but
from one of his peers. William Hornaday, the American wildlife preservationist, wrote of his Canadian friend in 1920: 'May heaven send to
wild life more men like him.'[17]

The second explanation why the national conferences were not inaugurated was the abolition of the Conservation Commission. A bill to

repeal the Commission was brought before Parliament in May 1921, where it sparked a lengthy and bitter debate. There were a number of reasons advanced by the Conservative government for abolishing the body. Arthur Meighen, the new Prime Minister and one of the Commission's most formidable opponents, charged that it overlapped and duplicated the work of other government bodies at great cost. According to James Lougheed, the government leader in the Senate and a member of the Committee set up in 1920 to investigate the work of the Commission, it had cost the Dominion (and the taxpayers) over $104,000 each year. During the eleven years of its existence, the Commission was charged with spending $560,000 on salaries; approximately $106,000 on members' travelling expenses, and $22,000 on the Commission library. Added to these figures was the cost of printing reports, publications, and 'publicity propaganda,' which came to more than $257,000. Lougheed believed that one (unnamed) staff member continued his private practice and maintained an office in Toronto which, reportedly, cost the Commission a further $500 a year. 'It seems extraordinary,' Lougheed wrote, 'that this condition of affairs should be permissible when the work for which this official is responsible could be more effectively and economically done at Ottawa.'[18]

The costly duplication of work formed the real basis of the Privy Council Committee's investigation and Lougheed examined each field – forestry, water power, agriculture, interior, marine and fisheries, mines, publicity, and even external affairs – to show how in each case the Commission had conducted almost the same investigations and experiments as had regular government departments. (It is important to note that 'wildlife' was not included in the resources listed by Lougheed. Either he did not consider it of major importance or he recognized that, in fact, the Commission had played a very large role in this new and important area.)

Of even greater concern to both Meighen and Lougheed, however, was the fact that the Commission had been set up in 1909 as an entirely independent body, responsible only to Parliament. 'I do not think it is consistent with our system of government,' Meighen exclaimed during debate on the bill, 'that there should be a body for which no one is answerable, and over which no one has any control, as is the case with this commission.'[19] Lougheed elaborated on the point still further in the Senate. Although the Commission reported to Parliament each year through the Minister of Agriculture, he argued, the latter had no effective control over the Commission. 'The intensity of rivalry which obtained between the Commission and the Departments had to be terminated,' he concluded, 'and the Government has taken this method of doing it.'[20] The Investigating Committee claimed the Commission was trying to perpetuate a separate and distinct extra-departmental organization which, if permitted to continue, would tend to still greater waste of public money. The Committee did not consider that Commission members constituted either a responsible or cohesive organization and found that 'matters are sometimes dealt with or statements made on their behalf of which they have little or no knowledge':

While nominally responsible to Parliament, to whom it must look for funds to carry on its work, the Commission is not a departmental body under ministerial control, but operates under the domination of the Chairman.[21]

Several of the charges made against the Commission in the Privy Council Report and in Parliament were, no doubt, valid. By 1921, there was a considerable overlapping and duplication of work being done by government departments but only, one suspects, because the Commission itself had brought so many matters of resource conservation to the government's attention. Since its inception in 1909, the Commission had conducted elaborate inventories of all Canada's natural resources, carried out special studies, and put forward recommendations for better and more efficient resource utilization. Committees annually carried out investigations and produced numerous publications and valuable reports on all phases of resource conservation, particularly in the areas of forestry and waterpower. Because many members of the Commission were also members of the dominion and provincial governments, Commission ideas and recommendations were taken up and acted upon promptly. As one author has noted, the Commission 'made it simple for governments to borrow ideas and programs from one another.'[22] It is small wonder that an overlap between the work of the Commission and that of other government departments began to appear.

It was Sifton, however, the former Chairman of the Conservation Commission, who provided the most thorough rebuttal to the Privy Council charges. Lougheed's report, Sifton contended in 1921, 'indicates very clearly that there has been placed in the Minister's hands a series of statements calculated to mislead him and to give a wholly distorted view of the Commission's activities and expenditures.' Sifton denied that Commission expenditures were increasing rapidly and he produced figures to show that in 1914–15 the funds voted to the

Commission were $136,000. Seven years later, the funds were $141,000, an increase of less than 4 per cent. 'It is questionable whether any other governmental organization can show such a record of economy and such a small increase in its expenditures as is shown by the funds granted to the Commission of Conservation since the outbreak of war.' Not only had there been no substantial increase in expenses, Sifton concluded, but it was safe to say that no other government expenditure 'has given greater returns to the people of Canada than the Commission of Conservation.' The reduction of forest fires alone, in which the Commission played a substantial role, he argued, represented a saving to Canada 'many times greater than the total outlay of the Commission since its inception.'[23]

Sifton also rejected Lougheed's accusation that the Commission was duplicating the work of other government departments. He noted that for the year 1920–1 the Commission had been given funds of $141,450 to carry out its work, while for the same year the government departments in question had at their disposal over $12,800,000, more than ninety times the sum granted to the Commission. 'If the Commission duplicated any substantial portion of the work of these departments, with less than two percent of the amount of money voted to the departments for that purpose,' Sifton concluded, 'it must have expended its funds with exceptional economy and efficiency.' Sifton admitted that the Commission's constitutional status was unique. But it had been established in 1909, he believed, to fulfil a need for an organization that could promote co-operation between the provinces and the Dominion, to give some degree of 'national solidarity' in confronting conservation problems that were national in scope. Such an independent, intermediary body was necessary, he pointed out, due to the divided jurisdictions over natural resource administration under the British North America Act. The Commission was given an independent status in order to 'ensure its strength as a link between governments that might or might not be of the same political colour':

At the same time, its independent status contains no menace to the principle of responsible government. The Commission has purposely been denied the administrative powers and authority which alone can be exercised in subversion to that principle. It exists only to advise, investigate, and inform – and it is responsible to Parliament in the fullest degree.[24]

It is difficult to read either the Investigating Committee's Report or the Senate and Commons debates for 1921 and correctly assess the charges and counter-charges made against the Conservation Commission. Any true evaluation of the accusations is obscured by the apparent bitterness, jealousy, and rivalry that permeate the record. Senator William Edwards, acting Chairman of the Commission after Sifton resigned, claimed that such jealousy had always been manifested towards the Commission.[25] There is little doubt that government members were jealous of the apparent freedom of action the Commission enjoyed. At the height of the controversy which raged between 1910 and 1913 over the American proposal to dam the Long Sault, a Committee of the Commission made a separate, independent representation to the International Waterways Commission on the proposal (the Commission had consistently opposed the project). Meighen, for one, resented this independent action. He complained to Parliament in 1921 that 'we found ourselves appearing before the International Joint Commission to state the position of the government and immediately alongside would appear the representative of the Conservation Commission who would also state the position of this country. If one can conceive of anything more anomalous than that, one's conception must be very lively.'[26] Sifton answered this charge in 1921 by stating that 'the records of the International Joint Commission ... clearly demonstrate that the stand taken by the Commission of Conservation upon all such issues has been in the best interests of Canada, and also, in accord with the contentions of other organizations which have striven to preserve the integrity of Canada's interest in international waters.'

The constitutional character of the Commission was bound eventually to put it at odds with the Conservative government. As Meighen charged, the Commission enjoyed virtual autonomy and was subject to no ministerial responsibility, something few governments would be prepared to tolerate for long, particularly in such a sensitive area as resource development and conservation. But the Conservatives could have restructured the Commission if, indeed, it was considered valuable, and placed it under a regular government department. The sad fact is that the government showed little interest or enthusiasm in 1921 to salvage an advisory body that had been created by Laurier and the Liberals in 1909. As Harrison Lewis recalled in 1971, 'accommodation in the national interest might have been reached in 1921 had the government not been of a different political kind from the government that had established the Commission.'[27]

The real reasons for the demise of the Conservation Commission will probably never be known. Few of its records or papers survive; most were destroyed in the years after the Commission was abolished and it is difficult to sort out the facts from all the rumours and stories that still circulate. It was common knowledge that Meighen and Sifton did not get on well together and were 'always at odds.'[28] One of James White's daughters remembers being told that a member of the Commission once remarked to Meighen's Private Secretary that the Commission 'would be around long after Meighen left the scene.' She claims this made Meighen 'terribly mad' and he resolved then and there to 'wind up the Commission.'[29] Still others recall that the Commission became unpopular with lumbering interests because of its advocacy of reforestation. Another story maintains that White found material in the United States regarding the Labrador boundary dispute that was 'politically embarrassing' to the government and that he quickly lost favour with the Conservatives.[30] But without documented evidence, it is impossible to judge the truth or merit of any of these claims and the real reason for the demise of the Commission remains shrouded in speculation.

When examined against the credit side of the ledger, however, the faults and shortcomings of the Commission, and the reasons for its abolition, become less important than what the Commission achieved in its eleven-year history. 'Conservation' was still a comparatively new concept in 1909, but the Commission grappled it head-on and stimulated an enlightened debate among the public and government on all aspects of resource conservation. It provided an essential public forum for discussions between government members, international figures, and concerned citizens, and initiated many conservation programs that were later taken up by the government. In many ways, the Conservation Commission was years, and even decades, ahead of its time.

The Commission made its most notable contribution in the field of wildlife preservation. Once the migratory bird protection issue came before government in 1913, the Commission took up the wildlife cause, advocating protection not just for migratory birds but for all endangered bird and mammal species. Government members and American representatives were frequently invited to address the annual meetings on all aspects of wildlife preservation, and each year valuable recommendations for greater wildlife protection were invariably found among the Commission resolutions. The Commission took much more than a passing interest in the establishment of parks and sanctuaries. James White, the Commission's Secretary, personally conducted several negotiations with the Quebec government over the acquisition of the Bonaventure Island and Percé Rock sanctuaries in 1918 and was appointed Chairman of the interdepartmental Advisory

Board on Wild Life Protection in 1916. (In 1920, the Investigating Committee charged that the Commission was claiming credit for all the work done under the Migratory Birds Convention Act merely because an official with the Commission [White] was the Chairman of the Advisory Board. Sifton denied the accusation, replying that the selection of White for the chairmanship 'is sufficient evidence of the manner in which the Commission's work has been regarded by authorities whose jurisdiction is said to be infringed.')

As far as wildlife conservation was concerned, however, the Commission had effectively completed its work by the end of 1919. It had acted as host for the first National Wildlife Conference and had been asked to arrange for similar wildlife conventions to be held annually. Although no records survive, the Commission likely was working on such a program at the time it was abolished. It also helped to establish a new type of federal involvement in wildlife conservation, for protection of wildlife resources was gradually becoming a part of regular government policy. In the words of Harrison Lewis, the Conservation Commission was 'the essential forerunner to wildlife protective legislation.'

Hewitt was dead and the Conservation Commission abolished, but James Harkin did not forget the proposal Hewitt made at the 1919 National Conference to hold annual wildlife conventions. The success of the 1919 meeting convinced him more than ever of their importance. He wrote to Manitoba's Deputy Minister of Agriculture in October 1922 that he had become 'more and more convinced' that it was of vital importance to hold meetings each year with provincial representatives. Indeed, Harkin was so firm in his conviction that he confided to the Minister that he had included a sum of money in his departmental estimates to 'help this scheme along.'[31] Harkin hoped the conferences would be characterized by friendly, candid, round-table discussions and that they would go far beyond the mere reading of formal papers. The Deputy Minister had written to Harkin about the damage caused to Manitoba's grain crops by wild ducks and Harkin replied that 'this is only one of many problems that can be discussed at such a conference to the mutual advantage of all participants.' Harkin must have persuaded his own Minister too, for in November 1922 a report was sent to the Privy Council by the Minister of the Interior recommending a game conservation conference be arranged by the

Parks Branch for 6, 7, and 8 December. The report stated that the object of such a conference was to discuss important wildlife matters with dominion and provincial representatives and 'to develop co-operation between the Federal and Provincial organizations.'[32] The expenses of the conference were to be paid for by the Department of the Interior.

In sharp contrast to the 1919 conference, which was open to anyone interested in wildlife conservation, the 1922 conference was restricted to those dominion and provincial officials directly involved with game administration. This restriction underscored the government's intention to work with provincial administrations in order to deal effectively with wildlife conservation throughout the Dominion. Many of the provincial delegates were familiar, having been present in 1919, but on the dominion side there were a number of new faces: Hoyes Lloyd, now Supervisor of Wild Life Protection in Canada; Chief Federal Migratory Bird Officers Harrison Lewis and Robie Tufts; Arthur Gibson, replacing Gordon Hewitt as Dominion Entomologist; Lieutenant-Colonel C. Starnes, Assistant Commissioner of the RCMP (police patrols were helping enforce provincial game regulations in the west); O.S. Finnie, Director of the Northwest Territories and Yukon; and Professor E.E. Prince, Dominion Fisheries Commissioner. And Elizabeth Hewitt, Gordon Hewitt's widow, also attended as the Convenor of the Conservation Committee, National Council of Women.

There was none of the fanfare and publicity that marked the 1919 conference; no visiting delegates from the United States attended; nor were local game organizations or citizens' groups represented. No formal papers were read and, indeed, the minutes of this first Dominion-Provincial Conference on Wild Life Protection were never even published.[33] After the opening address, delegates got down to the business at hand and for the next three days the conference was taken up with lengthy, detailed, frank discussions that covered the broad spectrum of wildlife conservation matters. The Migratory Bird Treaty and Convention Act were gone over once again, this time clause by clause, with suggestions made for provinces experiencing migratory bird crop damage. (Under the treaty terms and Convention Act regulations, provinces could obtain special permits to kill migratory birds out of season if they were harming agricultural crops.) The sale of game was discussed as well as the necessity for uniform bag limits all across the country. Delegates also debated the need for a gun licensing system, predator control, federal assistance to provinces in controlling illegal shipment of furs and game, the need to establish public shooting grounds as well as bird preserves, and the demand for an extensive educational campaign on wildlife conservation.

The debates at the 1922 conference were characterized, as Harkin had hoped they would be, by a high degree of frankness and informality. Recommendations that covered most of the topics discussed were framed and passed unanimously.[34] Many of them related to the regulations under the Migratory Birds Convention Act and in subsequent years were adopted by the government.[35]

One of the more significant resolutions was put forward by Professor Prince, relating to whales and walrus that were 'in danger of extinction in the near future.' Prince called for the reservation of sanctuaries in the major whale breeding grounds, the protection of female whales with calves, and a complete system of whale and walrus hunting licences. His resolution concluded by stating: 'This conference favours international co-operation to limit and effectively control the killing of these valuable and interesting animals.' Unfortunately, international co-operation was never achieved and commercial exploitation of declining whale species has continued, uninterrupted, down to the present day. The International Whaling Commission proposed a ten-year moratorium on all commercial whaling in 1973. Canada was a strong supporter of the measure, but the motion was defeated.

Wildlife conservation was still a relatively new concern for the government and at least one representative to the conference recalled that many members were hampered by inexperience in what they were attempting.[36] Not all government members were trained zoologists, ornithologists, biologists, or wildlife management theorists. But the chief accomplishment of this first Dominion-Provincial Conference was in acquainting participants with one another so that thereafter they could deal with each other in their official positions with confidence. The dominion-provincial conferences held after 1922 developed that level of confidence to a very high degree, and the co-operation that was achieved bore out what Hewitt had said in his opening address to the 1919 National Conference – that wildlife conservation was not a matter that any one province, state, or territory could handle alone. Co-operation had always been Harkin's goal and no doubt he found great personal gratification in one of the resolutions passed in 1922, which expressed to the Dominion Parks Commissioner an appreciation of his efforts to conserve the wildlife of Canada on behalf of the Canadian people:

This conference ... assures him of the continued hearty co-operation in this great work of all the provinces and territories here represented, and regards the calling of this conference as a very valuable step toward still closer co-operation and productive of a much better understanding between Dominion and Provincial officials entrusted with this work.

The 1922 Dominion-Provincial Conference, and the decision to hold regular wildlife conferences, marked the final acceptance by the federal government of its reponsibilities in the field of wildlife preservation. In many ways, therefore, 1922 marks the end of the beginning in the story of wildlife conservation in Canada. The efforts begun by a handful of dedicated civil servants in the late nineteenth and early twentieth centuries finally culminated in government recognition that wildlife was an important and valued natural resource, and that measures for its protection and wise conservation had to be adopted and carried out as part of regular government policy. In his final address to the 1922 conference, Harkin paid tribute both to the Deputy Minister and the Minister of the Interior, who had greatly assisted the Parks Branch in its wildlife work. Game would be an important asset to Canada for one hundred years, he said, and 'I have tried to work for the cause.' The conference had broken the ice and opened the way for more direct communication and close co-operation between dominion and provincial governments. Such co-operation was to lead to better administration and protection of Canada's precious wildlife resources in the years ahead. For Gordon Hewitt and James Harkin, and for all the other civil servants who had worked unstintingly towards these goals, 1922 was, indeed, the end of the beginning.

10
Epilogue

Although the 1922 Dominion Provincial Conference on Wild Life Protection had marked the recognition by government of wildlife's value, it was to be many more years before well-planned, well-funded government programs for wildlife conservation were to be developed. Public awareness of the importance of wildlife and a growing concern for the environment was also to take many more years to develop. In this respect, Americans were far ahead of Canadians. Both the conservation and preservation movements began in the United States at the turn of the century and since then American naturalists, conservationists, scientists, politicians, and concerned citizens have willingly taken up the cause. Part of the reason is that America's natural environment changed far more rapidly and to a far greater extent than Canada's. Forests were cleared, swamps drained, and fragile prairie sod broken for agriculture as the frontier quickly gave way to settlement. The consequences of habitat modification and overkill of many wildlife species became evident in the United States before the end of the nineteenth century. Faced with radical changes in the quality of the environment, the larger, better organized, and more vocal population below the border was ready to respond to a crusade for protection. The population of Canada was tiny in comparison and subtle changes in habitat modification and wildlife numbers aroused little concern among people to whom a wilderness frontier was still an everyday reality. Another sixty years were to pass before significant numbers of Canadians joined in a new conservation movement that articulated the modern pressures on wildlife, pressures far more dangerous and complex than the guns of yesterday: rising population, diminishing wild-

lands, deadly pesticide residues entering the food chains of wild creatures, and air and water pollution.

The few individuals whose story has been told in this book were, in a
very real sense, pioneers. They were there at the beginning, working to
shape government policy at a time when there was little understanding
of animal behaviour or the interrelationships between species and their
dependence on habitat. Douglas, Harkin, Graham, and Campbell were
not zoologists, and with the exception of Gordon Hewitt none of them
was schooled in the natural sciences. The only method of protecting
wildlife species that these men recognized was the establishment of
reserves; they had no knowledge of wildlife management techniques.
Today we know there are many other methods of maintaining the
health and numbers of wildlife that go beyond the simple establishment of sanctuaries, and greater insights have been gained into all of
those factors – biological, ecological, and environmental – that affect
wildlife.

Like most pioneers, these early civil servants made mistakes and
their arguments for preservation were not always founded on sound
judgement. For example, in 1925 it was decided to close down Wainwright Park, which housed the Pablo buffalo herd, and to ship the
animals to Wood Buffalo Park in the Northwest Territories. Harkin
supported the proposal, but it was a bad decision since the herd had
overpopulated and become infected with tuberculosis and brucellosis.
Hoyes Lloyd and Harrison Lewis argued against the move, pointing
out that the highly contagious diseases would infect the wood buffalo,
but the transfer was carried out regardless. Not only did the diseases
spread as predicted, but the pure-bred wood buffalo strain was hy-
bridized through the introduction of plains bison. The diseased animals should have been killed at Wainwright, but given the strong
public sentiment about buffalo at that time, this would have been
politically unpopular.

But such misjudgement does not detract from what these men accomplished in an age when wildlife conservation was still a comparatively new subject. Each wanted to protect and preserve Canada's
wildlife resources, from personal and professional standpoints. Because there was no active preservationist movement in Canada, they
knew that economic arguments were the most effective and, indeed,
the only means by which they could demonstrate wildlife's importance.
Howard Douglas used the argument of increasing tourist revenues to
justify park expansion and the costly purchase of the Pablo herd;
Harkin urged the establishment of parks both in terms of tourist

revenues and of the government's obligation to preserve wildlands and wildlife for future generations. And Harkin, Hewitt, and Graham pointed to agricultural losses suffered by farmers due to the decline of insectivorous birds. This was a convincing case for a migratory bird treaty but not a biologically sound argument, as Percy Taverner himself admitted at the time. Nevertheless, it did help to influence public opinion on the protection issue. As Harkin declared in 1922: 'We have, therefore, to stand very closely ourselves by the economic view in order to secure the whole-hearted interest of the people of Canada in the conservation of forests and the wild life that may be accommodated therein. We have to show that we are aiming at something more than the luxury of watching wild life at play.'

Harkin alone articulated the most complete philosophy for wildlands preservation. The values that he placed on wilderness and the need for recreation are as relevant and meaningful today as they were sixty years ago when he expounded them so eloquently in his departmental reports to the Minister of the Interior. Roderick Nash, author of *Wilderness and the American Mind*, declared at a National Parks Conference in Calgary in 1968 that when it came to an appreciation of wilderness and an understanding of wilderness values, Canadians were fifty years behind the Americans. For the vast majority of Canadians, this assertion may well be correct, but not for James Harkin. He was not fifty years behind the times, but fifty years ahead.

The accomplishments of these few civil servants is all the more remarkable in the light of their relatively brief involvement with wildlife administration. The Canadian Wildlife Service was not established until 1947, and by then all of them had long since left the scene. Douglas had left in 1912; Hewitt had died in 1920; Graham, who had worked so enthusiastically for pronghorn and wood buffalo protection, transferred in 1921 from the Parks Branch to the new Northwest Territories Branch of the Department of the Interior. Seven years later, he died in office. James Harkin had resigned from the government in 1936 and died in 1955 at the age of eighty. And Hoyes Lloyd, Canada's Supervisor of Wild Life Protection, took an early retirement in 1943 to pursue his ornithological interests across five continents. At the time of this writing, Mr Loyd is in his late eighties and resides in Ottawa. At a recent meeting, I asked him how it felt to have accomplished so much significant work on behalf of wildlife in these early years. He replied: 'We didn't know we were doing anything significant. We were just doing our jobs to the best of our abilities.'

By any measure, that is a very modest assessment. Fortunately for

Canada, the achievements of Harkin, Campbell, Graham, Douglas, Hewitt, as well as Hoyes Lloyd, Harrison Lewis, and Percy Taverner, not only lived on after them but also became the basis on which today's understanding of wildlife and national park values is founded. The tribute that William Hornaday paid to Gordon Hewitt in 1920 could perhaps be given equally to all of these dedicated civil servants: 'May heaven send to wild life more men like them.'

Appendix:
The Migratory Birds
Convention Act

An Act respecting a certain Convention between His Majesty and the United States of America for the protection of Migratory Birds in Canada and the United States.   [*Assented to 29th August, 1917*]

Whereas on the sixteenth day of August, one thousand nine hundred and sixteen, a Convention was signed at Washington respecting the protection of certain migratory birds in Canada and the United States, and ratifications were exchanged at Washington on the seventh day of December, one thousand nine hundred and sixteen; and whereas it is expedient that the said Convention should receive the sanction of the Parliament of Canada and that legislation be passed for insuring the execution of the said Convention: Therefore His Majesty, by and with the advice and consent of the Senate and House of Commons of Canada, enacts as follows:

1
This Act may be cited as *The Migratory Birds Convention Act.*

2
The said Convention of the sixteenth day of August one thousand nine hundred and sixteen, which is set forth in the Schedule to this Act, is hereby sanctioned, ratified and confirmed.

3
In this Act and in any regulation made thereunder, unless the context otherwise requires:
a 'close season' means the period during which any species of migratory game, migratory insectivorous, or migratory nongame bird is protected by this Act or any regulation made under this Act;
b 'migratory game birds' means:
Anatidæ or waterfowl, including brant, wild ducks, geese and swans;
Gruidæ or cranes, including little brown, sandhill and whooping cranes;

Rallidæ or rails, including coots, gallinules and sora and other rails;

Limicolæ or shorebirds, including avocets, curlew, dowitchers, godwits, knots, oyster catchers, phalaropes, plovers, sandpipers, snipe, stilts, surf birds, turnstones, willet, woodcock, and yellowlegs;

Columbidæ or pigeons, including doves and wild pigeons;

c 'migratory insectivorous birds' means:

Bobolinks, catbirds, chickadees, cuckoos, flickers, flycatchers, grosbeaks, humming birds, kinglets, martins, meadowlarks, nighthawks or bull bats, nuthatches, orioles, robins, shrikes, swallows, swifts, tanagers, titmice, thrushes, vireos, warblers, waxwings, whippoorwills, woodpeckers, and wrens, and all other perching birds which feed entirely or chiefly on insects;

d 'migratory nongame birds' means:

Auks, auklets, bitterns, fulmars, gannets, grebes, guillemots, gulls, herons, jaegers, loons, murres, petrels, puffins, shearwaters, and terns;

e 'Minister' means the Minister of the Interior;

f 'regulation' means any regulation made under the provision of section four of this Act.

4

1 The Governor in Council may make such regulations as are deemed expedient to protect the migratory game, migratory insectivorous and migratory nongame birds which inhabit Canada during the whole or any part of the year.

2 Subject to the provisions of the said Convention, such regulations may provide,

a the periods in each year or the number of years during which any such migratory game, migratory insectivorous or migratory nongame birds shall not be killed, captured, injured, taken, molested or sold, or their nests or eggs injured, destroyed, taken or molested;

b for the granting of permits to kill or take migratory game, migratory insectivorous and migratory nongame birds, or their nests or eggs;

c for the prohibition of the shipment or export of migratory game, migratory insectivorous or migratory nongame birds or their eggs from any province during the close season in such province, and the conditions upon which international traffic in such birds shall be carried on;

d for the prohibition of the killing, capturing, taking, injuring or molesting of migratory game, migratory insectivorous or migratory nongame birds, or the taking, injuring, destruction or molestation of their nests or eggs, within any prescribed area;

e for any other purpose which may be deemed expedient for carrying out the intentions of this Act and the said Convention, whether such other regulations are of the kind enumerated in this section or not.

3 A regulation shall take effect from the date of the publication thereof in the

Canada Gazette; or from the date specified for such purpose in any regulation, and such regulation shall have the same force and effect as if enacted herein, and shall be printed in the prefix in the next succeeding issue of the Dominion Statutes, and shall also be laid before both Houses of Parliament within fifteen days after the publication thereof if Parliament is then sitting, and if Parliament is not then sitting, within fifteen days after the opening of the next session thereof.

5

1 The Minister may appoint game officers for carrying out this Act and the regulations, and may authorize such game officers to exercise the powers of Justice of the Peace or the powers of a Police Constable. Such persons shall hold office during pleasure, and shall have, for the purposes of this Act and the said Convention, such other powers and duties as may be defined by this Act and the regulations.

2 Every game officer who is authorized by the Minister to exercise the powers of a Justice of the Peace or of a Police Constable shall, for all the purposes of this Act and the regulations, be *ex officio* a Justice of the Peace or a Police Constable, as the case may be, within the district within which he is authorized to act.

3 Every such game officer shall take and subscribe an oath in the form following, that is to say:
'I, A.B., a   of   do solemnly swear that to the best of my judgment I will faithfully, honestly and impartially fulfil, execute and perform the office and duties of such   according to the true intent and meaning of *The Migratory Birds Convention Act* and the regulations made thereunder.
So help me God.'

6

No one without lawful excuse, the proof whereof shall lie on him, shall buy, sell or have in his possession, any bird, nest or egg or portion thereof, during the time when the capturing, killing or taking of such bird, nest or egg is prohibited by law.

7

All guns, ammunition, boats, skiffs, canoes, punts and vessels of every description, teams, wagons and other outfits, decoys and appliances of every kind, used in violation of or for the purpose of violating this Act or any regulation, and any bird, nest or egg taken, caught, killed or had in possession, in violation of this Act or any regulation, may be seized and confiscated upon view by any game officer appointed under this Act, or taken and removed by any person for delivery to any game officer or justice of the peace.

8

Any game officer appointed under this Act who violates this Act or any regulation, or who aids, abets or connives at any violation of this Act or of any regulation, shall be liable, upon summary conviction before any recorder, commissioner of police, judge of the sessions of the peace, police stipendiary or district magistrate or any two justices of the peace, to a penalty not exceeding five hundred dollars and costs or six months' imprisonment and not less than one hundred dollars and costs or three months' imprisonment.

9

Any person who assaults, obstructs or interferes with any game officer or peace officer in the discharge of any duty under the provisions of this Act, or of any regulation, shall be guilty of a violation of this Act.

10

Any person who wilfully refuses to furnish information or wilfully furnishes false information to a game officer or peace officer respecting a violation of this Act or of any regulation, the existence of or the place of concealment of any bird, nest or egg, or any portion thereof captured, killed or taken in violation of this Act or of any regulation, shall be guilty of a violation of this Act.

11

Any game officer or peace officer may enter any place or premises in which he has reason to believe there exists migratory game, or migratory insectivorous, or migratory nongame birds, nests or eggs, or any parts thereof, in respect of which a breach of this Act or of the regulations may have been committed, and may open and examine any trunk, box, bag, parcel or receptacle which he has reason to suspect and does suspect contains any such bird, nest or egg, or any part thereof.

12

Every person who violates any provision of this Act or any regulation shall, for each offence, be liable upon summary conviction to a fine of not more than one hundred dollars and not less than ten dollars, or to imprisonment for a term not exceeding six months, or to both fine and imprisonment.

SCHEDULE

Convention

Whereas many species of birds in the course of their annual migrations traverse certain parts of the Dominion of Canada and the United States; and

Whereas many of these species are of great value as a source of food or in destroying insects which are injurious to forests and forage plants on the public domain, as well as to agricultural crops, in both Canada and the United States, but are nevertheless in danger of extermination through lack of adequate protection during the nesting season or while on their way to and from their breeding grounds;

His Majesty the King of the United Kingdom of Great Britain and Ireland and of the British dominions beyond the seas, Emperor of India, and the United States of America, being desirous of saving from indiscriminate slaughter and of insuring the preservation of such migratory birds as are either useful to man or are harmless, have resolved to adopt some uniform system of protection which shall effectively accomplish such objects, and to the end of concluding a convention for this purpose have appointed as their respective plenipotentiaries:

His Britannic Majesty, the Right Honourable Sir Cecil Arthur Spring Rice, G.C.V.O., K.C.M.G., etc., His Majesty's ambassador extraordinary and plenipotentiary at Washington; and

The President of the United States of America, Robert Lansing, Secretary of State of the United States;

Who, after having communicated to each other their respective full powers which were found to be in due and proper form, have agreed to and adopted the following articles:

ARTICLE I

The High Contracting Powers declare that the migratory birds included in the terms of this Convention shall be as follows:

1 Migratory Game Birds:
a Anatidæ or waterfowl, including brant, wild ducks, geese, and swans.
b Gruidæ or cranes, including little brown, sandhill, and whooping cranes.
c Rallidæ or rails, including coots, gallinules and sora and other rails.
d Limicolæ or shorebirds, including avocets, curlew, dowitchers, godwits, knots, oyster catchers, phalaropes, plovers, sandpipers, snipe, stilts, surf birds, turnstones, willet, woodcock, and yellowlegs.
e Columbidæ or pigeons, including doves and wild pigeons.
2 Migratory Insectivorous Birds: Bobolinks, catbirds, chickadees, cuckoos, flickers, flycatchers, grosbeaks, humming birds, kinglets, martins, meadowlarks, nighthawks or bull bats, nut-hatches, orioles, robins, shrikes, swallows, swifts, tanagers, titmice, thrushes, vireos, warblers, waxwings, whippoorwills, woodpeckers, and wrens, and all other perching birds which feed entirely or chiefly on insects.
3 Other Migratory Nongame Birds: Auks, auklets, bitterns, fulmars, gannets, grebes, guillemots, gulls, herons, jaegers, loons, murres, petrels, puffins, shearwaters, and terns.

ARTICLE II

The High Contracting Powers agree that, as an effective means of preserving migratory birds, there shall be established the following close seasons during which no hunting shall be done except for scientific or propagating purposes under permits issued by proper authorities.

1 The close season on migratory game birds shall be between 10th March and 1st September, except that the close of the season on the limicolæ or shorebirds in the Maritime Provinces of Canada and in those States of the United States bordering on the Atlantic Ocean which are situated wholly or in part north of Chesapeake Bay shall be between 1st February and 15th August, and that Indians may take at any time scoters for food but not for sale. The season for hunting shall be further restricted to such period not exceeding three and one-half months as the High Contracting Powers may severally deem appropriate and define by law or regulation.

2 The close season on migratory insectivorous birds shall continue throughout the year.

3 The close season on other migratory nongame birds shall continue throughout the year, except that Eskimos and Indians may take at any season auks, auklets, guillemots, murres and puffins, and their eggs for food and their skins for clothing, but the birds and eggs so taken shall not be sold or offered for sale.

ARTICLE III

The High Contracting Powers agree that during the period of ten years next following the going into effect of this Convention, there shall be a continuous close season on the following migratory game birds, to-wit:

Band-tailed pigeons, little brown, sandhill and whooping cranes, swans, curlew and all shorebirds (except the black-breasted and golden plover, Wilson or jack snipe, woodcock, and the greater and lesser yellowlegs); provided that during such ten years the close seasons on cranes, swans and curlew in the province of British Columbia shall be made by the proper authorities of that province within the general dates and limitations elsewhere prescribed in this Convention for the respective groups to which these birds belong.

ARTICLE IV

The High Contracting Powers agree that special protection shall be given the wood duck and the eider duck either (1) by a close season extending over a period of at least five years, or (2) by the establishment of refuges, or (3) by such other regulations as may be deemed appropriate.

ARTICLE V

The taking of nests or eggs of migratory game or insectivorous or nongame birds shall be prohibited, except for scientific or propagating purposes under such laws or regulations as the High Contracting Powers may severally deem appropriate.

ARTICLE VI

The High Contracting Powers agree that the shipment or export of migratory birds or their eggs from any State or Province, during the continuance of the close season in such State or Province, shall be prohibited except for scientific or propagating purposes, and the international traffic in any birds or eggs at such time captured, killed, taken, or shipped at any time contrary to the laws of the State or Province in which the same were captured, killed, taken, or shipped shall be likewise prohibited. Every package containing migratory birds or any parts thereof or any eggs of migratory birds transported, or offered for transportation from the Dominion of Canada into the United States or from the United States into the Dominion of Canada, shall have the name and address of the shipper and an accurate statement of the contents clearly marked on the outside of such package.

ARTICLE VII

Permits to kill any of the above-named birds which, under extraordinary conditions, may become seriously injurious to the agricultural or other interests in any particular community, may be issued by the proper authorities of the High Contracting Powers under suitable regulations prescribed therefor by them respectively, but such permits shall lapse or may be cancelled, at any time when, in the opinion of said authorities, the particular exigency has passed, and no birds killed under this article shall be shipped, sold, or offered for sale.

ARTICLE VIII

The High Contracting Powers agree themselves to take, or propose to their respective appropriate law-making bodies, the necessary measures for insuring the execution of the present Convention.

ARTICLE IX

The present Convention shall be ratified by His Britannic Majesty and by the President of the United States of America, by and with the advice and consent of the Senate thereof. The ratifications shall be exchanged at Washington as soon as possible and the Convention shall take effect on the date of the exchange of the ratifications. It shall remain in force for fifteen years, and in the event of neither of the High Contracting Powers having given notification, twelve months before the expiration of said period of fifteen years, of its intention of terminating its operation, the Convention shall continue to remain in force for one year and so on from year to year.

In faith whereof, the respective Plenipotentiaries have signed the present Convention in duplicate and have hereunto affixed their seals.

Done at Washington this sixteenth day of August, 1916.

(L.S.) CECIL SPRING-RICE
(L.S.) ROBERT LANSING

REGULATIONS

1 In these regulations, unless the context otherwise requires:
a 'Migratory game birds' means the following:
– Anatidæ or waterfowl, including brant, wild ducks, geese and swans;
– Gruidæ or cranes, including little brown sandhill and whooping cranes;
– Rallidæ or rails, including coots, gallinules and sora and other rails;
– Limicolæ or shorebirds, including avocets, curlew, dowitcheres, godwits, knots, oyster catchers, phalaropes, plovers, sandpipers, snipe, stilts, surf birds, turnstones, willet, woodcock and yellowlegs;
– Columbidæ or pigeons, including doves and wild pigeons;
b 'migratory insectivorous birds' means the following:
– Bobolinks, catbirds, chickadees, cuckoos, flickers, fly-catchers, grosbeaks, humming birds, kinglets, martins, meadowlarks, nighthawks, or bull bats, nuthatches, orioles, robins, shrikes, swallows, swifts, tanagers, titmice, thrushes, vireos, warblers, waxwings, whippoorwill, woodpeckers, and wrens, and all other perching birds which feed entirely or chiefly on insects;
c 'migratory non-game birds' means the following:
– Auks, auklets, bitterns, fulmars, gannets, grebes, guillemots, gulls, herons, jaegers, loons, murres, petrels, puffins, shearwaters, and terns.

2 No person shall kill, capture, injure, take, molest, sell or offer for sale any migratory game birds during the following periods:
– In Prince Edward Island, New Brunswick, Quebec, Ontario, Alberta, British Columbia, (northern district), Northwest Territories and Yukon Territory,
December 15 to August 31, both days inclusive.
– In Manitoba:
December 1 to September 14, both days inclusive.
– In Nova Scotia, Saskatchewan and British Columbia (southeastern district):
January 1 to September 14, both days inclusive.
– In British Columbia (southwestern district):
January 15 to September 30, both days inclusive.
– *Shorebirds or Waders*, including only the following:
Woodcock, Wilson or jack snipe, blackbreasted and golden plover, and the greater and lesser yellowlegs:

– In Prince Edward Island, Nova Scotia, New Brunswick, and in the counties of Saguenay, Rimouski, Gaspe and Bonaventure in Quebec:
December 1 to August 14, both days inclusive,
Except that on woodcock and Wilson or jack snipe the closed season in Prince Edward Island and New Brunswick shall be from December 1 to September 14, and in Nova Scotia from December 15 to August 31, both days inclusive.
– In Quebec, other than the aforementioned maritime counties, Ontario, Alberta, British Columbia (northern district), Northwest Territories and Yukon Territory;
December 15 to August 31, both days inclusive,
Except that on woodcock and Wilson or jack snipe, the close season in Ontario shall be from November 15 to October 14, both days inclusive.
– In Manitoba:
December 1 to September 14, both days inclusive.
– In Saskatchewan and British Columbia (southeastern district):
January 1 to September 14, both days inclusive.
– In British Columbia (south-western district):
January 15 to September 30, both days inclusive.
– Provided, however, that:
– Indians and Eskimos may take scoters or 'Siwash Ducks' for food at any time of the year, but scoters so taken shall not be sold.
– In this or any other regulation the southern limit of the northern district of British Columbia shall be, west to east, a line running by way of the middle of Dean Channel, Dean River, Entiako River, Nechako River and the Fraser River from Fort George to Yellowhead Pass; and the line of division between the southeastern and the southwestern district of British Columbia shall be the summit of the Cascade Range as defined by the British Columbia Interpretation Act, Revised Statutes, 1911.

3 The killing, capturing, taking, injuring, or molesting of migratory insectivorous birds, their eggs, or nests, is prohibited throughout the year, except as hereinafter provided.

4 The killing, taking, injuring, capturing or molesting of migratory non-game birds or their eggs or nests, except as herein or hereinafter provided, is prohibited throughout the year; Provided, however, that Indians and Eskimos may take at any season auks, auklets, guillemots, murres and puffins and their eggs for human food and their skins for clothing, but birds and eggs taken in virtue of this exemption shall not be sold or offered for sale or otherwise traded.

5 A close season shall continue until the first day of January, 1928, on the following migratory game birds: band-tailed pigeons, little brown, sandhill and whooping cranes, swans, curlew and all shore birds (except the black-breasted and golden plover, Wilson or jack snipe, woodcock, and the

greater and lesser yellowlegs). In the province of British Columbia during such period the close season on cranes, swans, and curlew, shall be made by the proper authorities of that province within the general dates and limitations elsewhere prescribed in these regulations for the respective groups to which these birds belong or greater restrictions on the hunting of these birds shall be made should the aforementioned authorities deem such further restrictions desirable as provided by Article III of the Convention between His Majesty and the United States of America, scheduled to chapter 18, 7–8 George v.

6 A close season shall continue until the first day of January, 1923, on the wood duck and eider duck, except that in the province of British Columbia, the wood duck shall be protected by such special means or regulations as the proper authorities of that province may deem appropriate, as provided by the convention referred to in clause 5.

7 The taking of the nests or eggs of migratory game, migratory insectivorous or migratory non-game birds is prohibited except as otherwise provided in the regulations.

8 Migratory game, migratory insectivorous or migratory non-game birds or parts thereof or their eggs or nests may be taken, shipped transported or possessed for scientific or propagating purposes but only on the issue of a permit by the Minister or by any person duly authorized by him. Such a permit shall terminate at the end of the calendar year in which it shall have been issued, it shall not be transferable and shall be revocable at the discretion of the Minister.

Such permits may, upon application, be granted to recognized museums, or scientific societies, and to any person furnishing written testimonials from two well-known ornithologists.

Applications for permits for propagating purposes shall be accompanied by a statement giving:

1 The species of birds or eggs that it is desired to take,
2 the number,
3 the place at which the birds or eggs are to be taken.

Any package in which such migratory game, migratory insectivorous or migratory non-game birds or parts thereof, or their eggs or nests are shipped or transported for scientific or propagating purposes shall be clearly marked on the outside with the number of the permit, the name and address of the shipper and an accurate statement of the contents.

No transportation company shall accept for transportation any package containing eggs, nests, or parts of migratory game, migratory insectivorous or migratory, non-game birds unless such package shall be marked as hereinbefore required, and shipment of the same through the mails is prohibited, unless marked as aforesaid.

9 The shipment or export of migratory game, migratory insectivorous, or migratory non-game birds or their eggs from any province during the close season in such provinces is prohibited except for scientific or propagating purposes and traffic between Canada and the United States in any such birds, or their eggs captured, killed, taken or shipped at any time contrary to the laws of the Province or State in which the same are captured, killed, taken or shipped, is likewise prohibited.

10 No person shall ship or offer for shipment from Canada to the United States any package containing migratory game, migratory insectivorous or migratory non-game birds or any parts thereof or their eggs unless such package shall have the name and address of the shipper and an accurate statement of the contents clearly marked on the outside of such package.

No transportation company shall accept for transportation to the United States, any packages of migratory game, migratory insectivorous or migratory non-game birds or any parts thereof or their eggs unless such packages bear the name and address of the shipper and an accurate statement of the contents, and shipment of the same through the mails is prohibited, unless marked as aforesaid.

11 If any of the migratory game, migratory insectivorous or migratory non-game birds should under extraordinary conditions become seriously injurious to agricultural, fishing or other interests in any particular locality the Minister may issue permits to kill such birds so long as they shall continue to be injurious. Applications for such permits shall include a full statement describing:

    1 the species and an estimate of the numbers of birds committing the damage.

    2 the nature and extent of the damage.

    3 the extent of the agricultural or other interests threatened or involved.

Such permits shall be revocable at the discretion of the Minister. On the expiration of the permit the person to whom it is issued shall furnish to the Minister a written report showing the number of birds killed, the dates upon which they were killed and the disposition made of the dead birds.

No birds killed under such permits shall be shipped, sold or offered for sale.

Introduction of Foreign Species of
Migratory Birds Without Consent
Prohibited.

12 No person or organization shall introduce for the purpose of sport or acclimatization any species of migratory birds without the consent of the Minister in writing.

Notes

CHAPTER 1: INTRODUCTION

1 Meighen, Commission of Conservation Annual Report (1919) 4
2 Udall, *The Quiet Crisis* 54
3 Mackenzie, *Voyages from Montreal on the St Lawrence through the Continent of North America to the Frozen and Pacific Oceans* 161
4 Harmon, *A Journal of Voyages and Travels in the Interior of North America* 45
5 Lewis and Clark, *Journals, 1804–6*, 3 volumes, I, 122
6 Palliser, *Explorations – British North America.* 14
7 Hind, *Narrative of the Canadian Red River Expedition and of the Assiniboine and Saskatchewan Exploring Expeditions, 1857 and 1858*, 2 volumes, I, 180
8 *The Canadian Handbook and Tourist Guide* 25
9 McGrath, *Authentic Letters from Upper Canada* 107
10 Doyle, *Hints on Emigration to Upper Canada* 36
11 Jameson, *Winter Studies and Summer Rambles* 71
12 Dawson, *Report on Route between Lake Superior and the Red River Settlement*
13 Tuttle, *Our North Land* 406
14 Dawson, ibid.
15 Palliser, ibid. 39–40
16 Hector Report, Palliser, ibid. 126
17 Ibid. 111
18 Ibid. 8
19 Clerk of Forestry, Report (1899) quoted in Lambert and Pross, *Renewing Nature's Wealth* 9
20 C.H.D. Clarke, 'Game Laws,' Fish and Wildlife Report, Ministry of Natural Resources, Ontario 18 (August 1954)
21 For a full examination of the psychological effects of wilderness on pioneer man see Nash, *Wilderness and the American Mind.*
22 Jameson, ibid. 96

23 *Emigration to Canada*, Ontario Department of Agriculture (Toronto: Queen's Printer 1871) 15
24 'Ontario Fish and Wildlife Headlines,' mimeograph, Ministry of Natural Resources, Ontario (nd) 2–3
25 *Report*, Royal Commission on Fish and Game, Ministry of Natural Resources (Toronto: Queen's Printer 1892) 189
26 A.D. Stewart, Secretary, Ontario Fish and Game Branch, address delivered to the International Conference on Fish and Game, 1903, Ministry of Natural Resources, Ontario
27 Hornaday, *Our Vanishing Wildlife* 1
28 *Canada: Its History, Productions and Natural Resources Handbook* (Ottawa: Department of Agriculture 1886)
29 Clarke, 'Wildlife in Perspective'
30 F.H.H. Williamson, address to the International Association of Game and Fish Commissioners, Ottawa, included in 1920 Report of the Association

CHAPTER 2: PARKS, RESOURCES, AND THE ROLE OF WILDLIFE

1 Brown, 'Doctrine of Usefulness' I, 97–8
2 PAC, Macdonald Papers, MG26 A-LB, Vol. 154, Thomas White to John A. Macdonald, 21 November 1885
3 Catlin, 'North American Indians, 1880,' in Nash, editor, *The American Environment* 8–9
4 Ibid. 9
5 United States Statutes at Large no. 17, 1872
6 Muir, *Our National Parks* 39
7 Ise, *Our National Parks* 17
8 Ibid. 19, 21, 23
9 Superintendent Norris, Report, 1880, quoted in Ise, *Our National Parks* 576
10 PAC, Macdonald Papers, Peter Mitchell to John A. Macdonald, 23 July 1885, Vol. 228, 99345–8
11 Pearce, 'The Establishment of National Parks in the Rockies'
12 PAC, Macdonald Papers, Vol. 229, Alexander Burgess to John A. Macdonald, 3 August 1885
13 Ibid., Thomas White to John A. Macdonald, 21 November 1885
14 Ibid.
15 Order-in-council, PC 2197, 25 November 1885
16 Canadian Pacific Archives, Montreal, J. Egan to Willian Van Horne, 26 April 1886
17 Department of the Interior, Annual Report, 1887
18 Ibid., Report of the Deputy Minister
19 Ibid.
20 Canada, House of Commons, Debates, 1887, Bill 16 Respecting Banff National Park
21 A. Roger Byrne, 'Man and Landscape Change in Banff National Park Area before 1911' 134

22 Canada, House of Commons, Debates, 3 May 1887, 232
23 Ibid. 228
24 Ibid.
25 Ibid. 227
26 Ibid. 232
27 Ibid. 229
28 Ibid. 232
29 Ibid. 238
30 Ibid.
31 Ibid. 238
32 Ibid. 233
33 Ibid.
34 Ibid. 243
35 Brown, 'The Nationalism of the National Policy' 162
36 Canada, House of Commons, Debates, 3 May 1887, 233
37 Bill Respecting Rocky Mountains Park, 1887
38 Canada, House of Commons, Debates, 3 May 1887, 241
39 Ibid.
40 Canada, Senate, Debates, 17 May 1887, 117–18
41 Ibid. 118
42 Act Respecting Rocky Mountains Park of Canada, 50 Victoria ch. 32, 1887, 40–51
43 Muir, *Our National Parks*; Ise, *Our National Parks*
44 The bill introduced in the house contained the clause 'preservation and protection of game and fish.' The phrase 'and wild birds generally' was added by members of the Senate.
45 Superintendent's Report, Department of the Interior Annual Report, 1888
46 Deputy Minister's Report, Department of the Interior Annual Report, 1888
47 Ibid.
48 Canada, Parliament, Sessional Papers (House of Commons) 1887, no. 7, Mr Whitcher's Report 86
49 Ibid. 87
50 Ibid. 93
51 Ibid. 92
52 Ibid. 87
53 Ibid. 86
54 George Stewart, Report, Department of the Interior Annual Report, 1887
55 Rocky Mountains Park, Annual Reports, 1887–93
56 Alexander Begg to Thomas White, 25 April 1887, Banff File 87154, National Parks Archives, Ottawa
57 Edgar Dewdney, Lieutenant-Governor's Report, Department of the Interior Annual Report, 1887
58 Deputy Minister's Report, Department of the Interior Annual Report, 1895

59 Rocky Mountains Park, Superintendent's Report, Department of the Interior Annual Report, 1895
60 Byrne, 'Man and Landscape Change' 140
61 Udall, 'The Raid on Resources,' in *The Quiet Crisis* 54–69
   Smith and Witty, 'Conservation, Resources, and Environment'
62 Smith, *The Politics of Conservation* 67–8
63 Udall, 'The Woodlands,' in *The Quiet Crisis*
64 Ibid. 108
65 Pinchot, *The Fight for Conservation* excerpted in Nash, editor *The American Environment* 59
66 Muir, *Our National Parks* 257
67 The controversy culminated in the fight over the proposal to dam the glacial carved valley, Hetch Hetchy, in Yosemite National Park. In the continuing search for water resources for San Francisco, the Hetch Hetchy was supposedly an 'ideal' dam site. The valley was claimed in 1901, but the preservationists bitterly opposed the project. Muir and Pinchot met head-on over the issue, but the preservationists lost the battle, and in 1913 construction of the Hetch Hetchy was authorized by Congress.
68 Clepper, editor, *Origins of American Conservation*; Smith, *The Politics of Conservation*
69 J.H. Morgan, appointed in 1884
70 Sir Wilfrid Laurier, opening address, Canadian Forestry Association, *Canadian Forestry Journal* (1906–7) 11
71 Ibid. 10
72 Pinchot, address to Canadian Forestry Association, 1906
73 Canada, House of Commons, Debates, 1 May 1906, 2832
74 Thorpe, 'Historical Perspective on the "Resources for Tomorrow Conference"' 2
75 PAC, Laurier Papers, MG26 GI Vol. 551, Theodore Roosevelt to Wilfrid Laurier, 24 December 1908
76 Pinchot also addressed the Canadian Club in Ottawa on the importance of conservation and the role of forestry in the conservation movement.
77 PAC, Laurier Papers, Vol. 551, Wilfrid Laurier to Theodore Roosevelt, 30 December 1908
78 Ibid., Wilfrid Laurier to Gifford Pinchot, 5 February 1909
79 Canada, Parliament, Sessional Papers (House of Commons) 1909; also cited in Thorpe, 'Historical Perspective' 3
80 PAC, Sifton Papers, MG 27 II C 15, Vol. 192, Robert Young to Clifford Sifton, 31 March 1909
81 Canada, House of Commons, Debates, 1 February, 1909, 368
82 Ibid.
83 Ibid., 27 April 1909, 4988
84 Ibid., 12 May 1909, 6364–5
85 Act to Establish the Commission of Conservation, 9 Edward VII, section 3, 8–9

86 Ibid., section 4
87 Clifford Sifton, opening address, Commission of Conservation, 1910, 3
88 Canada, House of Commons, Debates, 12 May 1909. Chief opposition on
    the question of cost came from Frederick Monk.
89 Ibid. 6366, 6370
90 Ibid. 6367
91 Sifton, opening address, Commission of Conservation, 1910, 2
92 Canada, House of Commons, Debates, 12 May 1913, 6467
93 Sifton, opening address, Commission of Conservation 3
94 Act to Establish Commission of Conservation, section 10
95 Sifton, opening address, Commission of Conservation 7
96 Ibid. 6
97 Clifford Sifton, address to Canadian Club, Ottawa, 7 December 1910
98 Ibid., Montreal, 1911
99 Sifton, opening address, Commission of Conservation, 1910, 27
100 Reports prepared by M.J. Patton. The Commission of Conservation pub-
    lished the reports in *Sea Fisheries in Eastern Canada* (Ottawa: The Mortimer
    Co. 1912).

CHAPTER 3: PRESERVATION: THE BEGINNING OF AN IDEA

1 The herd was donated to the park by a Mr Blackstock of Toronto.
2 Superintendent's Report, Rocky Mountains Park, Department of the In-
    terior Annual Report, 1906
3 Ibid.
4 PAC, Banff File RG 84, Vol. 224, Edwin Tinsley to William Magrach, 10
    March 1904
5 Superintendent's Report, 1903
6 Ibid.
7 Ibid., 1898
8 Deputy Minister's Report, Department of the Interior Annual Report,
    1906
9 Superintendent's Report, Department of the Interior Annual Report,
    1900
10 Deputy Minister's Report, Department of the Interior Annual Report,
    1899
11 Annual Reports, Department of the Interior, 1887–1900. Visitor numbers
    estimated from Banff Springs Hotel registration:

1887: 3000	1894: 4734
1888: 5822	1895: 4924
1889: 4000	1896: 3996
1890: 5000	1897: 5087
1891: 7250	1898: 5537
1892: 5394	1899: 7387
1893: 6826	

12 Zaslow, *The Opening of the Canadian North* 97
13 NWMP, Department of the Interior Annual Report, 1889
14 Assistant Commissioner's Report, NWMP, Department of the Interior Annual Report, 1889
15 Superintendent McIllree, Report, NWMP, E Division, Calgary, 1890
16 Report, NWMP, G Division, Fort Saskatchewan, 1890
17 Superintendent's Report, Department of the Interior Annual Report, 1892
18 Unorganized Territories Game Preservation Act, 57–8 Victoria, ch. 31, 1894
19 Canada, Senate, Debates, 26 April 1894, 286
20 Parks Canada, Banff File B2, Vol 1, Alfred E. Cross to Clifford Sifton, 21 January 1899
21 Ibid., William Pearce to Clifford Sifton, 7 February 1899
22 Ibid., Howard Douglas to Clifford Sifton, 23 March 1899
23 Ibid.
24 Deputy Minister's Report, Department of the Interior Annual Report, 1901
25 Act to Amend the Rocky Mountains Park Act, 2 Edward VII, ch. 31, 1902
26 Canada, House of Commons, Debates, 23 April 1902, 3305
27 Superintendent's Report, Department of the Interior Annual Report, 1904
28 Ibid., 1906
29 Ibid., 1904
30 Department of the Interior Annual Reports, 1897–1901
31 Superintendent's Report, Department of the Interior Annual Report, 1905
32 Ibid., 1908
33 Ibid., 1903
34 Ibid. Direct quotation from Muir, *Our National Parks*, quoted in Nash, editor *The American Environment* 72
35 Hornaday, 'The Extermination of the American Bison'
36 Rorabacher, *The American Buffalo in Transition* 34–49
37 Hornaday 393
38 Ibid. 434
39 Hind, *Narrative* ... II, 110
40 Palliser, *Explorations – British North America* 14
41 Denny, *The Law Marches West* 31–2
42 Ibid. 133, 143
43 Macoun, *Manitoba and the Great Northwest* 342
44 Roe, *The North American Buffalo* 467
45 Nelson, *The Last Refuge* 164–6
46 Grant MacEwan, *Chief Sitting Bull* (Edmonton: Hurtig Publishers 1973); also described in Denny, *The Law Marches West*
47 NWMP, Report to the Secretary of State, 1879

48 Denny 152
49 Anonymous, *A Holiday trip: Montreal to Victoria and Return via the Canadian Pacific Railway, Midsummer 1888* (CPR Archives; reprint, undated, Railfare Enterprises Ltd., Montreal)
50 PAC, Buffalo File, RG 84, Vol. 108, Howard Douglas to Deputy Minister William Cory, 4 February 1907
51 Ibid., J. Obed-Smith to W.D. Scott, 20 November 1905
52 Ibid., William Cory to Keyes, 8 January 1906
53 Ibid., Benjamin Davis to W.D. Scott, 6 March 1906
54 Ibid., Howard Douglas to Secretary of the Interior, 15 June 1906
55 Ibid., William Cory to Frank Oliver, 25 January 1907
56 Ibid., Howard Douglas to William Cory, 4 February 1907
57 Ibid., Benjamin Davis to William Cory, 2 April 1907
58 M.J. Elrod, 'The Flathead Buffalo Range,' American Bison Society Annual Report (1905–6) 45–6
59 Canada, House of Commons, Debates, 8 June 1908, 1202
60 Robert Froman, 'The Herd that Wouldn't Vanish,' Ontario Archives, undated mimeograph copy of article that appeared in *True: The Man's Magazine*. The magazine is no longer being published.
61 Ibid.
62 PAC, Buffalo File, RG 84, Vol. 108, Howard Douglas to Frank Oliver, 27 July 1907
63 Ibid., Wilfrid Laurier, memorandum, 12 August 1907
64 Canada, House of Commons, Debates, 20 March 1908, 5795
65 Ibid., 18 May 1908
66 Deputy Minister's Report, Department of the Interior Annual Report, 1907
67 Froman, 'The Herd that Wouldn't Vanish'
68 The American Bison Society was instrumental in having this reserve set aside.
69 Parks Canada, Buffalo File BU 209, Whyte to Frank Oliver, 2 February 1909; Robert Campbell to Frank Oliver, 5 February 1909
70 Commissioner's Report, Department of the Interior Annual Report, 1910
71 Deputy Minister's Report, Department of the Interior Annual Report, 1909
72 Order-in-Council, PC no. 1340, 21 June 1909, *Canada Gazette*, 3 July 1909, XLIII, 5
73 Commissioner's Report, Dominion Parks, 1912
74 Superintendent's Report, Rocky Mountains Park, Department of the Interior Annual Report, 1912
75 Douglas was dismissed from government service on 3 July 1912. The reasons for his dismissal are obscure. Frank Oliver stated in the House that it was because he was 'unreliable and using his official position to advance his personal interest.' A reference was made to Timber Berth no. 588, BC, and there was a rumour at the time that Douglas was involved in timber

speculation. However, A.R. Byrne in his study, 'Man and Landscape Change in Banff National Park Area before 1911' (1968), states that it was reported in a local Banff newspaper that Douglas had been dismissed for 'excessive partisanship' during the 1911 federal election (Byrne 145).

CHAPTER 4: TOWARDS BETTER ADMINISTRATION

1 Transcript, Nicholas Ignatieff, interview with Mabel Williams, Harkin's former secretary, in Ottawa, 1 July 1968
2 Dominion Forest Reserves and Parks Act, 3–4 George v, ch. 18, 19 May 1911
3 Under the Act, the entire eastern slope of the Rocky Mountains from the international boundary to a point 200 miles west of Edmonton was set aside. Park and Forestry jurisdictions were defined under the Act to Amend the Forest Reserves and Parks Act, 1911. James Harkin was appointed Commissioner by Order-in-Council, 10 August 1911.
4 Canada, House of Commons, Debates, 9 May 1911, 8611
5 E.A. Mitchner, 'William Pearce and the Federal Government's Activity in the West, 1882–1904,' unpublished PH D thesis (University of Alberta 1971)
6 Canadian Forestry Convention, 1906
7 This matter was discussed during the Commission's first annual meeting in 1910.
8 Parks were reduced by order-in-council, PC 1338, 8 June 1911.
9 Both Douglas and the Game Guardian at Banff had suggested a park reduction as early as 1908.
10 Canada, House of Commons, Debates, 9 May 1911, 8611
11 Stated during bill's first reading, 28 April 1911, 8614
12 Canada, House of Commons, Debates, 9 May 1911, 8616
13 Ibid., Frank Oliver's reply to J. Herron
14 Forestry Superintendent's Report, Department of the Interior Annual Report, 1909
15 PAC, Sifton Papers, Vol. 188, Robert Campbell to Clifford Sifton, 10 May 1909
16 Forestry Superintendent's Report, Department of the Interior Annual Report, 1909
17 PAC, Sifton Papers, Vol. 188, Robert Campbell to Clifford Sifton, 10 May 1909
18 Orders-in-council: PC 1382, 1909; PC 1553, 1910; PC 1551, 1910
19 Forestry Superintendent's Annual Reports, Department of the Interior, 1910–12
20 Under the same order-in-council, Howard Douglas was designated Chief Superintendent of Dominion Parks with headquarters based at Edmonton, Alberta.

21 Mabel Williams recalled that there were seven original members of the branch.

22 Mabel Williams, *The History and Meaning of National Parks* 5

23 Transcript, Ignatieff, interview with Mabel Williams

24 Commissioner's Report, Parks Branch, Department of the Interior Annual Report, 1912

25 National Archives, Washington, DC, USBS, Records, Canadian Papers, James Harkin to C.D. Ucker, 21 October 1912

26 Commissioner's Report, Parks Branch, Department of the Interior Annual Report, 1915

27 Ibid.

28 Williams 8

29 Commissioner's Report, Parks Branch, Department of the Interior Annual Report, 1914

30 Williams 13

31 Commissioner's Report, Parks Branch, Department of the Interior Annual Report, 1913

32 Ibid., 1914; Harkin quoted from Muir, *Our National Parks* 1–3

33 Commissioner's Report, Parks Branch, Department of the Interior Annual Report, 1915

34 Ibid. 4

35 Ibid. 4–5

36 Ibid.

37 Harkin, 'Our Need for National Parks' 105

38 Williams, *The History and Meaning of National Parks* 16

39 Transcript, Mabel Williams interview

40 Williams, *The History and Meaning of National Parks* 9

41 National Archives, Washington, DC, Records, Department of the Interior, correspondence between C.S. Ucker and W. Scheckebia, 17 February 1913

42 Ibid., correspondence between James Harkin and C.S. Ucker, 25 February 1913

43 Parks Canada Archives, Banff File B–2–1, cited in Robert Campbell to Deputy Minister William Cory, 9 November 1909

44 Ibid.

45 Ibid., Secretary, Alberta Game and Fish Protective Association, to the Minister of the Interior, 19 July 1911

46 Parks Canada Archives, Waterton Lakes File W–2–1, F.K. Vreeland to Robert Campbell, 14 December 1911

47 Ibid., Jasper File, J–2–1, James Harkin to C.R. Mitchell, 28 November 1913. Memo includes letters received by the Department in previous years from W. Wainwright, Vice-President, H.R Charlton, and W.E Davis, Grand Trunk Pacific Railway; W. Mackenzie and H. Fitzsimmons, Canadian Northern Railway; and A. Wheeler, Alpine Club of Canada.

48 Ibid., Banff File B–2–1, Howard Douglas to Secretary, Department of the Interior, 19 July 1911

49 Ibid.
50 Ibid,. Park Extension File U–2, Vol 1, James Harkin memorandum, 30 November 1912
51 Ibid., James Harkin to William Cory, 30 November 1912
52 Order-in-council, PC 646, 18 November 1913
53 Rodney, *Kootenai Brown*
54 Parks Canada Archives, Park Extension File U–2, Vol. 1, John Brown to James Harkin, 1 June 1913
55 Ibid.
56 Ibid., James Harkin to William Cory, 1 March 1913
57 PAC, Borden Papers, Vol. 156, James White to Robert Borden, 4 February 1914
58 Order-in-council, PC 1167, 24 June 1914
59 Parks Canada Archives, Jasper File J–2–1, Vol. 1, James Harkin to William Cory, 2 May 1912
60 Ibid.
61 Ibid.
62 Ibid., Waterton Lakes File W–2–1, Vol. 1, C.R. Mitchell, Treasurer, Alberta provincial government, to James Harkin, and reply, 9 and 19 March 1915
63 Ibid.
64 Commissioner's Report, Department of the Interior Annual Report, 1916
65 Williams 10
66 Harkin, 'Our Need for National Parks' 104
67 Commissioner's Report, Department of the Interior Annual Report, 1916
68 James Harkin, 'Conservation is the New Patriotism,' 1 September 1922, mimeograph, Parks Canada Library, Ottawa
69 Commissioner's Report, Department of the Interior Annual Report, 1916

CHAPTER 5: TAKING THE INITIATIVE

1 Einarson, *The Pronghorn Antelope*; Hewitt, *The Conservation of the Wild Life of Canada*; Mathiessen, *Wildlife in North America*; Seton, *Life Histories of North American Animals*, 4 volumes
2 Seton, *Life Histories of North American Animals* 1
3 Canadian Wildlife Service, Antelope Records, Thomas Willing to Robert Campbell, 11 May 1910
4 Ibid., Robert Campbell to William Cory, 21 July 1910
5 Ibid., 20 March 1912
6 Report of Chief Game and Fish Guardian, Department of Agriculture Annual Reports, Alberta, 1913
7 Personal information regarding Graham's life was given to the author by his two daughters, Mrs Olive Fetherstonhaugh and Mrs Naomi Thompson. Additional information also came from his granddaughter, Mrs Betty Salmon.
8 Parks Canada Archives, Buffalo Files, BU 211, J. Byshe to Robert Campbell, 25 March 1911

9 PAC, Records, Department of Northern Affairs and Natural Resources, RG 84, Vol. 74, Maxwell Graham to James Harkin, 3 August 1912
10 Canadian Wildlife Service, Antelope Records, James Harkin to William Cory, 9 March 1914
11 PAC, Records, Department of Northern Affairs and Natural Resources, RG 84, Vol. 74, Ernest Thompson Seton/Maxwell Graham Report, 10 May and 10 June 1914
12 Ibid., Vol. 22, Ernest Thompson Seton to James Harkin, 1914 memorandum
13 Ibid., Maxwell Graham to James Harkin, 17 June 1914
14 Canadian Wildlife Service, Antelope Records, Sgt Tom Stevens to Commanding Officer, NWMP, 14 February 1915
15 Ibid., James Harkin to William Cory, 26 February 1915
16 Ibid., Graham reports and cables to James Harkin, 10, 18, 20 March 1915
17 Ibid., James Harkin to William Cory, 20 March 1915
18 Ibid., James Harkin memo to William Cory, 31 March 1915
19 Ibid., Maxwell Graham to James Harkin, 19 April 1915
20 Ibid., James Harkin to Maxwell Graham, 27 April 1915
21 Maxwell Graham to Ernest Thompson Seton, 18 June 1915 (letter in possession of Betty Salmon)
22 William Hornaday, 'A Great Antelope Preserve in Alberta.'
23 Canadian Wildlife Service, Antelope Records, Maxwell Graham to Ernest Thompson Seton, 18 June 1915
24 James Harkin, 'Conservation Work in Canada's National Parks'
25 Seton, *Lives of North American Animals* III, 425–7
26 Northwest Territories Game Administration Records, MG 30 C 63, Vol. I, James Harkin to William Cory, 1914, 'Memorandum Regarding Dominion Parks – Their Values and Ideals'
27 Hearne, *Journey from Prince of Wales's Fort...*
28 Franklin, *Journey to the Polar Sea*
29 Mackenzie, *Exploring the Northwest Territory from Athabasca to the Pacific, 1789* and *Voyages from Montreal through the Continent of North America, 1789, 1793;* Harmon, *Journals of Voyages and Travels, 1820* 174; Archibald McDonald, *Peace River: A Canoe Voyage from Hudson Bay to the Pacific, by Sir George Simpson in 1828, journal of the late chief factor Archibald McDonald, who accompanied him;* edited, with notes, by Malcolm McLeod (Ottawa: J. Durie and Son 1872)
30 Soper, 'Mammals of Wood Buffalo Park, Northern Alberta and District of Mackenzie' 362
31 Butler, *The Wild North Land*
32 Macoun, *Manitoba and the Great Northwest*
33 Charles Mair and Robert MacFarlane, *Through the Mackenzie Basin* 177
34 William Ogilvie, Report, Department of the Interior Annual Report, 1889
35 Related in Raup, 'Range Conditions in Wood Buffalo National Park' 19
36 Hornaday, 'The Extermination of the American Bison'
37 Raup, 'Range Conditions in Wood Buffalo National Park' 20

38 Report of Select Committee of the Senate on Certain Documents Pertaining to the Resources of the Great Mackenzie Basin, 1891 Session (Ottawa: Queen's Printer, 1891)

39 NWMP Report, 1897, Sessional Papers, 1898

40 Inspector Arthur M. Jarvis, NWMP Report, 1898, 1899

41 Ibid., 1899 Report

42 *Ottawa Naturalist* XIV (1901) 228–9

43 PAC, Sifton Papers, Vol. 123, Madison Grant to Clifford Sifton, 26 May 1902

44 Raup, 'Range Conditions in Wood Buffalo National Park'

45 NWMP Reports, 1902–5, Sessional Papers

46 PAC, Records, Department of Northern Affairs and Natural Resources, RG 84, Vol. 74, Maxwell Graham to James Harkin, 22 July 1914; also related in Ernest Thompson Seton's *Arctic Prairies*

47 Inspector Jarvis, NWMP Report, 1907, Sessional Papers (1908)

48 Police Commissioner Perry, NWMP Report, Sessional Papers (1909)

49 Forestry Superintendent, Department of the Interior Annual Report, 1912

50 PAC, Records, Department of Northern Affairs and Natural Resources, RG 85, Vol. 664, Robert Campbell to George Mulloy, 25 March 1911

51 Ibid., Maxwell Graham to James Harkin, 22 July 1914

52 Ibid., George Mulloy to Robert Campbell, 31 May 1912

53 Ibid., Finlayson to Robert Campbell, 8 March 1914

54 Ibid., George Mulloy to Robert Campbell, 31 May 1912

55 Ibid., Maxwell Graham to James Harkin, 30 June 1912

56 George Mulloy, Report to Forestry Branch, 11 June 1912; quoted at length in Maxwell Graham's letter to James Harkin, 30 June 1912 (PAC Records, Department of Northern Affairs and Natural Resources, RG 85, Vol. 664)

57 A.J. Bell Report to Forestry Branch, also quoted in Graham to Harkin, 30 June 1912

58 Forestry Superintendent, Department of the Interior Annual Report, 1913

59 Deputy Minister, Department of the Interior Annual Report, 1913

60 Forestry Superintendent, Department of the Interior Annual Report, 1915

61 PAC, Records Department of Northern Affairs and Natural Resources, RG 85, Vol. 664, Maxwell Graham to James Harkin, 30 June 1912

62 Ibid., Maxwell Graham to James Harkin, 16 October, 7 December 1912

63 Ibid., 7 December 1912

64 Ibid., 6 July 1912

65 Commissioner's Report, Parks Branch, Department of the Interior Annual Report, 1914

66 PAC, Records, Department of Northern Affairs and Natural Resources, RG 85, Vol. 664, James Harkin to Minister of the Interior, 11 June 1914

67 Ibid., Maxwell Graham to James Harkin, 22 July 1914

68 Ibid., Minister of the Interior to Governor-General-in-Council, 30 June 1914
69 Ibid., James Harkin to William Cory, 18 April 1916
70 Ibid.
71 Ibid., Vol. 664, H.J. Bury, Report to Deputy Minister of the Interior, 13 April 1916
72 Ibid., James Harkin to Deputy Minister William Cory, 5 July 1916
73 Wood Buffalo National Park proclaimed 18 December 1922, *Canada Gazette* LVI 36 (3 March 1923). The boundaries of Wood Buffalo National Park were enlarged to 17,300 square miles in 1926.
74 PAC, Records, Department of Northern Affairs and Natural Resources, RG 85, Vol. 665, James Harkin to William Cory, 20 February 1913
75 Ibid., Summary, James Harkin to William Cory, 30 December 1914
76 Ibid.
77 Ibid., Robert Campbell to William Cory, 7 January 1915
78 Ibid., James Harkin to William Cory, 13 January 1915
79 Ibid., Maxwell Graham to James Harkin, 8 and 23 January 1915
80 Ibid., James Harkin to William Cory, 13 January 1915
81 Ibid., Deputy Minister to Robert Campbell, 5 March 1917
82 PAC, Northwest Territories Game Administration Records, MG, 30 C63, Vol. 1, James Harkin to Deputy Minister, 1914, 'Memorandum Regarding Dominion Parks – Their Values and Ideals'

CHAPTER 6: PROTECTING AN INTERNATIONAL RESOURCE

1 Mathiessen, *Wildlife in America*
2 Hornaday, *Our Vanishing Wildlife*, chs 11, 12
3 The Labrador duck became extinct before there was much recorded information about the species. Earl Godfrey states in *Birds of Canada* that the bird was not particularly good to eat and it is doubtful that hunting played a significant role in its extinction. It is also doubtful that a great deal will ever be known about the Labrador duck or the causes of its extinction.
4 American Ornithologists' Union, *Bulletin* no. 1 of the Committee on the Protection of Birds, 'The Destruction of Our Native Birds,' Special Publication, Supplement to *Science* (26 February 1887) 7
5 Phillips, *Migratory Bird Protection in North America*
6 Clara Thaxter, 'Women's Heartlessness,' *Audubon Magazine* I (1887) 13–14
7 Anonymous, 'Bird Banding in Canada,' *Forest and Outdoors* (1951)
8 American Ornithologists' Union, *Bulletin* no. 1, 3
9 For an excellent study of the feather trade in the United States, see Doughty, *Feather Fashion and Bird Preservation*.
10 Day, *North American Waterfowl*. Day was formerly Director of the US Fish and Wildlife Service.
11 Phillips, *Migratory Bird Protection in North America*

12 Buchanan, *The Life and Adventures of John James Audubon*, diary entry for 23 June 1833
13 C.D.H. Clarke, Ontario Fish and Wildlife Headlines, mimeograph (Toronto: Ministry of Natural Resources for Ontario)
14 National Library, Ottawa, Annual Report, North American Fish and Game Protective Association
15 Author's correspondence with Manly Miner, Jack Miner's son, May 1972
16 Harrison F. Lewis, 'The Canadian Wildlife Service: A Lively History,' unpublished manuscript (Ottawa: cws 1973)
17 Phillips, *Migratory Bird Protection in North America*; Pearson, *Adventures in Bird Protection*, ch. 16
18 Haskell, *The American Game Protective and Propagation Association*
19 J. Walter Jones, 'Fur Farming in Canada,' Commission of Conservation Annual Report 1913, 42–8
20 cws, Records, Migratory Bird Protection, Maxwell Graham to James Harkin, 18 March 1913
21 Ibid., Maxwell Graham to John Macoun, 20 March 1913 and reply, 22 March
22 Ibid., Percy Taverner to Maxwell Graham, 22 March 1913
23 Royal Ontario Museum, Toronto, Taverner Papers (uncatalogued), Percy Taverner to James Fleming, 24 March 1916
24 National Archives, Washington, dc, usbs, Records, Papers Relating to Canada, James Harkin to Secretary, American Game Protective and Propagation Association, 25 March 1913
25 cws, Records, James Harkin to William Cory, 2 April 1913
26 Ibid., James Harkin to James Fleming, 19 May 1913. the earliest record of systematic bird banding in Canada was on 24 September 1905, when Fleming banded a robin. Fleming reply to Harkin, 18 June 1913
27 Ibid., William Saunders to James Harkin, 5 December 1913
28 Ibid., reply, 16 December 1913
29 Transactions, North American Fish and Game Protective Association, Ottawa, 9 December 1913
30 cws, Records, Migratory Bird Protection, Edward Chambers to James Harkin, 26 January 1914
31 Ibid., Maxwell Graham to James Harkin, 19 December 1913
32 Ibid., James Harkin to Edward Chambers, 19 January 1914
33 Ibid., Edward Chambers to James Harkin, 26 January and reply, 26 January 1914
34 William Haskell, 'Protection of Migratory Birds,' Report, Commission of Conservation (1915) 66–8
35 Ibid. 214–15
36 pac, Borden Papers, Vol. 187, James White to Robert Borden, 14 May 1914
37 cws, Records, Maxwell Graham to James Harkin, 27 March 1914
38 Ibid., Lieutenant-Governor Langelier to Secretary of State, 13 July 1914
39 Ibid., Josiah Wood to T. Mulvey, Under-Secretary of State, 25 April 1914

40 Ibid., J.A. Knight, Chief Game Commissioner, Nova Scotia, to the Provincial Secretary, 27 May 1914

41 Ibid., Lieutenant-Governor Patterson to Under-Secretary of State, 28 July 1914

42 Ibid., James Harkin/Gordon Hewitt correspondence, 1916

43 Order-in-council, PC 1247, 15 May 1915

44 Elizabeth Hewitt, preface to C. Gordon Hewitt, *The Conservation of the Wild Life of Canada* vii–viii

45 G.J. Spence, 'A Century of Entomology in Canada,' *Canadian Entomologist* LCIV (1964)

46 National Archives, Washington, DC, USBS, Records Relating to Canada, Gordon Hewitt to Henry Henshaw, 17 February 1913

47 Dominion Entomologist, Annual Report, Department of Agriculture, 1915

48 Report, Commission of Conservation annual meeting (1916) 117–19

49 National Archives, Washington, DC, USBS, Records Relating to Canada, Gordon Hewitt to Theodore S. Palmer, 27 September 1915

50 Order-in-council, PC 503, 7 March 1916. Hewitt conducted two sessions of negotiations in Washington, in January and in March. There are no existing formal notes of the conferences. What transpired is contained in the Harkin-Hewitt correspondence.

51 CWS, Records, Migratory Bird Protection, Gordon Hewitt to James Harkin, 11 April 1916

52 Ibid.

53 No copy of the original draft treaty survives. What it contained can be understood by comparing the Hewitt-Harkin correspondence with the revised draft and the final treaty itself. The revised draft is with the CWS in Ottawa.

54 CWS, Records, Maxwell Graham to James Harkin, 20 January 1916

55 Ibid., Gordon Hewitt to James Harkin, 28 January 1916

56 Ibid., 11 April 1916

57 Reported in Pearson, *Adventures in Bird Protection* 285

58 Ibid.

59 CWS, Records, Gordon Hewitt to James Harkin, 11 April 1916

60 In the clause permitting birds to be shot 'when injurious to agricultural interests,' the BC government wanted the phrase 'or other interests' to be added. The change was made. Also, permission was given to west coast Indians to kill scoters for food in Article 2 Section 1 of the treaty.

61 Hewitt cable to Henry Henshaw, 2 June 1916; reply, 3 June

62 Phillips, *Migratory Bird Protection*; Hornaday, *Thirty Years War for Wildlife*, and John Burnham, 'A Great Victory for American Sport,' *Rod and Gun in Canada* (1918) 300–1

63 Ibid., Phillips 19

64 National Archives, Washington, DC, USBS, Records Relating to Canada, Gordon Hewitt to Edward Nelson, 17 August 1916

65 Ibid., William Hornaday to Gordon Hewitt, 2 September 1916
66 Ibid., Gordon Hewitt to Henry Henshaw, 2 September 1916
67 Ibid., Edward Nelson to Gordon Hewitt, 3 December 1916
68 Bill no. 82 Respecting Migratory Birds Convention
69 Canada, House of Commons, Debates, 21 June 1917, first reading of Bill 82, p. 3697
70 Ibid., 21 June 1917
71 National Archives, Washington, DC, USBS, Records Relating to Canada, Edward Nelson to Gordon Hewitt, 26 June 1917
72 US Statutes at Large, 1918, Vol. 40, Part I, 755–7
73 State of Missouri v Ray P. Holland, 19 April 1920, 40 *Supreme Court Reporter* 382
74 The King v Russell C. Clarke, 1920. National Archives, Washington, DC, USBS, Records Relating to Canada, James Harkin to Edward Nelson, 7 December 1920
75 Ibid., 12 July 1918

CHAPTER 7: NEW RESPONSIBILITIES

1 National Archives, Washington, DC, USBS, uncatalogued records relating to Canada, Gordon Hewitt to Edward Nelson, 2 May 1918
2 Canada, House of Commons, Debates, 7 May 1919, 2165
3 Ibid.
4 National Archives, Washington, DC, USBS, Records, Gordon Hewitt to Edward Nelson, 23 June 1919
5 Canada, House of Commons, Debates, 7 May 1919, 2165
6 National Archives, Washington, DC, USBS, Records, Gordon Hewitt to Edward Nelson, 23 June 1919
7 Canada, House of Commons, Debates, 11 May 1922, 1684
8 National Archives, Washington, DC, USBS, Records, correspondence between Gordon Hewitt and Edward Nelson, 19 December 1918–3 January 1919
9 Ibid., James Harkin to Edward Nelson, 27 May 1921
10 Ibid.
11 Royal Ontario Museum, Toronto, Report, Canadian Society for the Protection of Birds, 1915–17
12 Report, Province of Quebec Society for the Protection of Birds (Montreal: Lachine Museum 1918)
13 Report, Essex County Wild Life Conservation Association, in *Rod and Gun in Canada* (August 1917)
14 *Rod and Gun in Canada* (April 1917)
15 Interview with Harrison F. Lewis, Federal Migratory Bird Officer for Ontario and Quebec, appointed in 1920. Lewis was also a former Director of the Canadian Wildlife Service. He died in 1974.
16 Interview with Hoyes Lloyd, 18 December 1971 and 10 November 1974
17 Ibid.

18 Order-in-council, PC 3231, 28 December 1916
19 Entomologist's Report, Department of Agriculture Annual Report, 1917. Hewitt drafted the order-in-council creating the Advisory Board; CWS, Records.
20 Harrison Lewis, interview, 8 December 1971
21 Hewitt, 'The Conservation of Wild Life in Canada in 1917,' address given to the Commission of Conservation, Annual Report, 1918, 130
22 Commissioner's Report, Parks Branch, Department of the Interior Annual Report, 1918
23 Lewis, 'The Canadian Wildlife Service – A Lively History' (Ottawa: Canadian Wildlife Service 1973)
24 Hewitt, address to Commission of Conservation, 1918
25 Ibid.
26 CWS, Records, Migratory Bird Protection, James Harkin to William Cory, 14 December 1916
27 Canada, Senate, Journals, 1907, xiii
28 Ibid. 29–32
29 Ibid. 65–6
30 Zaslow, The Opening of the Canadian North, chs 9, 10
31 Seton, Arctic Prairies
32 Zaslow, The Opening of the Canadian North 242
33 Edward Nelson, Natural History Collection, Alaska, 1887. Quoted in Seton, Lives of Game Animals III, 130
34 Warburton Pike, The Barren Grounds of Northern Canada 82–4
35 Frank Russell, Explorations in the Far North (Iowa City, Iowa: University of Iowa 1898) 88
36 Tener, Muskoxen in Canada 112–14
37 Russell, Explorations in the Far North 117
38 Personal papers, Mrs Betty Salmon, Maxwell Graham to James Harkin, 23 June 1914
39 Ibid.
40 PAC, Sifton Papers, Vol. 123, Madison Grant to Clifford Sifton, 18 November 1902
41 Ibid., Northern Territories Administration Records, RG 18, Vol. 879, Fred White to Frank Oliver, 13 November 1907
42 Seton, Lives of Game Animals III, 602
43 PAC, Sifton Papers, Vol. 123, Lord Grey to Wilfrid Laurier, 12 November 1907
44 Vilhjalmur Stefansson, My Life with the Eskimo 13
45 Rudolph M. Anderson, 'Arctic Game Notes,' American Museum Journal (1913) 5–8
46 Ibid. 8
47 Stefansson, My Life with the Eskimo 55
48 PAC, Borden Papers, Vol. 185, Vilhjalmur Stefansson, report to Clifford Sifton, 8 February 1914
49 Ibid., William Roche to Robert Borden, 30 March 1914

50 Ibid., James White to Robert Borden, 6 July 1914
51 Ibid., Inspector Jennings, Report, 11 April 1914
52 Ibid., Sifton Papers, Vol. 201, Gordon Hewitt to Clifford Sifton, 16 July 1914
53 National Archives, Washington, DC, USBS, Records, Gordon Hewitt/Henry Henshaw correspondence, 16–27 July 1914
54 PAC, Sifton Papers, Vol. 201, Gordon Hewitt to Clifford Sifton, 16 July 1914
55 Gordon Hewitt, 'Conservation of Birds and Mammals in Canada,' address given to the Committee on Fish, Game and Fur Bearing Animals, published in Commission's Report (1915) 148–9
56 Hewitt, 'The Conservation of our Northern Mammals,' Report, Commission of Conservation (1916) 32–40
57 PAC, Records, Department of Northern Affairs and Natural Resources, RG 85, Vol. 666, H.J. Bury, Report, 6 November 1915, and Supplement, 1916
58 Ibid., Borden Papers, Vol. 185, Gordon Hewitt to James White, 14 November 1916
59 Ibid., Clifford Sifton to Robert Borden, 16 December 1916
60 Ibid., Robert Borden to Clifford Sifton, 27 December 1916
61 Northwest Game Act, 7–8 George v, ch. 36, 20 September 1917
62 Hewitt, 'The Conservation of Wild Life in Canada in 1917,' Report, Commission of Conservation (1918) 124

CHAPTER 8: THE SANCTUARY IDEA BROADENED

1 Commissioner's Report, Parks Branch, Department of the Interior Annual Report, 1914
2 Ibid.
3 Commissioner's Report, Parks Branch, Department of the Interior Annual Report, 1916
4 Ibid.
5 Parks Canada Archives, Northern Economic Development Records, File 148431, Box 480094, Accession 68C2, Edgar Dewdney to Thomas White, 12 March 1887
6 Gordon Hewitt, 'Protection of Birds,' Report, Commission of Conservation (1916) 119
7 William Wood, 'Our Kindred of the Wild,' address, Canadian Club, 30 November 1912 (Ottawa: The Canadian Club Report 1912) 50
8 Ibid. 51
9 University of Toronto Library, William Wood, 'Draft Plan for Beginning of Animal Sanctuaries in Labrador,' private publication and circulation, 1913
10 Report, Commission of Conservation, 1913; 'Game Protection, North Shore' 172–4. There is no record of what the Commission's executive committee did with Wood's recommendation.
11 Published separately as a 'supplement' to his original paper

12 Supplement 15
13 Ibid. 30
14 Ibid. 28
15 Ibid. 19–20
16 Linda McKeane, 'The Gannets of Bonaventure,' *Ontario Naturalist* IX (December 1971) 5
17 D.G. Pettie, editor, *Audubon's America* (Cambridge, MA: Riverside Press 1940) 231
18 Buchanan, editor *The Life and Adventures of John James Audubon*, diary, 23 June 1833
19 Ibid.
20 Godfrey, *The Birds of Canada*
21 'Gannet,' CWS monograph, Environment Canada Ottawa (1973); McKeane, 'The Gannets of Bonaventure'
22 National Museum of Canada, Taverner Papers, Percy Taverner to Theodore Palmer, 22 April 1914
23 John M. Clarke, 'The Saving of the Sea Birds in the Gulf of the St Lawrence,' Statement of the Permanent Wild Life Protection Fund, New York Zoological Society, New York, 1920. Clarke bases this belief on a personal correspondence he had at the time with Commander Wakeham.
24 National Museum of Canada, Taverner Papers, Percy Taverner to Theodore Palmer 22 April, 1914
25 Ibid.
26 National Archives, Washington, DC, USBS, Records, Gordon Hewitt to Theodore Palmer, 20 April 1914
27 National Museum of Canada, Taverner Papers, Theodore Palmer to Percy Taverner, 25 April 1914
28 National Archives, Washington, DC, USBS, Records, Theodore Palmer to Gordon Hewitt, 26 April 1914
29 CWS, Bonaventure Island Records, James Harkin to G. Heidmann, 10 June 1914
30 Percy Taverner, 'The Gannets of Bonaventure Island,' *Ottawa Naturalist* XXXII (May 1918) 26
31 National Museum, Taverner Papers, Percy Taverner to James White, 10 December 1914
32 Taverner, 'The Gannets of Bonaventure' 26
33 CWS, Bonaventure Island, Records, Percy Taverner to James Harkin, 28 November 1914
34 Percy Taverner to James White, 10 December 1914
35 Ibid., Gordon Hewitt to James Harkin, 14 December 1914
36 John M. Clarke, 'Protection of Sea Fowl in the Gulf of the St Lawrence,' Report, Commission of Conservation (1915) 108
37 Gordon Hewitt, 'Protection of Birds,' Report, Commission of Conservation (1915) 117
38 Appendix 3, Report, Commission of Conservation, 1915. Taverner also

recommended establishing Point Pelee, Ontario, as a national park and bird sanctuary.

39 National Museum, Taverner Papers, William Wood to James Harkin, 12 April 1915

40 Ibid., James Harkin to William Wood, 20 April 1915

41 cws, Records, John Clarke to James Harkin, 15 January 1915

42 National Museum, Taverner Papers, Percy Taverner to John Clarke, 4 March 1915

43 cws, Records, William Wood to James Harkin, 26 April 1915

44 Ibid., James Harkin to William Wood, 30 April 1915

45 Ibid. Clarke later conducted negotiations under the authorization of the Commission of Conservation.

46 cws, Records, F.H.H. Williamson to Percy Taverner, 21 May 1915

47 National Museum, Taverner Papers, Percy Taverner to James Harkin, 13 June 1915, report on the follow-up of recommendations for national parks

48 John Clarke, 'The Saving of the Sea Birds in the Gulf of St Lawrence (New York: Wild Life Protection Fund, New York Zoological Society 1920). Clarke might well have been referring to the Honourable Richard Turner. Turner was born in Quebec in 1843 and gained prominence in the business and industrial communities. He was president of the Turner Lumber and Pulpwood Company and Director of the Matane Railway Company. He was a member of the Quebec legislative council from 1897 to 1917 and died shortly thereafter.

49 cws, Records, Gordon Hewitt to James Harkin, 1917, Record of Negotiations

50 Canada, House of Commons, Debates, 18 May 1918, 2223

51 Taverner, 'The Gannets of Bonaventure Island' 26

52 National Museum, Taverner Papers, Percy Taverner to Gordon Hewitt, 13 December 1918

53 Clarke, 'The Saving of the Sea Birds' 174

54 cws, Records, James Harkin to William Cory, 27 November 1918

55 Ibid., Taverner to Harkin, 1914; Percy Taverner, Commission of Conservation address, 1915; Charles Townsend, Commission of Conservation address, 1916

56 Godfrey, The Birds of Canada 30

57 James Harkin, 'Conservation is the New Patriotism,' mimeograph, Parks Branch, Ottawa 1922

58 The Ontario government was also anxious to acquire a wildlife sanctuary on the point, and when Pelee was set aside as a dominion park under the Dominion Forest Reserves and Parks Act in 1918, the point was also declared a provincial game sanctuary under Ontario's game laws but subject to dominion park regulations.

59 Percy Taverner, 'Three National Parks,' Appendix 3, Report, Commission of Conservation, 1915

60 Author's correspondence with Manly Miner, Jack Miner's eldest son, 1971–2
61 PAC, Records, Point Pelee National Park, File 1509, Vol. III, Edward Kerr to James Harkin, 6 January 1919
62 Ibid., 6 January 1919
63 Ibid.
64 Ibid., Forest Conover to James Harkin, 22 January 1919
65 Ibid., James Harkin to Albert Girardin, 15 February 1919
66 Ibid., Rudolph Anderson, report to James Harkin, March 1919
67 The ten areas were Betchouane Island, Birch Islands, Washishow Island, Fog Island, Wolf Bay, Cape Whittle, St Mary Islands, Macatina, St Augustin, and Bradore Bay.
68 Harrison Lewis, 'The Canadian Wildlife Service – A Lively History,' unpublished manuscript (Ottawa: The Canadian Wildlife Service 1973)
69 The Canadian Society for the Protection of Birds, in Toronto, passed a resolution at their 1916 annual meeting for the reservation of Bonaventure and Percé, while the Société de Géographie de Québec published the full text of Clarke's Conservation Commission address in their 1916 bulletin, adding that public powers were 'inefficient' to enforce adequate seabird protection. The Société demanded reservation of the bird colonies and the initiation of 'well constructed and seriously applied laws to protect all bird life in the St Lawrence.' (F. Rouillard, 'Les Oiseaux de Mer,' Société de Géographie de Québec, *Bulletin*, 1916)
70 PAC, North West Territories Game File, Black Series RG 10, Vol. 485, James Harkin to William Hornaday, 17 October 1917

CHAPTER 9: WILDLIFE CONSERVATION COMES OF AGE

1 CWS, Records, Migratory Bird Protection, James Harkin to William Cory, 2 April 1913
2 National Conference on the Conservation of Game, Fur-Bearing Animals and Other Wild Life, 18–19 February 1919, Commission of Conservation Annual Report, 1919
3 Gordon Hewitt, 'The Need for a Nation-Wide Effort in Wild Life Conservation,' National Conference, 18–19 February 1919, Report 8–16
4 Discussions, National Conference, 18–19 February 1923, Report, 102–20
5 The cost of federal game officers and wardens for the Maritime Provinces in 1921 amounted to $10,674.34, a sum that did not include travelling expenses. Sessional Papers, departmental estimates
6 The suggestion was made by Dr Howard Murray, ex-officio member of the Conservation Commission.
7 James Harkin, 'Wild Life Sanctuaries,' National Conference, 18–19 February 1919, Report 47–50
8 A resolution was passed to this effect at the end of the conference by Ernest

Smith. In a footnote to the report it is stated that, since the conference was held, a 250,000-acre game preserve had been established by the New Brunswick provincial government in the western portion of Northumberland County.

9 Hewitt's suggestion followed an address by R.H. Coates, Dominion Statistician and Chief of the Dominion Bureau of Statistics. National Conference, 18–19 February 1919, Report 134–8

10 National Conference, 18–19 February 1919, Report 27–32. It was suggested at the end of the conference that the dominion government use officers of the RNWMP to help enforce provincial game laws. This suggestion was subsequently acted upon by the federal government.

11 William Hornaday, 'The Rational Use of Game Animals'; Edward Nelson, 'The Migratory Bird Treaty'; John Burnham, 'The War and Game,' National Conference, 18–19 February 1919, Report

12 Gordon Hewitt, 'National Organization for the Conservation and Protection of Wild Life,' National Conference, 18–19 February 1919, Report 150

13 Commissioner's Report, Parks Branch, Department of the Interior Annual Report 1919

14 Elizabeth Hewitt, preface, C. Gordon Hewitt, *The Conservation of the Wild Life of Canada*. Also reported in Arthur Gibson's article, 'Writings of the Late C. Gordon Hewitt,' extracts from *The Canadian Entomologist* LII (May 1920) 97–105

15 Hewitt, *The Conservation of the Wild Life of Canada* 309

16 Ibid., preface viii–ix

17 Statement, Permanent Wild Life Protection Fund, Gordon Hewitt obituary, 1920 (New York: New York Zoological Society 1920)

18 PAC, Department of Northern Affairs and National Resources Files, Vol. 6, Privy Council Sub-Committee Report (undated) 1920, 3

19 Canada, House of Commons, Debates, 26 May 1921, 3958

20 Canada, Senate, Debates, Bill F4 to Repeal the Commission of Conservation, 19 May 1921, 511

21 PAC, Department of Northern Affairs and National Resources Files, Vol. 6, and Meighen Papers, Extracts from Privy Council Report, prepared by Senator James Lougheed

22 Zaslow, *The Opening of the Canadian North* 197

23 PAC, Sifton Papers, Vol. 278, Memorandum Regarding Lougheed Speech in the Senate of Friday, 13 May 1921 on the Abolition of the Commission of Conservation

24 Ibid.

25 Canada, Senate, Debates, 19 May 1921, 511

26 Canada, House of Commons, Debates, 26 May 1921, 3968

27 Transcript, interview conducted by the author with Harrison Lewis, Ottawa, 8 December 1971

28 Reported by Allan Donnell, then editor of the Commission's monthly bulletin *Conservation*, during an interview with Nicholas Ignatieff in

Ottawa, 20 January 1970. This was also recalled by Kathleen Moodie, a government employee at the time, during a similar interview with N. Ignatieff.

29 Mrs Sydney Stevens, youngest daughter of James White. This was related to N. Ignatieff on 18 March 1968.

30 Moodie interview

31 cws, Records of 1922 Dominion-Provincial Conference, James Harkin to J.H. Evans, Deputy Minister of Agriculture, Manitoba provincial government, 20 October 1922

32 pac, Northern Affairs Administration Files, Advisory Board Records, Vol. 148, Privy Council Report, 18 December 1922, containing report of 24 November 1922

33 A draft copy of the minutes of the conference in note form is located among the Advisory Board records, cws, Ottawa. The minutes of the Dominion-Provincial Wildlife conferences are missing for most of the 1920s. During the 1930s, the minutes were published and circulated on a more regular basis.

34 Harrison Lewis, 'The Canadian Wildlife Service – A Lively History' unpublished manuscript (Ottawa: Canadian Wildlife Service 1973). Resolutions passed during the 1922 conference:
 – that daily and seasonal bag limits for migratory game birds be applied in each province and each state;
 – that existing migratory bird regulations with respect to bird damage to crops are inadequate and some better arrangement should be found and put into effect;
 – that a provision should be made in migratory bird regulations to deal with bird damage to fisheries, declared to be a serious matter in the Maritime provinces and Quebec;
 – that legislation be passed to prohibit sale or barter of game birds and animals in all the provinces;
 – that complete protection be given to Harlequin Ducks in Canada and the United States for five years;
 – that complete protection be given to black bellied and golden plover until numbers have increased sufficiently to warrant an open season;
 – extension of complete protection for eider duck in St Lawrence Gulf, Maritimes, and some United States states;
 – that provision be made under the Treaty whereby murres, auks and puffins would be classed as game birds;
 – that the Dominion Parks Branch carry on campaign of education in wildlife conservation through distribution of literature;
 – that all provinces require permits to shoot wildlife and such permits demand returns to be made setting forth the numbers and kinds of game killed in that season (this had been discussed at length during the 1919 conference);
 – that nonresident Canadians be charged less for hunting permits than nonresident aliens;

- that the Department of Indian Affairs endeavour to persuade Indians to observe game laws and to co-operate with game officials when increased restrictions are found necessary;
- that National Parks Branch and provincial representatives confer to propose suitable legislation for control of shipments of game and fur-bearing animals;
- that regulations be adopted restricting the use of sink boxes in Tadoussac Lagoon, New Brunswick.

35 A closed season on eider ducks was extended in 1922 and protection was increased for the species with the establishment of island bird sanctuaries along the north shore of the St Lawrence in 1925. A closed season for the protection of golden and black-bellied plover was also instituted in 1926. The Game Export Act was passed during the 1940s and eventually all of the provinces and territories prohibited the sale of game.

36 Author's interview with Harrison Lewis, 1970

Note on Sources

The American literature and historical bibliography on natural resource conservation and wildlife preservation is large and extensive. Both the conservation and preservation movements began in the United States at the turn of the century and it is not surprising that since then the conservation issue has become the focal point for study by American resource historians.

Americans became concerned about the state of their natural environment and diminishing wildlife long before Canadians. A skimming of titles of books written after 1900 tells a great deal about the high level of interest Americans were taking in the subject of conservation:

John Muir, *Our National Parks* (1901)
Gifford Pinchot, *The Fight for Conservation* (1910)
William Hornaday, *Our Vanishing Wildlife* (1913)
George Grinnell, *Hunting and Conservation* (1925)
William Hornaday, *Thirty Years War for Wildlife* (1930)
Gifford Pinchot, *Breaking New Ground* (1947)
Edward Graham, *The Land and Wildlife* (1949)
Aldo Leopold, *A Sand County Almanac* (1949)
Peter Mathiessen, *Wildlife in America* (1959).

During the sixties, American interest in conservation history intensified, heightened no doubt by the knowledge that modern man possessed the ability to impair and ultimately destroy his natural world. In 1962, Rachel Carson published *Silent Spring*, which illuminated, for the first time, the harmful and dangerous effects of chemical pesticides on bird, mammal, and marine life. As conservationists and environmentalists launched a new campaign in the sixties to save the environment, American historians turned to the past and poured forth numerous scholarly works on conservation history:

James Trefethen, *Crusade for Wildlife* (1961)
Elmo Richardson, *The Politics of Conservation* (1962)
Donald Swain, *Federal Conservation Policy, 1921–33* (1963)
Ira Gabrielson, *Wildlife Conservation* (1963)
Stewart Udall, *The Quiet Crisis* (1963)
Henry Clepper, *The Origins of American Conservation* (1966)
Frank Smith, *The Politics of Conservation* (1966)
Roderick Nash, *Wilderness and the American Mind* (1967)
Samuel Hayes, *Conservation and the Gospel of Efficiency* (1969)
Douglas Strong, *The Conservationists* (1970).
Robin Doughty, *Feather Fashion and Bird Preservation: A Study in Nature Protection* (1975)

Canadian concern for the environment and interest in conservation lagged far behind. Only since the sixties have Canadian historians begun to look back on their own conservation history. Paul Pross and Richard Lambert's *Renewing Nature's Wealth* (Ontario Department of Lands and Forests, 1967) and H.V. Nelles's *The Politics of Development* (1974) examine development and conservation at the provincial level (Ontario), but a major work on early federal resource conservation policy has yet to be written. More scholarly work has been accomplished in the area of early national park policy with A. Roger Byrne's *Man and Landscape Change in Banff National Park Area before 1911* (1968); Sylvia Van Kirk's 'Canada's Mountain National Parks and Federal Policy, 1885–1930' (unpublished MA thesis, University of Alberta, 1969), and E.A. Mitchner's 'William Pearce and the Federal Government's Activity in the West, 1882–1904' (unpublished PH D thesis, University of Alberta, 1971). Canadian geographer J.G. Nelson has added considerably to conservation studies with *Canadian Parks in Perspective* (1969) and *The Last Refuge* (1973). Canadian historian R. Craig Brown has illuminated early park policy with a paper on 'The Doctrine of Usefulness' presented to the Parks Conference at Calgary in 1968, while Robert D. Turner and William Rees published an excellent critical comparison between Canadian and American national park policy in the January/March issue of *Nature Canada*, 1973. Numerous short articles on the Commission of Conservation have been published in recent years. The best of these are Stewart Renfrew's critique of the Commission in the *Douglas Library Notes* (Vol. XIX, 1971) and Fred Thorpe's paper, 'Historical Perspective on the Resources for Tomorrow Conference' (1961).

A survey of Canadian wildlife conservation history is less rewarding. Historians have seldom ventured into this field of study and as yet there has been no legislative history written other than Gordon Hewitt's *The Conservation of the Wild Life of Canada* (1921). Biologists, of course, have published numerous works on specific wildlife species which contain detailed biological histories, notably Frank Gilbert Roe's *The North American Buffalo* and John Tener's *Muskoxen*. Anne Innis Dagg has also examined in general terms the historical relationship between man and wildlife in *Canadian Wildlife and Man* (1974).

The Canadian Wildlife Service regularly publishes short monographs with detailed information on birds and mammals, while Earl Godfrey's *The Birds of Canada* (1966) and A.W.F. Banfield's *The Mammals of Canada* (1974), published for the National Museum, contain good economic and historical descriptions.

Although a large volume of scientific literature is available on almost every wildlife species, neither biologists nor historians have examined the early political and legislative history of wildlife conservation in Canada. One of the major difficulties is that primary source material is neither readily available nor easy to find. Collections in various government departments are seldom well organized or catalogued. The Parks Canada file boxes at Tunney's Pasture in Ottawa contain extensive material on early park history, but access to those holdings is not automatically given to the general public. Papers at the Canadian Wildlife Service of Environment Canada relating to bird protection and pronghorn antelope protection are not catalogued. Nor, as yet, are the Percy Taverner Papers held at the Royal Ontario Museum in Toronto. The records of the United States Biological Survey at the National Archives, Washington, DC, contain some material relating to Canada but this is not catalogued either. One can only hope that as more scholars and writers become interested in Canada's wildlife conservation history and in the role played by individual Canadians, a more concerted effort will be made to collect and preserve what few primary sources still exist.

Bibliography

Aitken, Hugh, *American Capital and Canadian Resources* (Cambridge, MA: Harvard University Press 1961)

Alcock, Frederick James, *A Century of the History of the Geological Survey of Canada* (Ottawa: King's Printer 1947)

Alberta, Department of Agriculture Annual Reports 1908–16

Banfield, A.W.F., *The Mammals of Canada* (Toronto: University of Toronto Press 1974)

Belaney, Archibald ('Grey Owl'), *The Men of the Last Frontier* (Toronto: Macmillan Co. of Canada Ltd 1931, 1976)

– *Tales of an Empty Cabin* (Toronto: The Macmillan Co. of Canada Ltd 1935)

– *Pilgrims of the Wild* (Toronto: The Macmillan Co. of Canada Ltd 1975)

Benson, Norman Gustaf, editor, *A Century of Fisheries in North America* (Washington, DC: Special Publication of the American Fisheries Society 1970)

Berger, Carl, 'The True North Strong and Free,' in Peter Russell, editor, *Nationalism in Canada* (Toronto: McGraw-Hill Ryerson Ltd 1966)

Brown, Robert Craig, 'The Doctrine of Usefulness: Natural Resources and National Park Policy, 1887–1914,' in J.G. Nelson, editor, *Canadian National Parks: Today and Tomorrow* (Calgary: University of Calgary 1968)

Buchanan, Robert William, *Life and Adventures of John James Audubon* (London: J.M. Dent and Sons Ltd 1869)

Burroughs, Raymond Darwin, *The Natural History of the Lewis and Clarke Expedition* (East Lansing, MI: Michigan State University Press 1961)

Butler, William Francis, *The Wild North Land* (Montreal: Dawson Brothers 1874; reprint, Edmonton: Hurtig Publishers 1968)

– *The Great Lone Land* (Montreal: Dawson Brothers 1874; reprint: Edmonton: Hurtig Publishers 1968)

Byrne, A. Roger, 'Man and Landscape Change in Banff National Park Area before 1911,' in *Studies in Land Use History and Landscape Change*, Recreational

Park Series no. 1 (Calgary, Alberta: University of Calgary 1968)

Canadian Handbook and Tourist Guide, 1867 (Montreal: M. Longmore and Company 1867; reprint, Toronto: Coles Publishing Co. Ltd 1971)

Canada, Its History, Production, and Natural Resources, Department of Agriculture (Ottawa 1886)

Canada, National Parks Policy, National Parks and Historic Sites Branch, Indian Affairs and Northern Development (Ottawa 1971)

Carleton, R.A., 'Government's Historical Role in Conservation,' *Current History* (June 1970)

Catlin, George, 'North American Indians, 1880,' in Roderick Nash, editor, *The American Environment: Readings in the History of Conservation* (Reading, MA: Addison-Wesley Publishing Company 1968)

Chambers, Ernest John, *The Great Mackenzie Basin* (Ottawa: King's Printer 1910)

– *The Unexploited West* (Ottawa: King's Printer 1914)

Clarke, C.H.D., 'Wildlife in Perspective,' Resources for Tomorrow Conference, Montreal (23–8 October 1961)

Clepper, Henry, editor, *Origins of American Conservation* (New York: Ronald Press 1966)

Cook, G. Ramsay, 'Landscape Painting and National Sentiment in Canada,' *Historical Reflections*, University of Waterloo, I, 2 (1974)

Cross, Michael, 'The Lumber Community of Upper Canada, 1815–67,' *Ontario History* 52 (1960)

Dagg, Anne Innis, *Canadian Wildlife and Man* (Toronto: McClelland and Stewart Ltd 1974)

Dawson, Simon James, *Report on Route between Lake Superior and Red River* (Ottawa: 1868, 1869; published for the Minister of Public Works)

Day, Albert M., *North American Waterfowl* (Harrisburg, PA: Stackpole Company 1949)

Denny, Sir Cecil E., *The Law Marches West* (Toronto: J.M. Dent and Sons [Canada] Ltd, 2nd edition 1972)

Doughty, Robin W., *Feather Fashion and Bird Preservation: A Study in Nature Protection* (Berkeley: University of California Press 1975)

Doyle, Martin, *Hints on Emigration to Upper Canada* (London: William Curry, June, and Company 1834)

Edwards, R. Yorke, 'What is a Park?' *Canadian Audubon Magazine* (November–December 1965)

Einarson, Arthur S., *The Pronghorn Antelope* (Washington, DC: Wildlife Management Institute 1948)

Franklin, Sir John, *Journey to the Polar Sea* (London: J. Murray 1823)

Gabrielson, Ira, *Wildlife Conservation* (New York: Macmillan Co. 1963)

Glover, Richard Gilchrist, editor, *David Thompson's Narrative* (Toronto: Champlain Society 1962)

Godfrey, Earl, *The Birds of Canada* (Ottawa: Queen's Printer 1966)

Graham, Edward Harrison, *The Land and Wildlife* (New York: Oxford University Press 1947)

Grenfell, William T., editor, *Labrador, the Country and the People* (New York: Macmillan Co. 1909)

Grinnell, George Bird, editor, *Brief History of the Boone and Crockett Club* (New York: Forest and Stream Publication 1910)

– and Charles Sheldon, editors, *Hunting and Conservation* (New Haven, Conn.: Yale University Press 1925; reprint, New York: Arno Press 1970)

Haig-Brown, Roderick, 'The Land's Wealth,' *The Canadians*, Part 2 (Toronto: Macmillan Co. of Canada Ltd 1967)

Haines, Francis, *The Buffalo* (New York: Thomas Crowell Company 1970)

Harkin, James Bernard, 'Our Need for National Parks,' *Alpine Journal* IX (1918)

– 'Conservation Work in Canada's National Parks,' *Bulletin*, American Game Protective Association (New York: 1917)

Harmon, Daniel, *A Journal of Voyages and Travels in the Interior of North America* (Toronto: G.N. Morang 1904)

Haskell, William S., *The American Game Protective and Propagation Society: A History* (New York: Society Publication 1937)

Hayes, Samuel, *Conservation and the Gospel of Efficiency* (Cambridge, MA: Harvard University Press 1969)

Hearne, Samuel, *A Journey from Prince of Wales's Fort in Hudson's Bay, to the Northern Ocean, 1769–1772* (London: 1795; reprint, Edmonton: Hurtig Publishers 1971)

Henry, Alexander, *Travels and Adventures in Canada and the Indian Territories, between the Years 1760 and 1776* (New York: I. Riley 1809; reprint, Edmonton: Hurtig Publishers 1969)

Hewitt, Gordon C., *The Conservation of the Wild Life of Canada* (New York: Scribner's Sons 1921)

Hind, Henry Youle, *Narrative of the Canadian Red River Exploring Expedition of 1857 and of the Assiniboia and Saskatchewan Exploring Expeditions of 1858* (London: Longman, Green, Longman and Robert 1860; reprint, Edmonton: Hurtig Publishers 1971)

Hopwood, Victor, G., editor, *David Thompson, Travels in Western North America 1784–1812* (Toronto: Macmillan Co. of Canada Ltd 1971)

Hornaday, William Temple, 'The Extermination of the American Bison,' United States Museum of Natural History *Annual Report* (1889)

– 'A Great Antelope Preserve in Alberta,' statement of the Permanent Wild Life Protection Fund, New York Zoological Society, New York (1915–16)

– *Our Vanishing Wildlife* (New York: New York Zoological Society 1913; reprint, New York: Arno Press 1970)

– *Thirty Years War for Wildlife*, Statement of the Permanent Wild life Protection Fund (Stanford, Conn.: New York Zoological Society 1931)

Ise, John, *Our National Parks: A Critical Study* (Baltimore, Md: Johns Hopkins University Press 1961)

Jameson, Anna B., *Winter Studies and Summer Rambles in Canada* (New York 1837; reprint, Toronto: McClelland and Stewart Ltd 1965, Coles Publishing Co. Ltd 1972)

Kortwright, Frank W., *The Ducks, Geese and Swans of North America* (Harrisburg, PA: Stackpole Company 1942)

Laing, Arthur, 'Wildlife in the Canadian Society,' speech to BC Federation of Fish and Game Clubs, 1965

Leopold, Aldo, 'Wildlife in American Culture,' *Journal of Wildlife Management* 7 (1943)

– *A Sand County Almanac* (Oxford University Press 1949; reprint, Ballantine Books 1970)

Lewis, Meriwether and William Clark *Journals, 1804–6* (Toronto: George N. Morang 1814)

Lothian, W. Fergus, 'Brief History of National Parks Administration in Canada' (Ottawa: Parks Branch 1955)

Lower, A.R.M., *Settlement and the Forest Frontier* (Toronto: Macmillan Co. of Canada Ltd 1936)

Mackenzie, Alexander, *Exploring the Northwest Territories from Athabasca to the Pacific, 1789*, T.H. Macdonald, editor (Norman, Oklahoma: University of Oklahoma Press 1966)

– *Voyages from Montreal on the St Lawrence through the Continent of North America to the Frozen and Pacific Oceans* (London: T. Cadwell, Jr and W. Davies 1801; reprinted with additional material, Edmonton: Hurtig Publishers 1971)

Macoun, John, *Manitoba and the Great Northwest* (Guelph: World Publishers 1882)

– 'Report on the Peace River Region' (Ottawa: Geological Survey of Canada 1903)

Magrath, Thomas W., *Authentic Letters from Upper Canada*, Thomas Radcliff, editor (originally published in 1833; reprint, Toronto: Macmillan Co. of Canada Ltd 1953)

Mair, Charles and Robert MacFarlane, *Through the Mackenzie Basin* (London: Simpkin, Marshall, Hamilton, Kent and Co. 1908)

Martin, Chester, *Dominion Lands Policy*, L.H. Thomas, editor (Toronto: McClelland and Stewart 1973)

Marx, Leo, *Machine in the Garden* (New York: Oxford University Press 1964)

Mathiessen, Peter, *Wildlife in America* (New York: Viking Press Inc. 1959)

Merk, Frederick, *Fur Trade and Empire: A Journal of Sir George Simpson* (Cambridge, MA: Harvard University Press 1968)

Miner, Jack, *Wild Goose Jack* (Toronto: Simon and Schuster of Canada Ltd 1971)

– *Jack Miner and the Birds* (Toronto: Simon and Schuster of Canada Ltd 1976)

Muir, John, *Our National Parks* (Boston: Houghton, Mifflin and Co. 1901)

– *The Yosemite* (New York: The Century Co. 1912)

Nash, Roderick, 'Wilderness and Man in North America,' in J.G. Nelson, editor, *The Canadian National Parks: Today and Tomorrow* (Calgary: University of Calgary 1968)

– *Wilderness and the American Mind* (New Haven: Yale University Press 1969)

Nelles, H.V., *The Politics of Development: Forests, Mines, and Hydro-Electric Power in Ontario, 1849–1941* (Toronto: Macmillan Co. of Canada Ltd 1974)

Nelson, J.G., *The Canadian National Parks: Today and Tomorrow* (Calgary: University of Calgary 1968)

– *Canadian Parks in Perspective* (Montreal: Harvest House 1970)

– 'Some Reflections on Man's Impact on the Landscape of the Canadian Prairies,' in P.J. Smith, editor, *The Prairie Provinces* (Toronto: University of Toronto Press 1972)

– *The Last Refuge* (Montreal: Harvest House 1973)

Palliser, John, *Explorations – British North America. The Journals, Detailed Reports, and Observations Relative to the Explorations … of the portion of British North America which, in latitude, lies between the British boundary line and the height of land or watershed of the northern or frozen ocean respectively, and, in longitude, between the western shore of Lake Superior and the Pacific Ocean, during the years 1857 and 1858, and 1859 and 1860* (London: Queen's Printer 1863)

Pearce, William, 'The Establishment of National Parks in the Rockies,' report to Calgary Historical Society, 16 December 1924

Pearson, T. Gilbert, *Adventures in Bird Protection*, Special Publication, American Committee for International Wildlife Protection (1937)

Penick, James L., *Progressive Politics and Conservation: The Ballinger-Pinchot Affair* (Chicago: University of Chicago Press 1968)

Phillips, John C., *Migratory Bird Protection in North America* (Washington, DC: Special Committee for International Wildlife Protection 1934)

Pike, Warburton, *The Barren Grounds of Northern Canada* (London: Macmillan Co. 1892)

Pimlott, Douglas H., 'The Migratory Birds Convention: A Special Problem,' background study for Science Council, *Scientific Action in Fisheries and Wildlife Resources* no. 15 (June 1971)

Pinchot, Gifford, *The Fight for Conservation* (New York: Harcourt, Brace and Co. 1910)

– *Breaking New Ground* (New York: Harcourt, Brace and World Inc. 1947)

Polk, James, *Wilderness Writers* (Toronto: Clarke, Irwin and Co. Ltd 1973)

Preble, Edward A., *North American Fauna* Washington, DC: United States Biological Survey 1908

Pross, Paul and Richard Lambert, *Renewing Nature's Wealth* (Toronto: Queen's Printer 1967)

Rasporich, Anthony W. and Henry C. Klassen, *Prairie Perspectives* (Toronto: Holt, Rinehart and Winston of Canada Ltd 1973)

Raup, Hugh M., 'Range Conditions in Wood Buffalo National Park,' Special Report no. 2, American Committee for International Wildlife Protection Washington, DC (1932)

Renfrew, Stuart, 'Commission of Conservation,' *Douglas Library Notes* XIX (Kingston: Queen's University 1971)

Rorabacher, J. Albert, *The American Buffalo in Transition* (St Cloud, Minnesota: North Star Press 1970)

Richardson, Elmo, *The Politics of Conservation* (Berkeley: University of California Press 1962)

Rodney, William, *Kootenai Brown: His Life and Times* (Sidney, BC: Gray's Publishing Ltd 1969)

Roe, Frank Gilbert, *The North American Buffalo: A Critical Study* (Toronto: University of Toronto Press 1951; 2nd edition 1970)

Salt, W. Ray and A.L. Wilk, *The Birds of Alberta*, 2nd edition (Edmonton: Queen's Printer 1972)

Scace, Robert C., *Banff: A Cultural and Historical Study of Land Use and Management in a National Park Community* (Calgary: University of Calgary 1968)

– The Management and Use of a Canadian Plains Oasis: The Cypress Hills (unpublished PH D thesis, University of Calgary 1972)

Schwartz, William E., *Voices for the Wilderness* (New York: Ballantine Books 1969)

Scott, Anthony, *Natural Resources: The Economics of Conservation* (Toronto: McClelland and Stewart 1973)

Seton, Ernest Thompson, *Wild Animals I Have Known* (New York: Charles Scribner's Sons 1900; reprint, New York: Bantam Books 1957)

– *Arctic Prairies* (New York: Charles Scribner's Sons 1912)

– *Life Histories of North American Animals* I–IV (New York: Doubleday and Page 1925)

Sharpe, P.F., Whoop-Up Country (Minneapolis: University of Minnesota Press 1955)

Simpson, Sir George, *Peace River: A Canoe Voyage from Hudson Bay to the Pacific in 1828* (Ottawa: J. Durie and Son 1872)

Smith, C. Ray and David R. Witty, 'Conservation, Resources, and Environment,' *Plan Canada* XI, 1 (December 1970)

Smith, Frank, *The Politics of Conservation* (New York: Harper and Row 1966)

Soper, J. Dewey, 'Mammals of Wood Buffalo Park, Northern Alberta, and District of Mackenzie,' *Journal of Mammalogy Report* XXIII (May 1942)

– *The Mammals of Alberta* (Edmonton: Hamly Press Ltd 1964)

Spry, Irene, *The Palliser Papers* (Toronto: Champlain Society 1968)

Stefansson, Vilhjalmur, *My Life with the Eskimos* (New York: Macmillan Co. 1913)

Strong, Douglas, *The Conservationists* (Toronto: Addison-Wesley Publishing [Canada] Ltd 1971)

Swain, Donald C., *Federal Conservation Policy, 1921–33* (Berkeley: University of California Press 1963)

– 'Passage of the National Park Service Act,' *Wisconsin Magazine of History* XL (1966)

Taverner, Percy A., 'The Gannets of Bonaventure,' *The Ottawa Naturalist* XXXII 2 (May 1918)

– *Birds of Eastern Canada* (Ottawa: King's Printer 1919)

– *Birds of Western Canada*, Victoria Memorial Museum Bulletin no. 41 (Ottawa: King's Printer 1926)
– *Birds of Canada* (Toronto: Musson Publishing 1937)
Tener, John S., *Muskoxen in Canada* (Ottawa: Queen's Printer 1965)
Theberge, Elaine, 'The Untrodden Earth: Early Nature Writing in Canada,' *Nature Canada* III 2 (April–June 1974)
Thorpe, Fred J., 'Historical Perspective on the Resources for Tomorrow Conference,' Resources Division, Department of Northern Affairs and National Resources (Ottawa 1961)
Townsend, Charles W., *In Audubon's Labrador* (Cambridge, MA: Houghton, Mifflin Company and University Press 1918)
Trefethen, James B., *Crusade for Wildlife: Highlights in Conservation Progress* (Harrisburg, Pennsylvania: The Stackpole Co. 1961)
– *Wildlife Management and Conservation* (Boston: P.C. Heath Publishing Ltd 1964)
Turner, John P., *The Northwest Mounted Police 1873–1893* (Ottawa: King's Printer 1950)
Turner, Robert D. and William Rees, 'A Comparative Study of Parks Policy in Canada and the United States' *Nature Canada* II, 1 (January–March 1973)
Tuttle, Charles R., *Our North Land* (Toronto: C. Blackett Robinson 1885)
Udall, Stewart, *The Quiet Crisis* (New York: Holt, Rinehart, and Winston 1963)
Warkentin, John, *The Western Interior of Canada* (Toronto: McClelland and Stewart 1964)
Williams, Mabel B., *Through the Heart of the Rockies and Selkirks* (Ottawa: Parks Branch 1921)
– *The History and Meaning of National Parks in Canada* (Saskatoon: H.R. Lawson Publishing 1957)
Zaslow, Morris, *The Opening of the Canadian North* (Toronto: McClelland and Stewart Ltd 1971)

Index